JAN   2006

WHERE
HELL
FREEZES
OVER

Lt. (j.g) William H. Kearns, Jr., USNR co-pilot

WHERE HELL FREEZES OVER

A Story of
Amazing Bravery
and Survival

David A. Kearns

Thomas Dunne Books
St. Martin's Press 🙢 New York

THOMAS DUNNE BOOKS.
An imprint of St. Martin's Press.

Frontispiece: Lt. (jg) William Henry Kearns, Jr., USNR (circa 1946), youngest PBM plane commander to pilot Northwest Passage route during Operation Nanook, co-pilot on *George 1* during Operation Highjump. Official U.S. Navy photo courtesy of the Kearns family collection.

www.stmartins.com

Design by Phil Mazzone

Library of Congress Cataloging-in-Publication Data

Kearns, David A.
    Where hell freezes over / David A. Kearns.— 1st ed.
        p. cm.
    ISBN 0-312-34205-5
    EAN 978-0-312-34205-0
    1. Survival after airplane accidents, shipwrecks, etc. 2. Aircraft accidents—Antarctica. 3. Antarctica—Discovery and exploration—American. 4. Byrd Antarctic Expedition (4th : 1946–1947) I. Title.

TL553.9.K43 2005
613.6'9'09116—dc22

2005045526

First Edition: November 2005

10   9   8   7   6   5   4   3   2   1

To Maxwell Lopez, Fred Williams, and Wendell K. Hendersin,
you are not forgotten.

CONTENTS

PREFACE
ICE AND SILENCE

In bright yellow primer over navy blue, written on *George 1*'s broken wing, are the words "Lopez, Hendersin, Williams DEAD." The lettering in six-foot bold was visible from the air in 1947. There's a vertical line beside the names as if the author was making a statement: "Here we draw the line. There will be no more names added to this roll." The wing is buried beneath perhaps two hundred feet of ice at the bottom of the world. Three bodies lie in wait beneath it.

To my family, Bill, Donna, Fiona, Emily, and Sean, thank you for supporting these efforts.

WHERE
HELL
FREEZES
OVER

1   THURSTON ISLAND

LATITUDE 71 DEGREES 33 MINUTES SOUTH, LONGITUDE 98 DE-
GREES 45 MINUTES WEST, ANTARCTICA, 0617, DECEMBER 30,
1946   The airplane detonated around him, and yet he was still
alive.

With a roar in his ears, twenty-two-year-old naval aviator Bill
Kearns was hurled through the windshield of his twenty-ton seaplane
George 1 into a hail of ice, glass, and frigid air. Without the aid of a
parachute, without the slightest hope of survival, the copilot plummeted toward an icy mountain slope on the coldest, highest, driest,
most vacant place on earth, Antarctica.

His first thought was, *Here I go into the starboard prop.* The prop was
attached to a massive engine grinding away just ten feet or so to his
right. But the blades never touched him. Instead, the central wing

buckled in the explosion, which shook the engines loose from their mounts. They sawed into the after portion of the flight deck, sparing the cockpit, as well as pilot Ralph "Frenchy" LeBlanc and copilot Bill Kearns.

The brutal ripping and tearing of the props, in that second of mayhem, ignited aviation fuel and popped the forward observation bubble and the right-hand glass canopy of the cockpit in a gush of burning air moving through the bow of the seaplane. The extremely low temperatures slowed the explosion just enough to prevent the remainder of the crew from dying instantly.

Kearns, who had just walked through the plane on a safety check and failed to fasten his seat belt again, found himself alive, tumbling into the freezing air as what remained of *George 1* descended behind him in a cascade of burning metal.

The fall was just long enough to allow him to consider the irony of the situation: having survived World War II and dangerous flights around Greenland the previous summer, he would now die on his first peaceful survey mission over Antarctica.

As his body cartwheeled and bounded downslope, snow and ice sandpapering his face and eyes, arms and legs akimbo in their ridiculous flopping motions, it seemed to Kearns that the brutal descent would go on forever.

He came to rest with his body buried from head to waist in three feet of snow. He had three broken ribs, a broken nose, and a small chipped bone in his skull. His right arm was broken in several places, like splintered cordwood, his mind was blank from the violent landing, and he didn't know if any of his eight fellow crew members had survived the explosion.

The group included radioman James Robbins, crew chief Bill Warr, pilot Ralph "Frenchy" LeBlanc, the captain of the seaplane tender USS *Pine Island*, Henry H. Caldwell, along as an observer, navigator Ens. Maxwell A. Lopez, radioman Wendell Keith Hendersin, photographer Owen McCarty, and flight engineer Fred Williams.

Only Robbins and Warr were alert immediately following the crash. As Kearns lay unconscious, Warr checked for survivors, crying as he sifted through the debris with tears in his eyes. He came upon Robbins genuflecting in a bewildered daze.

2 OPERATION HIGHJUMP: TASK FORCE 68

The security of the United States for the next one hundred years lies in the polar regions.

–Rear Adm. Richard E. Byrd.

WASHINGTON, D.C., NOVEMBER 1946   A young lieutenant in the U.S. Naval Reserve was summoned to the offices of Rear Adm. Richard E. Byrd. Riding down Constitution Avenue in a cab, he was pretending he wasn't nervous.

He would later recall a mixture of emotions, from apprehension to extreme pride. How had he rated such an interview? What was so special about Bill Kearns from Boston?

Easy does it, he decided, *just like landing on an aircraft carrier.*

Growing up, Bill admired the hell out of Richard E. Byrd the way other kids loved Tom Mix or the entire roster of the Boston Red Sox.

William Henry and Lillian Rose Kearns taught their boy from an early age to be proud of America's heroes, men like Byrd—people with the guts and the courage to break new ground. Lillian married a naval engineer. She loved the sea as much as her husband did.

Just before she died in the winter of 1936, she had taken her son Bill down to a local radio station to sing "Anchors Away" for a chance to win a turkey. Another tenor collected the prize, having selected a more appropriate holiday song. Lillian swelled with pride nonetheless.

That following year William Henry took the motherless boy to watch a muster of the Atlantic fleet off Marble Head to try and shake him out of his blues. During the same year Richard Byrd spoke at the Lexington Rotary, due partially to William's finagling. Bill had sat right up front.

Byrd was all patrician charm and smooth Annapolis in his delivery in those days, with a barely detectable Virginia drawl. His clear blue eyes missed nothing.

For a rare second, sitting there listening to the explorer, the sting of losing his mother abated, and Bill was bowled over by the stories. Stories about the rough landings on ice, tales of sled dogs, seals, penguins, and bitter cold. Byrd recounted his 120 days alone, bivouacked in a small Quonset hut slowly submerging in the drifts of the Ross Ice Shelf near Roosevelt Island.

"Little America," he called it. What a brilliant joke! It had been nothing more than a collection of huts, sleds, radio antennae, and stovepipes, literally at the edge of the world, sinking into the eternal freeze. Byrd was the first man to spend the astral winter that close to the pole.

Now, as he entered the navy department, Bill had to remind himself that he was part of all that. He was going with Byrd as one of his aviators, and this was an invitation especially extended to reserve fliers—"Byrd's Boys"—to size up the potential participants and go over the details of the mission.

It would be called Operation Highjump, and it would be colossal, bigger than anything Byrd had ever attempted before. Byrd wasn't speaking at Rotary engagements to drum up the funding this time. Rather, Byrd had the backing of the entire U.S. Navy and, for the moment, the full support of President Harry S. Truman.

Highjump was to involve 13 ships, 23 aircraft, including at least 6 Martin PBMs (Patrol Bomber Martin), and 6 Douglas R4D transports, with a remainder in Sikorsky helicopters and single pontoon seaplanes, and as many as 4,700 sailors, Seabees, Coast Guardsmen, and scientists, along with more than 24 veteran aviators. The combined crew also consisted of 25 civilian observers and 11 radio and press correspondents.

Bill was a small part of those flight crews now training at the Norfolk Naval Base in Virginia. Though he was thrilled to finally be meeting the admiral, it was taking precious training time out of his schedule. He needed to get back to his ship as soon as possible.

The purposes of the operation have been debated since 1946, but the acquisition of territory for the United States of America—the whole continent if possible—rated second to the top of the list. The concept was simply to go to Antarctica, take a gigantic picture of it, and claim ownership to whatever parts had been photographed, charted, and deemed desirable for future bases and/or resources.

The best way to establish that you had seen a piece of territory was to photograph it for the record and establish its place on a map. Up to that point, the United States had recognized no formal claim made by any nation on Antarctica.

The actual costs for Highjump would obviously stretch into the millions, but the countless line items were buried in post–World War II surplus budgets for the ships and detachments involved.

But it was costly enough that on November 14 President Truman hauled the navy department's top brass, along with his military budget officers, into his office for an afternoon meeting and reportedly threatened to shut down the whole show, not only because of the cost but also because of the foreign policy aggravation Highjump was causing him.[1]

At that time, Bill was ignorant of the hubbub surrounding his mission. He was only vaguely aware that these gestures of Byrd's were designed to keep a slowing ball rolling forward, to keep morale and motivation up, to maintain the ongoing saga of adventure and exploration. Bill was a disciple in training. The aircrews risking their lives had to be the biggest converts to the mission.

Not everyone was pleased about Highjump. Great Britain, Chile, Argentina all had made claims on Antarctic territory, and they demanded to know what American intentions were.[2] "Exploration," Truman had said to the world through his Undersecretary of State, Dean Acheson. For the moment the world wasn't buying this. Exploration was obviously one answer but not the total story.

Not much was known about this landmass larger than the continental United States and Europe combined. The United States, at Byrd's protracted urging, wanted to put an end to that ignorance. In contrast with the North Pole, there was actually terra firma in Antarctica, roughly 5.6 million square miles of it there for the taking beneath all that ice.

Antarctica had been part of a massive supercontinent that peeled off from its siblings more than eighty million years ago. The scientific world was only beginning then to see evidences of the new theory of plate tectonics, and proof for that theory would be found in the ancient rocks of the sleeping continent. So there was a bona fide scientific reason for going.

In its geologic wandering, Antarctica ambled on down to the coldest corner of the planet, covering the absolute South Pole. Since water remains on average warmer than land, the huge landmass over the extreme south built up a massive ice sheet reflecting back into space more than 80 percent of the solar energy that reached it. Antarctica was also known to be one of the highest continents, with average elevations exceeding a baseline of six thousand feet. And it was the driest, with less than two inches of precipitation per year. So the gathering of meteorological data would be another excellent reason for going, in that more would be learned about the world's fickle weather patterns and steering currents.

But more to the nail of the matter, was the fact that every conceivable mineral found upon every other landmass on earth was also to be found in Antarctica, beneath the ice that had been slowly accumulating for more than eighty million years.

Those minerals included uranium. The United States was actively hunting for this element as it bolstered its growing nuclear arsenal.

As luck would have it, Antarctica was the last place on Earth where no one owned the land. Would the valuable resources be available given the limitations of geography? Who knew?

A race was on. Navy bases and resources were being decommissioned all across the country. Yet the U.S. Navy still had the gear, the energy, and the time to advance upon Earth's last continental frontier. Depleted from the war, the other nations could only watch as preparations got underway.

Military strategists were convinced that the battlegrounds of a coming Third World War between the superpowers would be in the polar regions. Plans of attack and defense in the age before intercontinental ballistic missiles focused primarily on the northern Atlantic and the Arctic Oceans.

American armed forces needed to know how to live, fight, and, if necessary, die in the cold and how to mount bombing and defensive operations from Greenland, which was thought of as similar to Antarctica in many ways. The military also needed a buildup of men, forces, and supplies toward that end—one that did not alarm the Soviets.

One of the U.S. Navy's greatest assets, retrieved out of mothballs at that time, was Byrd himself. He was reactivated as a rear admiral in the naval reserve and named leader for Operation Highjump in late 1945.

It would be the fourth of five journeys to the Antarctic he would eventually make. For years Byrd had been trying to persuade President Franklin D. Roosevelt that it was imperative to bring men, ships, and supplies to Antarctica on a massive scale in order to advance U.S. interests. Now Roosevelt's successor, Harry Truman, was listening.

Byrd graduated from the U.S. Naval Academy in 1912. He commanded a naval air station during World War I, and in 1925 he and other pilots pioneered Arctic aviation, flying seaplanes attached to the McMillian Expedition.

In May of the following year, Byrd made the first recorded flight over the North Pole, accompanied by Raymond Fosdick and Floyd Bennett. This claim is still in dispute because of today's advanced capabilities of global satellite telemetry, but the flight was close enough for credit back then, especially in light of the risks.

In 1927, Byrd, accompanied by U.S. Navy lieutenant George O. Noville, Bert Acosta, and Bernt Balchen, crossed the Atlantic in a small aircraft, water-landing in Ver Sur Mer, France, one month behind Charles Lindbergh's solo flight in the *Spirit of St. Louis*. The venture was designed to show the world that commercial flights between the continents would become a reality.

In 1928 Byrd established a base camp along the Bay of Whales at the edge of the Ross Sea in Antarctica, calling it Little America—the first of five encampments that Byrd would thus designate, all of them lying in the region of the Bay of Whales. The cost of the expedition, complete with mobile weather-observation platforms and several treks into the interior, had been a staggering one and a half million dollars in 1928 currency.

The next year Byrd and a team of as many as 125 explorers, including Balchen and an eager young meteorologist, Paul Siple, recorded having seen more square miles of Antarctic territory than previously seen in the history of the world. It was thus an area never before claimed by any country.[3]

On November 28, 1929, Byrd had flown the first recorded flight over the South Pole. In 1930, the explorer was made a rear admiral, and from 1933 to 1935 word of his bravery spread as he gained even more territory for the United States. He was lauded for spending more than four months alone in the Antarctic wilderness, about one hundred miles from his base camp at Little America II. That exploit, the basis for his firsthand account, aptly titled *Alone*, almost cost him his life when he suffered the prolonged effects of carbon monoxide poisoning.

Roosevelt created the U.S. Naval Antarctic Service in 1939 and immediately appointed Byrd to run it. Byrd also maintained a cordial relationship with President Harry S. Truman and had close working relations with navy secretary James Forrestal. Another fan was the chief of naval operations, Adm. Chester W. Nimitz.

The young Kearns was far removed from the circles of gigantic public figures like Truman, Byrd, and Nimitz. But he had his own accomplishments to bolster him as he approached the admiral's office.

He had fought in World War II. His skills as a Hellcat pilot earned him a slot as an instructor of single-engine fighters in Corpus Christi, Texas, before moving on to Banana River, Florida, where he fell in love with the big twin-engine Martin Mariner PBM patrol bombers.

Now a copilot in squadron VPB-19, just the previous summer he had become the youngest plane commander to fly the Northwest Passage route from Thule, Greenland, to Point Barrow, Alaska. He was considered a seasoned PBM pilot when it came to cold-weather conditions, and someone who rated an introduction to the admiral.

Neither Kearns nor other similarly rated aviators were aware of the stark differences between a summer in Greenland and a summer in Antarctica. Byrd was about to clue them in as best he could.

When Kearns arrived at the admiral's outer office, he was slightly disappointed to see two other fliers also waiting there, other young reservists who were being considered for Highjump and who had either been summoned to consider it or had volunteered as Bill Kearns had.

Byrd had deliberately set a ferocious-looking, but obedient,

Yukon sled dog stretched out across his office threshold prior to their appointment.

The admiral waited to see what the three young pilots would do when told to enter the office. Bill gingerly stepped over the animal, passing the test despite the dog's fanged snarl and low growl.

Byrd rose from his seat, smiled, extended his hand, and said, "Lieutenant, you never would have done that if you had ever seen him eat seal meat."

When the three pilots were settled in his office, Byrd clued them in to the project. "We know more about the dark side of the Moon than we do about Antarctica," he told them. They would be filling in the information gaps for the entire world.

The resources for Operation Highjump were divided into three groups. Central Group (TFG 68.1), Western (TFG 68.2), and Eastern (TFG 68.3). All three were to depart from ports from Norfolk, Virginia, to San Diego, California, and descend southward to the continent during the late fall of 1946 and January of 1947 like three well-coordinated swarms.[4]

They would be joined later by a newly commissioned aircraft carrier, the USS *Philippine Sea* (CV-47), on its maiden operational voyage. The *Phil Sea* would be ferrying six R4D aircraft down to the northern limit of the ice pack, and after the men of the Central Group had built a base camp at Little America IV on the edge of the Bay of Whales, these planes would lift off the carrier, fly over more than three hundred miles of ice pack, and land on a newly constructed airstrip built on the ice shelf. Nothing like this had ever been done before.

R4Ds were much larger than Captain Doolittle's B-25 raiders; in April 1942 the B-25 was the largest aircraft to ever take off from a carrier. The R4Ds, literally the same reliable aircraft as the DC-3, were also fitted with ski attachments to their wheels. The plane was chosen for a number of reasons, but near the top of the list was the landing-gear configuration. Any large aircraft with nose gear would likely capsize front end over as soon as it touched down on the ice, Byrd said. R4Ds had the third wheel in the tail. The nose stayed up.

The Eastern Group putting in at Norfolk would be first to set sail just after Thanksgiving weekend, making it through the Panama Canal about seven days later, escorting the command vessel USS *Mount Olympus* (ACG-8).

This armada would battle waves in the "Roaring 40s" and days of spine-softening war with record ice floes, which would keep them from penetrating the calm waters near the continent.

The Central Group under the operational command of Rear Adm. Richard Cruzen would form the main brunt of the effort. Cruzen had overseen Operation Nanook the previous summer and had traveled with Byrd on his 1938–39 mission.

The Central Group was comprised of the communications and command vessel *Mount Olympus* and the supply vessels USS *Yancey* (AKA-93) and USS *Merrick* (AKA-97), as well as the icebreakers USCGC *Northwind* (WAG-282) and USCGC *Burton Island* (AG-88), which were scheduled to arrive later in the mission. The Central Group also included a submarine, USS *Sennet* (SS-408), skippered by Capt. Joe Icenhower, who was appropriately named for the trip. He was about to get more ice than he could handle. The navy had included the *Sennet* to test the underwater limits of polar navigation— limits that would be abundantly delineated in the next few weeks.

However, the Central Group wouldn't arrive in the area until after the Eastern Group had begun their flights. After fighting through four hundred miles of pack ice, the Central Group would set up base camp and survey and photograph the central portion of the continent, using the R4D aircraft when they arrived with Byrd. They would also establish meteorological-data-collection stations radiating out from newly established Little America IV.

In practice, command for Highjump was to flow from Byrd, Rear Admiral Richard Cruzen, USN, and base camp commander Clifford

Campbell, working in conjunction from the command carrier *Phil Sea*, the communications vessel *Mount Olympus*, and at Little America IV, respectively.

The Western Group, under seaplane tender USS *Currituck* (AV-7), along with the destroyer USS *Henderson* (DD-785) and the tanker USS *Cacapon* (AO-52), was to explore first the unknown coast from the magnetic pole, then on the continent, near Commonwealth Bay, clocking around to an area near the Amery Ice Shelf. Command for the Western Group would rest on the shoulders of Capt. Charles Bond. His three seaplanes were thus designated B-1, 2, and 3.

The Eastern Group, under the direction of USS *Pine Island* (AV-12), including Kearns and his crewmates, was to photograph the coast of Antarctica, clocking around the continent from the area of Thurston (then thought a peninsula), all the way to the western limits of the Weddell Sea. The area was known then as the Phantom Coast, and included James Ellsworth Land, Marie Byrd Land, and Thurston. They would fly over the area and photo-map it along known coordinates. They would be joined by the destroyer USS *Brownson* (DD-868) and the tanker USS *Canisteo* (AO-99) in support roles for fuel and for gathering weather data. *Brownson* would also strike out on her own to collect bathymetry readings at several locales when not needed to backstop air operations.

Capt. George J. Dufek would lead the Eastern Group as the commodore. The three giant PBMs were named for him—*George 1, 2, and 3.*

The men of the *Pine Island* saw Dufek as a curious mix. He was an Annapolis graduate and an officer, and he was also pure sailor at heart. Aviation Radioman Second Class James Haskin Robbins, who observed Dufek on Operation Nanook, knew him as a "man [who] rarely smiled unless he was above the Arctic Circle or below the Antarctic Circle." Dufek had joined Byrd and Cruzen during the 1939 expedition to Antarctica and served there with great distinction as navigator of the RV *Bear*, a small navy research vessel that surveyed near the coast of Palmer Land.

Capt. Henry Howard Caldwell would skipper the 550-foot seaplane tender *Pine Island*. Caldwell had spent the war in command of Air Group 12 during heavy fighting in the Pacific. He had nearly been shot down while directing a major air attack on the Japanese stronghold of Rabaul. A 1927 graduate of the naval academy who knew Dufek before Highjump, Caldwell was also a former assistant football coach for the navy team after he distinguished himself as a standout fullback during his own midshipman days.

The overall task of the Eastern Group was to photo-map the coast of the continent from Thurston Island clocking all the way around to the far side of the Weddell Sea.

This was to be accomplished within the three-month timetable, hopefully linking up coastal photo images of the opposite coast, obtained by the Western Group. Byrd's goal was to gain a complete photo survey of the entire coast of the huge continent in that time frame. He also wanted to survey as much as one million square miles of the interior territory, if possible. The coastline alone was daunting enough.

It was like trying to photograph the entire combined coastline of the United States and Central America by flying low-survey missions with spotter seaplanes and DC-3s. At least one seaplane from each seaplane tender expected to be in the air at all times. Both tenders had three crews. The schedule entailed keeping seaplanes in constant rotation, either landing or in flight, and one on standby twenty-four hours a day, seven days a week. Flight quarters could be sounded at any time.

Byrd warned the Eastern Group that the vicinity of Thurston edged out Siberia for having some of the worst weather in the world, due to the vicious katabatic winds escaping the continent along that particular coast. The *Pine Island* flight crews would find the first few flights as tricky as they had been warned. Skies could change in less than two minutes from sunny and clear to whiteout conditions, with winds in excess of one hundred miles per hour. Still, they remained optimistic.

The plane chosen for the photo assignments operating out of the command ships was the Martin PBM. The men who flew these planes loved them, though at first glance they were ugly as sin. "Big ugly fuckers," some of the men called them—BUFs for short.

Kearns was warned at Banana River that the Martin PBM was a flying gas can. Fully loaded, she carried more than five hundred gallons of aviation fuel split between her two wing tanks located in the armpits and nacelles, which also housed the engines. Just over twenty-one hundred gallons of fuel were divided among seven self-sealing tanks in the hull, and seven hundred gallons could be loaded in the droppable "bomb bay" tank in the forward section of the plane. The hull was just over ten feet wide and was divided into five watertight compartments by bulkheads. Two feet or so above the hull tanks, deck plating afforded solid footing through the gangways.

But on the bright side, she had a flight range of two thousand miles at 118 nautical miles an hour for a flight time of about twenty hours. Her flight ceiling was about fifteen thousand feet, given normal conditions. She could go higher, but she wasn't equipped yet with onboard oxygen, although modifications would come.

With a full load of about fifty-five thousand pounds, under non-combat conditions and without jet-assisted takeoff (JATO), it would take her approximately thirty-five seconds to lift off the water from the time full throttle was applied. But JATO would be used in the Antarctic to overcome those bergs. She was a smooth airplane once aloft.

Lt. Comdr. John D. Howell, who would eventually lead Kearns and other members of Task Force 68's Eastern Group, said driving the PBM was like "flying around your living room sitting in a barber chair."[5]

Glenn L. Martin Company of Baltimore produced more than thirteen hundred of these planes in 1944 under contract for the navy. Easily carrying a crew of nine, the Martin Mariner variants had been designed as submarine bombers and reconnaissance spotters during the war and also used as rescue planes for downed pilots.[6]

With a wingspan of 118 feet, and just over 80 feet long, she stood about 20 feet off the ground if you wheeled her up on dry land and balanced her on the centerline of her hull.

Split horizontal stabilizers, cocked at about a 130-degree angle with rudder paddles, stuck into the air like dual shark fins, her "gulled" wings with their bulbous pontoons on the end as though drafted by a cartoonist.

On the good side, there were power and strength to the airframe. Heavy-rimmed gangways, galvanized ribs and dogged-doors, the battery banks, radio and radar gear all exposed on metal racks, the miles of electric cable, the massiveness of those huge propellers whirring on either side of the flight deck. Taken as a whole, she was, Kearns decided, a beautiful ship.

Martin produced several Mariner PBM variants until late 1944, when two Pratt and Whitney Supercharged Radial 2800s, one nestled in the crook of each gull wing, were settled on to power a pair of seven-foot quad Curtiss propellers.

The flight deck was located below her giant tear-shaped radar dome, which stuck up like a shark's dorsal fin just forward of the crook of her shoulders. Pilot and copilot were backstopped by a radioman located aft of the copilot's starboard side seat, a radar man behind the pilot, and a navigator's station just aft of radar and facing inward; a flight engineer's station, for controlling fuel tanks and plane trim, was tucked in a corner aft of the navigator.[7]

Pilot and copilot shared a duel yoke and a dash consisting of twenty-eight dials, gauges, and controls, as well as a common throttle column in the middle of the cockpit above the windscreen. They each had redundant gauges for gyro horizon, barometric altimeter, air-speed, and turn and bank indicators. These were joined by a dual tachometer and syncronoscope keeping the props in sync, wing flap indicators, autopilot indicators and charging switches, and a temperature gauge. A radio compass, a Mark Nine compass, a twelve-hour clock, and a radio altimeter joined the assortment of round displays on the dash. The radio altimeter was set in front of the pilot, and its warning indicator lights were facing the copilot. These were important in that they provided a backup for the standard altimeter should climate or other unforeseen circumstance affect the barometric reading. The yoke was of the wheel-type familiar to transport pilots. The hydraulic autopilot and pump had functioned well during the balmy Pacific war.

On the port side of the flight deck, there was a ladder leading below to a bow compartment containing a small galley on the port side, with racks of radio gear, below the radioman on the starboard bulkhead.

Forward of this, within the nose, there was an observation station capped with a glass blister forward of the galley. This had been where the bombardier did his deadly work during the later part of the war. The machine gun mounts had been removed, as had the bombardier's trigger and sighting gear. Thus the bubble had been converted into an observation post for work in the Arctic and Antarctic.

From the waist of the aircraft, two machine gun hatches with port-holes could be opened to the outside air and secured to the bulkhead or dogged shut. The navy had removed the machine gun mounts, but the cylindrical slots on the outside of the doors for the placement of JATO bottles were there for a purpose.

Aft of this there was a gangway leading to a smaller tunnel that sloped upward to a Plexiglas porthole within the tail. From this tunnel, which formerly held the rear gunner, the trimetrogon cameras would be mounted in place, pointing downward through the hull and operated by a photographer's mate.[8]

These triple cameras, with fields of view that overlapped at the adjoining sides, had been used to make relief maps of enemy cities and ports during the war, and could now be trained on land to make topographic maps. They took photos—hundreds of them an hour—as the plane traveled, and they would be used to make stereographic projection-based images. All seaplanes had been armed with highly advanced trimetrogon camera banks, each capable of a swath of three overlapping photographs covering twenty-four miles "horizon to horizon," and the 250 pounds of film expended on each flight would be used by cartographers over a five-year period to make relief maps of Antarctica.

They involved a Rube Goldberg–type system in which they photographed not only the topography below the aircraft, but also the timers adjacent to the working cameras, so that each photo's place in the sequence could be matched with the position of the plane throughout the course of its mission.

Consequent to their role in topography work, trimetrogon cameras also required that the photos themselves be calibrated against known ground points of reference, and that the elevations of these ground points and the distances between them be preestablished—a difficult task when there are shifting coastal zones, where the only surface feature is miles and miles of indistinguishable icy plain, and where the positions of "known" landmarks were often approximate. The men who operated them could be a smug, if extremely competent, bunch.

All operations would take maximum advantage of a ten-week period from late December through mid-February, when the sun would shine nearly continuously over the Antarctic.

By the time Lieutenant Kearns understood the mission and his vital part in its massive structure, his head was swimming in glory.

He shook the admiral's hand and left the building asking himself if he was equal to this historic task.

3   USS *PINE ISLAND*

"She's One Helluva ship, Bill."

–Lt. (jg) Ralph P. "Frenchy" LeBlanc, USNR

NORFOLK NAVAL BASE, THANKSGIVING WEEKEND   A day or two before departure, the docks became alive with the sound of Yukon huskies. The dogs were loaded in crates aboard the task force command vessel, USS *Mount Olympus*. It was only one of the aspects of this very strange cruise that distinguished it from every other naval mission in history. That evening a party was given for NCOs within walking distance of the ships, which included the Eastern Task Group USS *Brownson*, USS *Canisteo,* and USS *Pine Island.* Officers and "Airedales" (also known as fliers) made their own arrangements for weekend leave.

    USS *Pine Island* was dropped into the water at Todd Shipyard, Alameda, California, on February 26, 1944. She was commissioned in April the following year. At more than 550 feet in length, and nearly

70 feet of beam, she cruised along at about fifteen knots—an exemplary version of the *Currituck*, seaplane tender class.[1]

In 1942, when her forerunner, the lead ship for the Western Task Group, USS *Currituck*, was commissioned, the idea was to produce as many of these state-of-the-art sea bomber launching platforms as were needed in support roles to help end the war as soon as possible. The concept behind this class of tender was simple: they had to be beamy enough to accommodate the mass of long-range seaplanes, sufficiently sturdy to cart these planes across the Pacific, and maneuverable enough to steam into position while bearing loads exceeding 150 tons or more on the stern. Would they serve well in the Antarctic?

Pine Island normally carried a complement of four five-inch guns. But the two forward guns had been removed to make way for a spacious new helicopter deck that had been constructed with Antarctic work in mind.

"*PI,*" as the men called her, had a pilot's ready room, air plot and combat information centers, a meteorological lab, and spacious quarters located below decks for flight crews. The air-maintenance division was afforded their own living and working areas within the stern compartments as well.

The deep hangar deck was about the size of a college basketball gymnasium. In fact, this made it perfect for showing movies or as a setting for athletic competitions like "smokers," as boxing matches were called.[2]

Planes were prepared for flight inside the hangars, then transitioned to the afterdeck, which was seventy feet wide and one hundred yards long. When the planes checked out, they were hoisted by two enormous cranes—one located atop the hangar at about port midships, and another on the stern quarter—and then they were lowered to the water through a heavy-duty steel cable fastened to two eyebolts located at the balancing center of mass point on the spine of the air ship.

As the plane was hoisted and lowered, one or two men usually stood where the strap and the eyebolts were joined. Two additional crewmen stood or knelt on the wing, fastening guide ropes there so that the men on the deck of the tender could maneuver the airplane into position as it slowly descended to the water. It was dangerous work, and depending on conditions, it wasn't uncommon for eight-to-ten men to find themselves atop the slippery metal skin of the aircraft as it was hoisted and lowered. One false move could result in the death of one or more crewmen. Everyone was expected to participate as needed. This ensured steady cooperation and trust between flight crews and the men of the regular navy hauling them over the side.

The shallow-drafted, open-hull rearming boats, or "whaleboats," were also hoisted over. They carried the ends of the fuel lines, which were suspended by lines and the cranes. They drove the high-octane aviation gas aboard the plane. The boats also ferried supplies, JATO bottles, and crew members and could be used to rescue crew members who had fallen into the water.

Like Kearns, *Pine Island* had been sent out to the Pacific in time to catch the final stages of World War II. She served as a tender for Martins and Catalina PBYs in the waters near Okinawa, and contributed to seaplane flight operations during the occupation of Japan. Some of her crew saw the chilling aftereffects of nuclear war when they toured devastated areas of Nagasaki in the late summer of 1945. Following this, *PI* returned to the States via a western route, passing through the Suez Canal and on through the Mediterranean, and crossing the Atlantic to Norfolk in July of 1946. Preparations and refitting for Operation Highjump had been rushed.

But there was a remarkable esprit de corps aboard her that echoes throughout the accounts of several men who served on her during Highjump. They enjoyed working there. Not that there weren't rough spots in the chain of command. There were.

A few days before departure, Kearns met Captain Caldwell. Everyone liked him. He was a football player and a war hero, and he looked you straight in the eye. To Kearns's recollection, Caldwell was the sort of man who had you pegged down to your shoes instantly—what type of man you were and what motivated you. With a few kind words to get your gums batting while he eyed you up and down, his mind took a picture of you. Yet, if you voiced willingness to prove yourself in action, he forgave you for whatever silly faults you obviously had. At about forty-one, with a deep gravely voice reminiscent of the movie actor Ward Bond, he had something fatherly about him. According to everyone who knew him in those days, he was stern but forgiving and protective—the kind of man who hated to see a younger officer lose privileges or advancement opportunities, but who was able to recognize that sometimes it was necessary, and when it happened, he was able to issue the order himself.

The executive officer, Comdr. Isidore "Izzy" Schwartz, was originally from Brooklyn, and he had served during the war. Many saw Schwartz as more concerned with process than outcome and possessing an extreme prejudice toward Airedales.

It should be noted that Caldwell was a pilot, a heroic air-group commander in the Pacific war. Schwartz was not. The fact that he had an enlisted seaman's disdain for pilots shouldn't be surprising given the time during which he served.

By design or by coincidence the combined effect of their management was in the classic "good cop, bad cop" style that was surely as common in 1946 as it is today. Sometimes this approach is vital when it comes to dealing with youngsters—as with companies, as with sports teams, as with ships at sea. In Kearns's recollection, Schwartz was hard, by the book, and as socially inept as they came, which was unfortunate because he obviously was devoted to the U.S. Navy. The story on Schwartz was that he slept with a copy of the Navy Regulations by his bunk.

If Caldwell was Tom Landry, cool and collected, Schwartz was Bobby Knight, prone to outburst, meeting fallibility with scorn.

Both coaching styles have their uses. Only one engenders lingering resentment.

Schwartz warned his young officers immediately that he had a laser eye for infractions. Everything had to be regulation, from the type of shoes you wore aboard ship to the proper tilt of a hat to hair length. Beards were out despite the fact that they were not only going to be tolerated but encouraged among the Western Group of the task force, since they were scheduled to hold a "beard derby" somewhere south of the Antarctic Circle. Mustaches were to be neatly trimmed.

Not only could fliers in the navy of 1946 be vengeful toward a superior officer who was seen as a ball-buster, but their swashbuckling independent nature made them skilled at covert malice. Which was why a flier could coin a particularly cutting singsong verse like "Izzy, Izzy, are you busy?,"[3] and the enlisted man would actually get caught saying it by the hardened XO himself.

But Schwartz was a workaholic, and Caldwell needed one. From a purely tactical standpoint, Caldwell and Schwartz were dealing with a crew inexperienced with cold weather, and they all were scheduled to travel into the worst of it and carry out flight operations. Many of the men who would be hoisting, fueling, loading, and repairing the seaplanes had never even seen one before stepping aboard for this mission. In a few short weeks Schwartz had to train his crew how to troubleshoot the seaplanes inside and out, and how to hoist them off the water, take them apart, and put them back together again, all like clockwork. He didn't know precisely how to do it himself. It was rough going. They weren't ready at all, and he knew it. During the rigorous preparation before the December 2 departure, even Caldwell put the brakes on his ambitious commander, according to the memories of several crewmen.

During the weeks of training leading up to the cruise, Schwartz let his Brooklynese slip over the bullhorn to one of the young coxswains working a whaleboat. He called him a cocksucker. The word brought progress aboard the 550-foot ship to a standstill. Hardened seamen stood with jaws wide open and muttered, "Did he just say what I think he said?"[4]

The young coxswain thus abused flatly disobeyed a direct order to pick up a rope leading to his rearming boat. He kicked it into the water instead.

"No man can call me that, sir, you hear? No man."

Caldwell immediately called Schwartz, and not the coxswain, forward to the bridge for a fatherly chat and, according to crew accounts, issued orders preventing the commander from wandering near the fantail for an unspecified period of time, as much for Schwartz's own protection as for keeping the peace.

Twenty-year-old pilot navigators Ens. Maxwell Lopez and Ens. Martin Litz were also berated publicly, if less bitterly, for being late to their first 8 A.M. briefing in the ship's hangar. Litz remembered it well in later years.

"I couldn't stand the guy from the get-go, particularly after he dressed down Lopez and me in front of the entire ship's crew because we were a couple of minutes late for morning quarters on our first day out to sea. His remarks implied that we were in the "real navy" now and not at some cushy air station."

Kearns recognized Lopez from his time on *Norton Sound*. Lopez began his training as flight navigator in LeBlanc's outfit, Flight Crew 3 of *Pine Island*, which would be responsible for flying the *George 3*.

At some point before their departure, the young men began debating the logistics of going without liquor or beer for months on end. Having liquor aboard *Pine Island* was strictly against regulations, and Commander Schwartz would be hunting for miscreants who attempted to get around the rules. The cost benefit of spiriting liquor aboard in small caches would have to be weighed.

Lopez practically made Litz lean in as he shared a state secret with him. On *Norton Sound*, as on her *Currituck*-class sister ship, *Pine Island*, every officer from ensign to commodore was afforded a tall hutch in his quarters, at the bottom of which there was a rectangular lockbox for storing personal items.

"Those safes can hold exactly five bottles of Johnny Walker," Lopez said with a smile.

The ship could list to port or starboard, roll, and pitch, and as long as that lid was locked down tight, the bottles wouldn't break. They wouldn't even budge, so precise was the fit. Around this time Kearns began to realize how much he liked Lopez and enjoyed his company. He was a tall, good-looking kid from Newport, Rhode Island. Lopez's father, Maximo, was in the navy, serving in the Philippines. His mother, Clarice, still lived in Newport.

He liked to be called Val by his buddies, so Val he became to Kearns, who found himself on friendly terms with this fellow New Englander almost immediately.

Kearns couldn't precisely remember where the name Val came from, unless it was in reference to Rudolf Valentino. Lopez certainly looked the part. From a purely pragmatic view he was a perfect wing-man for evenings out. He attracted some beauties, but he was also kind of shy around the girls, and Bill just outranked him.

Kearns and Lopez shared a common interest in Antarctic history as well as in adventure reading in general. Like Kearns, Lopez was a big fan of Robert W. Service's poetry of the Yukon. One of his favorite pieces by the Bard of Canada was "Spell of the Yukon."

> The winter! The brightness that blinds you,
> The white land locked tight as a drum.
> The cold fear that follows and finds you,
> The silence that bludgeons you dumb.
> The snows that are older than history,
> The woods where the weird shadows slant;
> The stillness, the moonlight the mystery,
> I've bade 'em good-bye—but I can't.[5]

Kearns felt like he was back home chatting with his father. The very verses he found amusing, yet brilliantly telling of life in the wilderness, Lopez could reel off without a hitch. Then he would flash this enormous smart-aleck grin, pleased with himself to no end.

But Lopez wanted to go farther in his career than just Highjump. He was a confirmed, dyed-in-the-wool believer in the words of Richard Byrd. Either during his boyhood or during one of the briefings, Lopez had heard Byrd speak about Antarctica—about a heroic new age of discovery that was happening right now. Kearns knew what it was like to be in Byrd's presence, and he could relate. The man was like quicksand in Kearns's recollection—you listened to him long enough, and you would follow him anywhere. Apparently Byrd said something to the effect that all a young man had to do was acquit himself admirably on one or two expeditions, and before he knew it, more doors would open to him than he could possibly close.

Lopez talked about joining the Finn Ronne Expedition being planned for the year following Highjump, during the Antarctic summer of 1947–48. Captain Ronne was a Norse immigrant with a distinguished U.S. naval service career.

Ronne had served Byrd in two previous missions to the white continent. He had recently retired from the navy, and he would be looking hard for young recruits from the members of the Highjump mission. One of Ronne's goals was to determine whether the continent was a single landmass or were eastern and western Antarctica divided by a channel of frozen water connecting the Weddell and Ross Seas. Like his predecessor, Byrd, Ronne possessed a keen eye for publicity. He was garnering his own resources for the privately funded expedition to Antarctica.[6]

If a young man played his cards right, he could get his name on some charts demarking newfound coastline somewhere, or maybe even a mountain. Lopez, like many young explorers, wanted his name forever linked with Antarctic history, bonded with the landscape the way names like Amundsen and Byrd had become, and the way the name Ronne was surely going to be. Lopez was very serious about this, and he apparently had been given the word that he stood a good chance to do exactly as Byrd had done when he was much younger, which was take extended leave from his commitment to the navy to participate in an important expedition.

Litz reluctantly informed his friend that while spending a life on expeditions might be good for him, he didn't think that he, Gene Litz, would ever become a great polar explorer. It just wasn't in him. Litz enjoyed the good life far too much to even consider going back after Highjump.

Bill hadn't known Litz previously, but Litz and Lopez had received basic pilot training in North Carolina together. Litz warned Kearns right away that their flight group leader, Lt. Comdr. John D. Howell, was someone not to be trifled with.

Bill had already met Howell and liked him immediately. He had also heard the stories. John D. Howell's heroic bearing went much deeper than two dimensions. It wasn't a put-on. The guy was the real article, through and through. Silently, quietly, he exuded steely-eyed good sense and logic. To Kearns, having Howell aboard as the flight group commander was sort of like having a surrogate big brother in a box with a glass lid that had the words BREAK GLASS IN CASE OF EMERGENCY written on it in big, fifteen-point bold. You just knew he was ready to go. If you got in a jam, he'd get your butt out. You might not like what he had to say afterwards, but you'd be damned glad he'd been there.

Howell, born in 1918 in West Orange, New Jersey, graduated from the naval academy with the class of 1940. He had served as a fire-control officer aboard the light cruiser USS *Boise* (CL-47) during the battles of the Pacific.[7] There he earned the Navy Cross by walking into a flame-ringed ammunition bunker after an unexploded Japanese shell hit the ship. John D. carried out some of the ammunition that would have otherwise detonated, saving a number of crewmen still trapped in the flames and wreckage.

Returning stateside, Howell completed the navy's fighter-pilot training in Pensacola in 1943 and went back out to the Pacific carriers for air time just as the war ended. Howell then took an assignment as an executive officer for the PBM squadron based in San Juan, Puerto Rico, shortly before volunteering for Operation Highjump.

Litz was Howell's pilot-navigator from as far back as Puerto Rico. To Litz, Howell was Iron John, which is what the men in the San Juan squadron called him. Litz, then newly assigned to his crew and getting his flight hours up as a pilot-navigator, had enjoyed a grand-opening party at the new Don-Q rum distillery located just outside of town. His landing the next day was far from stellar.

"I'm walking back to the hangar, hoping he's not going to say anything about the landing. Iron John comes up and places an iron grip on my shoulder and says, 'If you ever screw up like that again, Litz, I'll have you court-martialed.'"

Litz was put in "hack" for a day. Hack was a humiliating nonadministrative punishment that included confinement to quarters and meals brought to the accused by grinning enlisted men. Thus began an uneasy relationship of give-and-take between Litz and Iron John.

The flight department of *Pine Island* consisted of more than thirty men. Some men of the regular crew were also qualified aviation machinists mates or radiomen as well. Each crew was assigned one of the PBMs aboard, *George 1, 2, or 3.*

The flight crew of *G3* was to be led by Lt. (jg) Ralph "Frenchy" LeBlanc, a former enlisted man who got into naval aviation by way of surviving the battle for Guadalcanal at the radio and rear observation position in a TBF-Avenger.

He could not get enough of flying. As a reward for his volunteering spirit he became a "ninety-day wonder" through the navy's program at the University of Southern California, trained on PBMs at

Banana River, and even saw a little Pacific action in the "Nightmare," the night bomber patrol mariner squadrons, before the war ended.

He had an eleventh-grade education and was from Breaux Bridge, Louisiana. He dated a movie starlet named Anna Wiman, daughter of Broadway producing legend Dwight Wiman. He could cut you up inside with his jokes, which were so seasoned with Cajun it would be a miracle if you understood half of them. Everyone loved having Frenchy around. He was a fearless and extremely skilled pilot.

With Kearns and Lopez, copilot and navigator positions respectively, Crew 3 also included Aviation Radioman Second Class James H. "Robbie" Robbins, who served as radar operator. Kearns knew Robbins from Operation Nanook, but until Highjump they had not crewed on the same plane together.

Robbins was a big, strapping kid with a ready smile and a thick head of hair that was always too long for navy regulations. LeBlanc often said Robbins was a dead ringer for Burt Lancaster. He couldn't understand why the kid hadn't done the more lucrative thing and, rather than enlisting in the navy, driven ten minutes to Hollywood, where they were still waiting for him.

Schwartz gave Robbins grief about the need to trim his coif more than once, and Robbins, meaning none of it, promised he would see to it.

Robbins was perfect for LeBlanc's team, with his gift of gab and his boundless energy. It seemed he never stopped moving, and like LeBlanc he had a joke or a story for every occasion.

Some of the men were considered less than desirable by their shipmates in that they contributed nothing when it came to actual work. Robbins carried out orders to a T. He also greased wheels and acquired things not normally obtained, like tubs of peanut butter and cans of apricots and other sweets from the mess. His twenty-year-old metabolism had its demands, and he had his ways and wiles.

Everyone aboard *Pine Island*, from the commodore to the mess cook, and even Schwartz, knew him and addressed him as Robbie.

In Robbins's eyes Kearns had enviable charisma and magnetism and the classic aviator's panache. Kearns was a northeasterner with a college professor's vocabulary, which could be infuriating. The man could argue up was down, and lesser combatants were forced to agree with him.

Crew 3's radioman was quiet Wendell K. "Bud" Hendersin. He had dark brown eyes, a pleasant smile, and a pencil-thin moustache. The look he often had made it seem as if he was thinking about six things at once. A pleasant look, but one that let you know the waters ran deep. He was the sort of fellow who read a lot, Kearns guessed—a "cool dude."

Like Robbins, Bud Hendersin was ambitious and thrilled to be in the navy. He wasn't bothered by Schwartz and all his harping on uniforms and regulations, because he himself took extreme pride in his bearing and appearance.

Hendersin, twenty-five, was one of six kids who grew up on a dairy farm in the rolling hills of Sparta, Wisconsin. Like Kearns, he was attracted to naval aviation at an early age as a means of seeing the world, of "getting out there." Like LeBlanc, Hendersin had been at Pearl Harbor when the Japanese attacked.

But color blindness took him only as far in aviation as radio operator. He had been physically disqualified for flight status, so he settled on operating the communications stations inside the PBYs and the big PBMs, and he never ran into an admiral or anyone else who could help him get around this deficiency in his vision.

If he couldn't fly them, he would ride in them, and this suited his needs, although he chaffed for an officer's post, propelled by his wife, Lillian, who saw in her husband much greater potential than the navy would currently allow, given his eye chart scores. He was thrilled to tell his parents, Walter and Marie, as well as his brothers, Ellwood and Bobby, and his sisters, Betty, Nancy, and Joanne, about the opportunity to work with Admiral Byrd.

Crew 3's crew chief was a stocky young boxer and affable machinist's mate from Georgia named J. D. Dickens. The crew chief's job—he was also called "the plane captain," in that he was responsible for anything amiss on board in the strictest naval sense—was to step into any role on the aircraft at a moment's notice and to fix anything that needed repairing. Dickens was also a flight engineer. He and Aviation Machinist's Mate Second Class William G. Warr—Bill—of Reading, Pennsylvania, spelled each other at this post during flights that could last from ten to twelve hours, just as Robbins and Hendersin spelled each other at radar and radio, and just like Kearns, LeBlanc, and Lopez, who were all qualified pilots, could fill in for each other at their posts as needed.

Dickens may have been selected for an additional skill: he seemed to have an uncanny ability to avoid death. Like LeBlanc and Hendersin, he had survived two crashes, and he had avoided several others by using his head. Once or twice he just plain got lucky when it came to the draw of fate's cards.

But he never backed down from a fight or mission. In fact, the more dangerous a mission was, the more apt he was to sign up for it. He just sort of figured out how to survive if things went bad. If he felt something was wrong, he'd say so, and pilots usually listened to him.

If LeBlanc had overcome an eleventh-grade education, Dickens had him beat on the "poor boy makes good" angle. Born in November 1921—one month later than LeBlanc—Dickens left the rolling pecan, peach, and peanut-farming country of middle Georgia with only an eighth-grade education and an innate ability as a mechanic, combined with a strong desire to join the military.

He and eleven buddies from his hometown drove up to Atlanta to enlist in the U.S. Marine Corps. They were sent back down to stay overnight in a hotel in Macon and begin enlistment paperwork. But the next day something in his recruiter's manner and attitude put Dickens off. So he walked across the hall and enlisted in the U.S.

Navy. He asked the navy recruiter what job or division he should apply for.

He said, "Son, take a fool's advice and sign up for the patrol squadrons. The worst they got is better than the best of the rest."

His perfect score on the mechanical-aptitude examination made him an aviation machinist's mate in the VP squadrons.

He found a home in the navy. His first brush with death occurred in Deland, Florida, while training as a flight engineer on the patrol bombers. On a night-training flight his pilot cut power to the starboard engine when it appeared that it was on fire.

The plane never made it back to the runway, and Dickens ended up in a canopy of pine trees. He hitchhiked back to the base, the only survivor among seven.

When he arrived, a young man said, "Boy, they got you down as dead!"

"Not hardly," was his response.

He eschewed the usual counseling. At the suggestion of a veteran pilot, he also denied himself any opportunity to change jobs or even take bereavement leave, feeling it would hamper his ability to ever get back into an airplane. He got back on the earliest training flight and kept going.

He survived several scrapes in bombers during the war.

By 1946 his time was up. Everything after December 2 was considered voluntary service by the U.S. Navy. He'd get paid the same, but he could walk away whenever he wished. This was fun—icing on the cake after World War II. His boxing record was forty wins and one loss. He might even get the chance for one more fight aboard *PI*. He'd married his hometown sweetheart and had been willed a plot of land in Thomaston. Marital bliss, children—the so-called rest of his life awaited him.

The men were joined by Chief Photographer's Mate Owen McCarty, from Sonoma County, California—wine country. But the hefty twenty-six-year-old McCarty was quiet, reserved—even a little stand-offish. His husky stature should have said otherwise, but mostly he was good at his job, and that was about it. He didn't socialize.

But, as usual, there was more to it. Mac, as he was known, had been among the first brave photographers in the Pacific pioneering the use of color film in the midst of action. He had likely gazed upon the aftermath of the worst of the war. Likely he had seen and filmed enough death to last a lifetime. Now he was off on this adventure.

LeBlanc's crew was scheduled to fly *George 3*. *George 1* was Howell's plane, and *George 2* was Lt. (jg) James Ball's. Ball was a great guy from Anson, Texas.

Ball's copilot, Lt. (jg) Bob Goff, also had a terrific sense of humor, according to shipmates. Goff was doodling on *Pine Island*'s ready room chalkboard one morning, just shortly before departure. The caption read, "Naval Aviation's Most Ancient and Honored Maneuver" below a diagrammed flight path of a plane in 180-degree, full-retreat mode. It had been pretty funny stuff—especially the lasting image of Goff furiously erasing it before Commander Schwartz could see it and gain more ammunition against his crew of "fair-weather Airedales."

4 PANAMA AND THE RIDE SOUTH

Ciudad Panama, a first stop for the explorers on their way to the Antarctic, had been a crossroads between the Pacific and Atlantic fleets during the war, and sometimes it resembled Dodge City, only more so. Street performers would do everything from the more common juggling and singing to the lewdly impossible, all for spare change in U.S. money.

The boys were about to get a taste of it. Kearns, who spent 1941, his first year out of school, as an engineer's helper and crew supervisor in the Naval District, knew all about this place. Father William, then chief engineer of the Naval District, had pulled the strings to give him that experience. Now Bill was back in town for a day or two.

The PBM-5s *George 1* and *George 2* had been flown over the canal locks from Coca Sola Naval Air Station to the Balboa submarine base, enabling the five-hundred-foot ship to just squeak through the canal without the obstruction of the seaplanes' wingtips fouling on the walls of the canal.

The *G3* already had its wings clipped. They had been dismounted from the engines and stored within the hangar, and the *G3* had already been secured to its position on the aftermost portion of the flight deck.[1] So the crew were not afforded the additional hop over the Canal Zone at the controls of their aircraft, although later Crew 3 aided in placing the *G1* and *G2* back aboard.

Saturday evening, Ensigns Litz and Lopez caught a raunchy *exibición*-style show in the ballroom of one of the finer hotels; the show was called "Beauty and the Beast." It was a tamer version of what was available to servicemen on liberty, and, though held in a finer setting, it was certainly not something Walt Disney would have approved of. In this one-act play, accompanied by a ten-piece band, a voluptuous Panamanian woman pantomimed coerced love with a gorilla. It started with a dance. The embracing, artificial gorilla was sewn into her belly dancer's costume at the hip.

These were some of the last moments Lopez would spend on earth as a free man. He was twenty years old. Yet still he had a brush with fame to look forward to.

At 3 A.M. Sunday morning, Litz and Lopez sat in plush chairs in the hotel lobby, smiling and laughing at the absurd, comic spectacle they had just witnessed, trying to wrap their minds around it. They grinned and smoked cigarettes into the mellow hours. Then who should stroll through the hotel lobby but the movie actor Errol Flynn. The actor was spending a day or two in Panama on his way through the canal to Jamaica, a trip he frequently made.

"Howya doin, fellas?" the original swashbuckler said to Litz and Lopez.[2]

The astonished men smiled, nodded, and managed a few barely intelligible words to the actor, who graciously extended his huge paw to each of them and asked why they were in town. They told him they were headed south, way south. Byrd's mission had been well publicized. Flynn understood. Litz recalled that he looked as fresh as a sweaty actor with a couple rums under his belt could look in all that heat and humidity. It was comical on a number of levels, not the least of which was the fact that Flynn played the doting fan to the young naval aviators, who at the moment were more intoxicated than the roving rogue himself.

By sunup both Litz and Lopez wondered whether they had indeed seen the actor at all. They couldn't really trust their eyes after their "Beauty and the Beast" incident.

Kearns, LeBlanc, and Lopez were having lunch in a notorious downtown bar called Kelley's Ritz Monday afternoon. Lopez here spurned the advances of several women so that he, Bill, and Frenchy could get through their meals in peace.

Years later the men who knew him would wonder with sadness whether Lopez died a virgin despite the fact that women and girls seemed to fall over in front of him. In Kearns's recollection, Lopez was so devoutly Catholic, and so desirous of doing nothing his mother would not approve of, that he refused to give into his natural proclivities.

On the other hand, Litz, arguably Lopez's best friend in the world, later claimed to know for a fact that Lopez enjoyed the full embrace of a woman before dying: he said that he and Lopez shared a room and both managed to sneak company into barracks before leaving Norfolk.

On Tuesday, December 10, flight crews gained an hour of air time on a short hop out to sea. This gave support crews a chance to train on pulling the large airplanes off the water and hauling them inboard on rolling seas.

All hands from the flight department participated in getting the birds back inboard. Kearns watched in horror from atop one of the planes as twenty members of the unseasoned crew manned the lines, trying to haul the unruly PBM through the breeze and swing it aboard the *Pine Island* as it was being hoisted off the water. It was ridiculous to have that many men disjointedly tugging on the ropes, and indeed their handling of the bird nearly cost a wingtip and pontoon as the PBM swung wildly and barely missed smashing into the hull of the *Pine Island.*

They could all get killed if the plane struck the side of the ship.

"Bill, set those guys straight, will ya?" bellowed LeBlanc from a porthole. LeBlanc then muttered something to the effect that this was a complete and total "up-fuck," his and Bill's favorite term for an unsafe situation in the making. Before Kearns knew what he was saying, the stream of words was flowing out of his mouth like a river.

"Christ almighty, fellas! Will some of you get off that damned line before you kill one of us? It only takes five or six of you—no more. Whose up-fuck is this, anyway?"

Immediately, Commander Schwartz blasted Kearns for insubordination and foul language over a bullhorn. He informed him that the men were acting on his orders, and told him to shut up immediately and report to the bridge when the plane was secured.

Kearns fired back, "Commander, this is all ass backwards! Someone's going to get killed up here. You need five or six guys on those ropes at most!"

"One more word, Lieutenant, and you're on report."

At his dressing down later in the day in front of Captain Caldwell, Schwartz told Kearns the crew was training for Antarctic operations en route. They were anticipating working in rough conditions with larger groups of men, and he wanted them prepared for it, at least as well as a rushed training schedule permitted. Many of the young men had no idea what they were doing, he said. The crew members would have to be patient with each other. Additionally, junior flight officers were expected to remain calm and to respect commands.

Schwartz told Caldwell that he wanted the lieutenant written up for insubordination. Caldwell paused for a moment and asked Kearns if he thought that was necessary.

"No, sir. I got it."

Caldwell nodded and dismissed him.

Kearns got the message. He had screwed up. He should never have argued with Schwartz or shot his mouth off. Looking back, Kearns felt that it was amazing that he hadn't been put in hack or written up. Schwartz was well within his rights to ask for it. But Caldwell obviously liked Kearns, not to mention the fact that a devout gutter mouth like Schwartz decrying foul language rang more than a little hollow.

That afternoon, *Pine Island* was rigged for running, with *George 3*'s wing attachments removed from the outward sides of their engines and stowed in the hangar deck. The *G3* was set at amidships on the very aft portion of the deck.

On December 11, *Pine Island* clipped the equator at longitude 28 degrees 47 minutes west shortly after 1 P.M.

Lt. Comdr. John D. Howell read descriptions on some of the more noteworthy pollywogs in his flight crew for the benefit of the assembled men of *Pine Island*.

Many veterans of the Pacific war had been through this before and were considered hardened seamen, or "shellbacks." A large portion of the crew had yet to endure the humiliating equatorial regime and were still considered neophytes, or "pollywogs." One can only imagine the dark origins of the lighthearted hazing, masked as naval tradition in the "King Neptune's court" proceedings that occur whenever a ship crosses the equator. In the navy of the 1940s, the games involved running around on deck in your shorts, having your T-shirt sprayed with shaving cream, and being flailed with switches and other objects before being summoned to King Neptune's court for more verbal abuse and remonstrations and further rituals of reduced dignity, which tested a man's mettle while pushing the boundaries of good taste.

Pine Island was a friendly ship, however. Records show that Caldwell abbreviated the usual shenanigans in expectation of rough seas.

But afterwards the cruise southward proved tame and uneventful—pleasantly so for Task Group 68.3. The *Pine Island*, with Captain Caldwell in command and Captain Dufek aboard as task group commodore, was escorted all the way down by the three-hundred-foot destroyer *Brownson*, skippered by Comdr. H. M. S. Gimber, as well as the 550-foot tanker *Canisteo*, under the watchful hand of Capt. Edward K. Walker. The ships remained about fifty miles apart, only drawing alongside to refuel while keeping an eye out for incoming storms on each other's behalf. The air grew increasingly chilly.

And just as the temperature began to cool, Dickens noticed that a draining abscess in his tooth was giving him trouble. He'd had it operated on shortly before departing Norfolk, and now a sharp, stabbing pain told him that he needed to have his jaw looked at again by the ship's doctor. It was later discovered the abscess needed to be reopened and cleaned. Infection had spread from his jaw up into his sinuses and began stopping up his ears.

Around the same time, Kearns dumped eight Panamanian coconuts overboard. No one saw him do it. Someone came up with the idea of stowing cheap Panamanian rum inside the coconuts by using paraffin wax to hide and seal the crease in the husk. This officer, who will go nameless into history, asked Bill to be the one to hold the smuggled rum in his locker, and he reluctantly agreed. It didn't take long for the concoction of rum and coconut milk to rot and begin to stink up the place. It was rancid by the time *Pine Island* reached the so-called Roaring 40s.

Despite due diligence Commander Schwartz hadn't discovered the coconuts during a shipwide check for concealed booze. That was the only fortunate aspect of this miserable affair. Trying to get them on deck, unseen by members of the crew and the officer of the deck, had been difficult.

As *PI* chugged southward, Bill wondered how long it would be until he saw coconuts again.

Shortly after reaching Antarctic waters, *Pine Island* took on fuel from *Canisteo*, and Ensign Litz planted seeds of revenge against his commander.

From his experience he knew that sometimes prior to flight operations men on board "avoided their razors" for a few days and began sporting beards. Learning from Litz that Captain Walker on the *Canisteo* was going to relax prohibitions against beards, the men on *Pine Island* took their cue. There was the very practical reasoning as well that beards kept the face warm against Antarctic windchill, which could be expected to generate frost nip on exposed skin. The men would be on deck in all weather. It seemed reasonable, so the men of *PI* assumed beards would be okay.

Seeing these scraggly beards, Schwartz told his men through the *PI*'s onboard publication, *Pine Knot*, that beards would not be tolerated. Schwartz said *PI* was a fighting ship and not a "beef boat." The men of *Pine Island* would remain clean-shaven. Litz, who had befriended the mailroom clerk aboard ship—a young man who was also from Baltimore—made sure a copy of *Pine Knot* was passed via breeches buoy over to *Canisteo* atop other items and packages in ship-to-ship transfer.

Litz stood on deck and watched through binoculars as a young seaman began reading the publication then handed it to a young officer, who immediately began making his way toward *Canisteo*'s bridge. It wasn't long before Captain Walker himself was shouting over a bullhorn to the *Pine Island*'s bridge, "Hey, Schwartz, so my ship is a beef boat, huh?"

And that wasn't all, apparently. Such a slight toward the commander of a vessel traveling the seven seas was not taken lightly back in 1946. Walker was not quelled by an easy apology until he expressed his displeasure to Caldwell personally, according to Litz.

"I don't recall if it was the same day or the next when the skipper of the *Canisteo*, Dufek, Caldwell, and Schwartz met in Dufek's quarters, and I like to think that Schwartz's navy career ended there. . . ."

SOMEWHERE NORTH OF THE ICE PACK, DECEMBER 23, 1946, 9:30 A.M.   In 1943, the U.S. Navy's hydrographic office produced an in-depth reference guide to Antarctic waters called *Sailing Directions for Antarctica*.[3]

Within the hardbound volume there's a ninety-word glossary of terms used to describe ice in its various states. Some of the words are recognizably Norse or Norse-sounding, such as *tarn*, *firn*, *névé*, and *Bergschrund*. Some, like *nunatak* and *gonga*, are Inuit words for Arctic features. Still others such as *pack ice*, are good old descriptive English.

According to this guide, pack ice is "sea ice which has drifted from its original position in (1) Field Ice (2) Close Pack, (3) Open Pack, and (4) Drift Ice."

At the moment the *Pine Island*, followed by *Canisteo* and shouldered by *Brownson*, was traveling eastward just over the horizon from "close pack," in a kind of area called "loose or open pack." It is comprised of flat, intermittent expanses of floe ice that has cracked loose from the denser pack and drifted northward on the currents.

The men stood on deck, marveling at all of it. The ship was heading south-southeast by now. So it was gradually making the transition between loose pack and close pack, with increasingly thick fields of white approaching from the starboard bow. What was sea and what was ice could be determined from the clouds well over the horizon. Patches of dark blue interrupted by reflected white from the surrounding pack were mirrored in the sky and called "ice blink." The navigators used these signs as a guide.

The task group hadn't yet encountered the fields of looming icebergs, but thicker patches of floe ice were commonplace by this point, as was the eerie phenomenon of the Antarctic twilight. During the austral summer in Antarctica, the sun shines continuously throughout the day. North of the Antarctic Circle it only dips below the southern horizon for a few hours of twilight, when the sky is clear and pastel blues and pinks dominate over the violet blue of the calm waters.

The change in lighting often plays hell on sleep patterns, and the men were told to get used to the feeling that they were going to bed in the middle of the day. It was either that, or they would run the risk of remaining active twenty-four hours a day until exhaustion took them out. Temperatures had descended to about thirty degrees. Foul-weather gear, including fur-lined parkas and winter boots, were broken out of storage.

The only surprise encountered by the ships along the way was the fact that they hadn't found Swain Island, their first rendezvous point, which reportedly was located somewhere along the Antarctic Circle. Task Force 68.3 wrote off the island as nonexistent after searching for it.

This was the first inkling of the problems with charts they were about to encounter. Their charts had placed the island at or near longitude 90 degrees 30 minutes west. Not only were the charts wrong, the tops of icebergs, under shimmering waves of moist, warmer air, rising through cracks in the ice, could appear to be solid landmasses. That could be where those vanishing islands had gone.

They were called ghost islands because having been seen once, they were later missing and were scratched off charts, only to be relocated in the future. Sometimes a cloud on a blurred horizon was enough to complete the optical illusion of land. These ghost islands had made it onto the British charts that the task force was using. They were the most accurate record extant at the time, since the United States had some catching up to do when it came to pioneering hydrographic intelligence below the Antarctic Circle.

Another phenomenon curbed that self-assured sense of dead reckoning these pilots and sailors had developed in the lower latitudes. It was the absence of perspective. Here there were no visible points of reference. Things that appeared to be up close were in fact miles away. There were no buildings on any stretch of jagged shoreline, no houses, no trees to give perspective to all that distance between the ship and the coast; there were just massive extrusions poking through the veil of mist. Men stood on deck for hours, passing strange white objects and debating exact distances. Only the man with his eyes glued to the radar screen on the bridge knew for sure.

The Eastern Group steamed along toward Peter I Island, sighting its first massive iceberg on the morning of Christmas Eve. By afternoon the icebergs were commonplace.

The planes *George 1* and *George 2* had been secured on the aft deck of the *Pine Island*, with *George 3* centered amidships farthest back behind them all, its huge wings still stored inside the hangar. This not only saved space, it also kept the ship in trim, as the men soon discovered. It was impossible to operate otherwise when the periodic swell would roll in, forcing them to move constantly to keep away from icebergs.

Task Group 68.3 had planned to be on station just west of here, before beginning their Christmas celebrations.

The fields of rolling slushy brash and so-called bergy bits (chunks of icebergs, each roughly the size of a house) had become denser, finally giving way to cakes of cracked white lily pads of ice that stretched to the horizon on the south. Here was the northern limit of the ice pack. The dense, eternal field of ice—some chunks as thick as twenty feet above and below the waterline—ran all the way to the continent.

Ice pack is a formidable barrier to ships, especially ships without the protection of a double-skinned U.S. Coast Guard icebreaker blocking their way. The Central Group, which before then had not encountered a similar four-hundred-mile wall blocking them from the Ross Sea, was expected to muscle through the pack ice by using USCG *Northwind*'s reinforced bows and beamy bulk to lead the way.

But the seaplane groups, the western and eastern, had no icebreakers. So, penetrating into pack ice without a blocker bulling the way for them would endanger the crews. To remedy that, two Sikorsky helicopters on board were each seaplane tenders. Ascending aloft, these aerial spotters would find weak passages, or "leads," in the dangerous ice, thus enabling ships to creep closer to shore to begin their air operations still hundreds of miles from the coast. In the case of the Eastern Task Group, the copters would be needed to find a passage to Peter I Island.

Planners in Washington had decided to use Peter I Island as that aerodrome. By 11 A.M. Christmas Day, Captain Dufek was losing ground on the timetable for operations, and also losing patience. The Eastern Task Group commander ordered the crew to prepare one of the Sikorskys. He would look for leads in the pack ice.

Lt. Comdr. Walt Sessums and Dufek took off shortly thereafter in one of the aircraft some of the pilots lovingly referred to as eggbeaters. Caldwell ordered one of the launches over the side to stand by, just in case the eggbeater's blades quit on takeoff or landing. About an hour later Dufek and Sessums reported back to the ship that they were low on fuel and returning as planned. They had located several cracks in the ice pack, but nothing very promising.

But as they approached, the engine quit suddenly. There was no wind, seas had been calm, and temperatures had been favorable. That shows on the film footage: the men are standing comfortably around on deck in jackets and caps. One witness on deck later said that the Sikorsky sounded like it simply "ran out of gas."

Quick-thinking Sessums heeled the eggbeater over and crash-landed her in the smooth water on the starboard side of the *Pine Island*, rather than cracking her up on the forward helicopter deck. As the heart-stopping weight of the water prevented the side doors from opening, and as the water then gushed into the cockpit around Dufek's chest, he calmly said to Sessums, "Well, Walter, what do we do now?" To which Sessums breezily replied, "Use my head, sir," and with that the pilot rammed his head into the glass windshield, smashing a hole just large enough for him and the captain to scramble out of before the helicopter disappeared below the surface of the sea.[4]

They were in the cold brine for less than two minutes when Caldwell's boys dragged them to safety aboard the rearming boats. Sessums suffered a sore head and neck for the remainder of the week. But Christmas celebrations, captured in photographs later in the day, showed Dufek apparently unaffected by his first brush with death. He was to have two more. It is interesting to note that in less than a week from the time the photo was taken, it would be Dufek fighting to save LeBlanc and Caldwell from death.

5

THE *GEORGE 1*'S
LAST FLIGHT: A RIDE THAT
WOULD COST THEM PLENTY

There are strange things done in the midnight sun, by men who moil for gold....

**–Robert W. Service, Bard of Canada, from
"The Cremation of Sam McGee"**

LEEWARD OF "OLD BESSY," 350 MILES NORTH OF ELLSWORTH LAND, BELLINGSHAUSEN SEA, DECEMBER 29, 1946   The Eastern Group was not much closer to Peter I Island than they had been on Christmas Day. Rather than fight the ice southward, Dufek and Caldwell opted to begin air operations from the side of the sheltering iceberg that Aviation Radioman Second Class James H. Robbins nicknamed Old Bessy.

He said something like, "Old Bessy ain't gonna let us go, boys!" This garnered a laugh, and the moniker stuck. When the wind blew from the southeast, Bessy, some fifty feet high, a mile long, and three football fields wide, not only baffled the rolling swells before they reached her wayward boys aboard the tiny ship, she also created a relatively ice-free lake that could allow air operations to proceed on schedule. *Canisteo* and *Brownson* stood off to offer aid and rescue if needed, and waited for further orders.

Exploring one last chance to get free of Bessy before changing plans, Caldwell ordered his crew to fire a shot at her with a forward flak gun. Then he had the ship's whistle blown for ten seconds to see if this would miraculously split her in half where the shell had struck the island of ice. It had no effect.[1]

So the men decided they could make up the distance at a later time and work with Bessy rather than against her. They were well within reach of the continent and the coast of Thurston. But the first two attempts to get started met with dismal results.

George 1 had been hoisted over the side on December 26, only to be hoisted right back up again after a swell sent one of the launch boats into a wing pontoon, damaging it. The following day, as the *George 1* was being repaired with spare parts from *George 3*, *George 2* was lifted by the onboard crane, hauled over the starboard side, and plopped in the water, where it was promptly met by a slow, rolling swell and incoming wandering pack ice and bergs. By the time the airships were securely lashed to the deck again, it was snowing and blowing hard.

The Western Group had lost one of their three PBMs overboard in the "Roaring 40s," which were roaring indeed by the time they encountered them, perhaps a day after the Eastern Group did. *Currituck* rolled thirty degrees on a rogue wave, and the shrouds of one of her three PBMs snapped as it upended and fell off into her wake. Luckily no one died, but a photographer's mate had his leg badly crushed by debris as he filmed the mayhem.[2]

Dufek and company were well aware that the entire operation was getting more expensive than had been predicted. The men of the Eastern Group wanted to get started immediately to ensure the survey's success. Chances were, the weather wasn't going to improve. They would have to take what they could get from Mother Nature and Old Bessy and be the first in the air.

Finally, on December 29, things were looking up, slightly. Weather improved.

With the men's fingers crossed, the *George 1* was again lowered over the side, complete with repair parts scavenged off *George 3*, and fueling began. The flying boats had to be fueled in the water. They would be too heavy to hoist on deck with fuel tanks full.

Lt. Comdr. John Howell had a crew of eight: copilot Dale Mincer, navigator Martin Litz, crew chief and first flight engineer George Mark, second flight engineer William Hills, William Smith and Vernon Hlubeck, first and second radar radiomen, photographer Richard Simpson, and third radioman Phillip Wexford were inside the plane as it was lowered to the surface of the sea. Most of the *Pine Island*'s crew was watching, with several filming and snapping cameramen, sensing that today was the day operations would commence in earnest.[3]

Topping off the tanks took the better part of an hour, at which time they were accustomed to often hearing the dreaded words, "Bad weather is rolling in. We're a no go." After scrubbed missions, fuel had to be dumped and the planes hauled back aboard. It was an agonizing, arduous, and frustrating process that was to be repeated countless times in the shifting waters of the Bellingshausen Sea before Highjump was over.

So, when on this occasion radar showed continued favorable climate to the south, and it appeared finally a flight was not going to be scrubbed, morale aboard ship climbed.

Dufek spoke with Caldwell. He had communicated with Cruzen previously, and they came to the conclusion that all flight crews were considered green in that none of them had flown over Antarctica before; it did not matter how much air time they had put in over Greenland. Dufek and Caldwell both wanted to see how the men performed under pressure and what kind of conditions they would face in the air. This was also to be the first flight of the entire task force, and it was considered very historic. If the first crew was going out into the unknown, then so was their leader, Capt. George Dufek. Caldwell would be in another flight when Dufek's party returned.

Checklists completed, *George 1* took off shortly after 1 P.M. The men on deck cheered and waved as the spent JATO bottles were jettisoned into the sea below the ship. She was finally headed off toward the continent.

Caldwell and Schwartz told the crew of the *George 2* to get ready and wait for word from the *George 1* that clear sky stood between the continent and *Pine Island*. Good news continued to flow back to the ship every fifteen minutes or so.

George 2 was lowered over the side with her crew for fueling. The crew included plane commander Lt. (jg) James Ball, copilot Bob Goff, navigator and second pilot Robert Jones, crew chief and first flight engineer John Shafer, second flight engineer Murray Schmidt, first radio-radarman Milton Blake, Jr., third radio-radarman Jeremiah Riley, and photographer on the trimetrogons James B. Payne.

The crew remained cautiously optimistic until about 6:30 P.M., when Howell's crew reported that conditions were favorable over the continent itself with CAVU (ceiling and visibility unlimited). He gave them the green light.

Soon afterwards, *George 2* took off for the continent with great fanfare. At that point Caldwell waited for Howell and Dufek to return before taking a flight himself.

But by the time Howell turned around after photographing part of the Thurston Coast, he reported that the weather was changing. As they moved eastward, taking their photos, they were buffeted by strong winds and periodic whiteout conditions. Howell and his crew landed and sidled up to the *Pine Island* just as Ball and company began to turn around from their run.

A launch was sent out just after midnight on December 30, 1946, to take Howell's crew back aboard the *Pine Island* after their historic flight. Spirits were high, but Howell urged caution.

According to Kearns, a rolling two-foot swell started pumping in from the south, as fog banks began forming, broken up intermittently by clear air showing stripes of blue.

The news from Ball by 1 A.M. December 30, was not great, but it was not bad enough to scrub the next flight. Ball and his crew were encountering rough air and blizzard bands as they headed back to *Pine Island*.

By this time Dickens had come up to the hanger deck to join his crewmates and offer moral support. It had already been decided that he would not go on Crew 3's first flight. His abscessed tooth had been removed, but the infection in his sinuses and ears remained.

According to Dickens, Lt. Comdr. H. E. "Doc" Williamson, the ship's surgeon and physician, told him that two things could happen to him if he went on the flight. His wound could bleed profusely at high altitude, or his impacted sinuses could prevent his ears from equalizing as he ascended and descended. Either eventuality could force the crew to turn back, unless luck was on his side and nothing happened at all. So Williamson did not explicitly ground him.

The only question was who would replace him. Dickens suggested William Warr. He was more than ready to serve as the crew's flight engineer and crew chief. He knew precisely when and how to switch tanks to keep the plane in trim, Dickens said. He would sit at the flight engineer's post and train a new guy as he went. Fred Williams was a soft-spoken, husky young fellow from Huntingdon, Tennessee. Dickens had worked with him on board ship, making sure the engines were up to snuff during the cruise, and he had found him to be a very competent mechanic. Robbins knew him in passing. Williams had hoped for a ticket aboard one of the big planes. He hadn't thought he'd get another shot at it, and here was his chance.

But shortly after the decision was made, and Williams was suited up, more discouraging news came: conditions weren't improving, and the two-foot swell lapping against the *Pine Island*'s hull earlier had

risen to three feet, with a light chop crinkling its surface. Now icebergs and the bergy bits began a slow, deadly dance, threatening continued operations. Conditions for takeoff were rapidly approaching
borderline, and LeBlanc said as much to Caldwell and Schwartz
within earshot of other pilots.

According to the children of Ralph LeBlanc, who were told the
story often by their father, Crew 3's plane commander was then
goaded by Commander Schwartz by the following remark:

"What the hell are you drawing flight pay for if you're not going
to fly?"

While neither Kearns nor Robbins remembers the remark specifically, they both admit this statement would not have been out of character for Schwartz. If indeed the commander said this, the best
anyone can make of such a statement is that it was meant as a joke, designed to motivate a young pilot. Coming from another aviator, it
might have even done the trick and rolled right off LeBlanc's back like
rainwater.

But Frenchy LeBlanc was not fond of Izzy. He took the remark as
an insult, an order, and a challenge. Schwartz was reminding the crew
that a substantial investment had been made to put the birds in the water. From an operational standpoint the crew was still firing on a "go,
go, go, while the getting is good" mentality. Men were in forward mo-
mentum, locked and loaded.

By this time, nearly 1:30 A.M., plane number 59098, the *George 1*,
was halfway gassed up again. All she needed was a crew, and Crew 3
was on deck. They were asked to step up to the plate.

LeBlanc assembled his crew again and told them he would not order them to go aloft. He was looking for volunteers. It was going to be
"a rough one," he said.

Sensing Dickens wanted to replace Williams again, LeBlanc cut
the crewman off before he could even get the words out of his mouth.

"Dick, you ought to get below. There's nothing you can do here," he said to Dickens. He pointed out that Williams was suited up and ready to fly and despite weather reports seemed excited about the prospect of going, while Dickens was full of medication, had a groggy head, and could scarcely speak in anything but garbled "Southernese" muffled by the cotton balls in his swelled mouth. So, in a decision that would save his life but quietly haunt him for years, J. D. Dickens did just as pilot Frenchy LeBlanc directed him to do: he went below.

He later said, "I knew if I'd a stayed up on deck a second longer, I was going to go. I don't know how it would have turned out."

A fellow photographer, hearing the conversation before the men departed, jokingly asked Chief Photographer's Mate Owen McCarty, "Hey, Mac, can I hold your wallet? Nice knowin' ya."[4] McCarty laughed off the remark at the time, and everyone climbed aboard the launch being roped down to the sea surface.

Just then Captain Caldwell came bounding down the ladder into the launch. He opted to join the crew in the observation dome, so that he could at least get a look at the coast. The way he said it made Kearns think that it was an honor he wanted to share with his children and grandchildren someday—no big deal.

The men made small talk as they headed out to the seaplane together. Once aboard, Caldwell asked what he could do to be useful getting the bird into the air. Captain or no, he said it was a sin to be "dead weight."

Robbins was taken aback by his captain's self-effacing manner. He hesitated for a second, and the captain said, "Can I at least help you lift those? Tell me what to do." Robbins nodded and showed him how to set the JATO bottles in their slots on the waist hatch doors. Without Dickens, who usually helped with this chore, and without Warr, who had taken Williams up to the flight deck and was showing him the ropes at the engineer's post before takeoff, this job—usually reserved for a true ordinance man—was up to radar man Robbins and the skipper of the *Pine Island*.

Caldwell lifted the eighty-pound JATO bottles unaided and held them in place while Robbins secured them into their slots. He had never seen a captain who could do that, and he never would again.

LeBlanc and Kearns began going over their checklist. Hendersin was checking his radio gear, following the last mission, as Lopez went over the navigation charts, picking out the best route to the *G2*'s last reported radio contact with the coast.

As Lopez knew from his two years of training, the gyrocompass would be their lifeline in the Antarctic, where navigation is complicated by the unique conditions at the bottom of the globe.

Magnetic compasses all point toward magnetic north, 180 degrees away from magnetic south. But magnetic north and true, or geographic, north don't coincide. Neither do magnetic south and the South Pole we know on the map. The effect is barely noticeable at mid-latitudes. But when you get near the poles, it plays hell with navigation.

Compound this problem with a mathematical one: as you get closer to either pole, the lines of longitude converge, and the closer you get, the faster they come to one another. Pilots used a combination of techniques in polar navigation, namely the gyrocompass and a grid system, and also an astrocompass to check calculation results. Every fifty to sixty miles southward, the gyrocompass had to be reset to account for the fact that the lines of longitude were converging. The angles of those resets were gained from a grid system that polar aviators laid down on the charts. The grid covered everything inside the Antarctic Circle. Also, at every fifty to sixty miles southward an increasing correction factor had to be added for the magnetic variation. Then the whole mess was dialed into the gyrocompass and checked with an astrocompass when a good bead could be taken on the sun over the horizon (which was next to never in these parts since it was cloudy much of the time).

The process required constant communication between the pilot and the navigator. If the pilot changed course, the navigator had to know heading speed and time immediately so that his calculations jibed with the actual position. Once bearings were lost, there was a mess of logic, angles, deviations, and speeds to sort through, and all the while the aircraft would be moving in the wrong direction. It was dicey and nerve-wracking.

Lopez had just completed training with this navigation system for polar exploration during Operation Nanook, and he had come through knowing his stuff with flying colors, as far as Kearns was concerned. But the problem of having incomplete and totally inaccurate charts was about to compound things for the crew in ways they couldn't yet fathom. And they were about to be introduced into the world of flying without reference points or land features on the ground—sometimes without even a distinguishable horizon.

When the tanks were topped off and all the checks had been made of the systems, Caldwell moved forward to his position in the observation bubble, just forward of the galley. Robbins held the rafters just below and aft of the flight deck in the waist section. His job at takeoff would be to notify the pilot in case anything threatened the ship structurally from below.

Robbins refused to sit until he absolutely had to. The men were all plugged into the common interphone system through a series of wall jacks that could be connected to their headsets. Ridiculously, and rather uncomfortably, Robbins remembered that these and the electric heating elements inside the flight suits plugged into the wall jacks with cords running from the hole in the rear end of the suit.

There were unseen chunks of ice all throughout these waters. If one tore through the hull on takeoff, the pilot needed to know immediately. Robbins would remain below, watching and listening during takeoff. McCarty curled up in a sleeping bag in the tail section after making preparations for his cameras, and plugged in his flight suit and his earphones so he could listen to onboard chatter.

The bigger swells now moving in had the fliers green around the gills as the fuel lines were retracted. LeBlanc gave the coxswain in the nearby launch a thumbs-up through his porthole window. After all the checks had been made, LeBlanc raised his hand to the throttles over the dash and inched her forward into the wind and water. It was immediately clear that the swell in front of her would have to be tamed, so Kearns asked for *Pine Island* to swing around in front of the *George 1* and plow through the rough sea. It took about ten minutes of taxiing to set it up.

Schwartz, with Dufek by his side at the bridge, issued the orders, and the broad side of the massive ship blocked the pilots' view of the sky for a moment. Then, turning into the wind and steaming forward to twenty knots, *Pine Island* cut to port, circling out of the way for the taxiing aircraft.

Even after the seaplane tender had cut most of the big stuff for them, *George 1* slapped and pounded in the ship's wake as though she were being abused. Headphones, calipers, and other gear jumped from desks, along with charts and wax pencils, as the pilots throttled up and she slugged forward.

Suddenly stress seams opened up, and water pulsed inwards along cracks near the waist hatches like jets from a ruptured fire hose. The icy water spilled at Robbins's feet as the bird gained speed. He called his plane commander over the intercom.

"Mr. LeBlanc, can we take all this pounding?"

"She'll take this and much worse, Robbie—don't you worry about a thing. As long as the water doesn't rise above the decking, we'll be fine," said LeBlanc.

Robbins shrugged and held on. Obviously the man knew the limits of his aircraft. But at that moment Kearns and LeBlanc were both fighting with the plane's dual yoke to keep her from burying her nose into oncoming swells. Neither man knew if the ship could take this punishment. Neither had attempted a takeoff in such seas and at these low temperatures.

LeBlanc had more than nine hundred flight hours in this model alone, but he had never attempted a takeoff in these conditions. Could the hull take it? Who knew? He guessed they would all find out soon enough. Within a few seconds the slapping on her underbelly grew gentler as *George 1* rose up on her step and began brushing aside the embrace of the sea.

Full throttle was applied, and the JATO bottles were ignited. As the plane skipped over the last few peaks like a stone skimmed onto the water, LeBlanc pulled her gently into the sky and banked. He had just negotiated the longest and toughest takeoff in his career as a pilot. It was also to be his last.

Robbins gave a sigh of relief as the icy water subsided and flowed out through the scuppers. He slowly made his way to the flight deck as the bird circled *Pine Island*, turned to true south, and climbed to four hundred feet. It was 2:44 A.M.[5]

Hendersin radioed back to the *Pine Island*, reading off the plane's heading as 180 degrees true and zero drift, and also noting wind speed and direction. They were heading directly into the twelve-knot breeze. Visibility was about two miles. The sky was broken up by bands of snow and fog.

At first, things really did seem to be looking up. Perhaps the air would be clearer over the continent, Kearns thought.

Hendersin, Lopez, and LeBlanc began working to code the first messages, giving the airplane's course and speed, and also outside conditions every thirty minutes or so. Every fifteen minutes course was again noted and flashed back to the ship, thereby allowing the ship to track them as they went. Robbins, who reached his post just aft of LeBlanc a minute after takeoff, began hunting for signals.

The men were scheduled to head due south and begin photographing inland when they reached the coast, then head east to link up the images taken by Ball's team.

But by this point it was difficult to climb much higher than eight hundred feet. A ceiling of dense fog began descending on them. They couldn't tell how high it extended. Also, the clouds were thick with moisture. Climbing up above them could result in success, or the plane could ice up and go out of control.

Although they avoided this blanket of clouds, ice began building up on the wings. Deicing boots were working, but they didn't cover the entire wing, not to mention all the other control surfaces which soon assumed the increasing burden. LeBlanc announced that she was answering sluggishly to yoke and rudders.

The engine temperatures for the big Pratt and Whitneys only read as high as two hundred degrees, which was about the lower limit at which they functioned normally, according to Kearns. The fliers had to increase power above eighteen hundred rpm just to keep from descending. Kearns cranked down the cowlings around the engines to retain as much heat as possible.

Outside air temperatures had dropped rapidly by the time they reached their cruising altitude of around six hundred feet. Staying beneath the clouds meant that they could at least cut down on the amount of ice building up on the wings while keeping an eye on the dense ice pack below.

At one point, when they descended to about four hundred feet, Kearns noticed groups of penguins and seals diving into steamy holes and cracks in the ice. It was interesting to see them, but more than a little chilling to remain that close to the sea's surface.

The sun was at a low angle this time of night at this time of year. Kearns and LeBlanc kept looking into space, hunting for clear air.

After an hour of continuous southerly flight, the interior of the *George 1* began to get very chilly. As the crew breathed, their exhalations turned to ice dust, which soon covered everything from instrument dials to navigation charts. It got so cold inside the ship, "your teeth hurt," Kearns would later recall. It was a cold that had power to it—energy in reverse, sucking the life and strength out of the air. Af-

ter a while, it hurt to even breathe deeply. All exertion was to be min-
imized at this point. Every now and again ice would build up on the
propellers; only to be flung off, striking the sides of the ship like rip-
ples of flak, reminding the men of warmer times.

All that broke the crew's silence was the murmuring sound of Warr
explaining the fuel-transfer process to Williams at the flight engineer's
station, but soon even that subsided.

Williams stood up beside Warr, hung close to a rafter with a
gloved hand, and listened. But he must have been fascinated with what
was going on in the windshield of the PBM. Natural curiosity would
have made him cock his eye to the right, through the doorway, and
over the dash, for a peak out at the yellow gray, three-hour dawn.

Periodically Lopez would call out their position. Frenchy would
answer with speed and heading. Kearns would check temperature
gauges, and the final coded report would go through Hendersin, back
to the *Pine Island.*

Sometime before reaching the coast, according to Kearns, Robbins
got up, went down into the galley, and poured a cup of coffee for Captain Caldwell. Robbins does not recall this detail, but Caldwell's observation dome had essentially become a frosty little meat locker with
a frozen glass bubble that he couldn't see out of anymore. Someone on
the flight deck had gone down to check on him. Since they were still
over the vast expanse, it might have been Lopez or Robbins who had
been sent to check on Captain Caldwell.

When Robbins returned to his seat at radar and began hunting for
signals from the coast, LeBlanc asked Kearns to make a check of the
entire aircraft. He also wanted Kearns to review Lopez's work at the
navigation table and make sure he was on target. Kearns unfastened
his seat belt and did just that.

McCarty was awake, bundled in his station, looking out a porthole
at the stern stretching out below and at the broad, flat expanse of ice
between the continent and the icy waters of the Bellingshausen Sea.

McCarty's cameras needed altitude to operate effectively. The crew was scratching just to find a mere one thousand feet of clear air above the pack. They still weren't even over the continent, where average elevations could be six thousand feet above sea level, or more. The way things were going, the mission might turn out to be a bust after all, and McCarty's camera skills would go unused.

Caldwell was in his freezing little dome, drinking coffee, smiling, waiting for things to clear. Kearns later recalled that the captain had a chart out and was attempting to track the progress of the ship on his own by listening in on intercom chatter. He and Kearns exchanged pleasantries as Kearns climbed the ladder back to the flight deck.

Kearns then reported to Lopez's position. The men were headed toward a point of land on Lopez's chart. This point, located on the northwestern tip of Thurston, was called Cape Dart at the time; it is now called Cape Flying Fish, probably, like Cape Dart, after the exploring vessel that claimed to have visited it first.

Thurston was the land on the border between James W. Ellsworth Land to the east and Marie Byrd Land to the west. This area also was known as the Phantom Coast, and in 1946 it had countless other names as well, depending on which charts one consulted.

The name Phantom Coast came from the fact that pack ice and the snowpack covering the land mixed so seamlessly in places, and covered everything so completely that it had been impossible to define with any certainty what was sea, what was island, and what was continent. In 1946, Thurston Island was also called Thurston Peninsula. Cartographers had been completely unaware that an arm of icebound sea ran between Thurston and the Antarctic mainland. It was one of the reasons the men were flying this mission—to sort all this mess out and establish what was what. To the east of Thurston there is an equally icebound collection of islands known as the Fletcher Islands; they bear a striking resemblance to parts of Thurston.

Thurston itself is also divided up by peninsulas jutting northward into the sea, as many as ten of them are attached to the main island. These rounded white peninsulas are ten miles long and are bordered by fjords of solid ice and camouflaged by snow and shelf ice that is two miles wide in places.

Were this area not covered so thoroughly in ice, it would all probably resemble the jagged, rocky coast of Maine. It might even be called charming one day, 6 million or 600 million years in the future, after the continent drifts to warmer climes. But not in 1946. All you could say about it back then was that each one of Thurston's ten white-coated peninsulas could appear, if a pilot approached it at the right angle, to be the northern end of a large landmass, or that it was Cape Dart, or Cape Flying Fish, or "somewhere along the Phantom Coast." Or it could seem like an empty white patch of sky, as indistinguishable from the ice pack as it was from the clouds covering it.

Charts from 1946 were also devoid of detail when it came to the topography of these landmasses, and the latitude and longitude coordinates did not always conveniently cross at the points of reference where they were supposed to cross.

The men were headed toward the intersection of 71 degrees 22 minutes south latitude, 98 degrees 30 minutes west longitude, which was close enough to the Antarctic coast to see Cape Dart due south. They crossed this point as planned—only the first point of land they saw was not Cape Dart, it was the northern end of the Noville Peninsula.

Kearns resumed his seat and said that Lopez's work checked out. He was unaware of anything but that they had hit their mark as far as lines of latitude and longitude were concerned. They were on course. There was no drift, because the wind they encountered came straight on. Tanks were balanced and in trim, so they hadn't slipped from course at all.

He was handed "the con," or the controls. LeBlanc, in Kearns's recollection, "needed to hit the head" momentarily. When he returned to his pilot's seat, he was more than willing to allow Kearns to continue at the controls for a while. He had recently concluded that he had never flown with a better instrument pilot than Kearns, and with fog banks rolling in, that meant the best instrument man should take the controls.[6] Also, LeBlanc needed to code the next position report. And the third reason, but not the least, was that LeBlanc said his arms were tired. The hydraulic pumps, designed for work in the balmy Pacific, were not functioning properly due to the frigid temperatures and required continued strained manhandling of the yoke. Frenchy had been at it for three hours, and he needed a break.

Just after crossing their checkpoint, shortly after 6:10 A.M., the men radioed back the following message to *Pine Island:*

CEILING 600 TO 1000 FEET. SKY COMPLETELY OVERCAST. OBJECTS NOT VISIBLE TWO MILES. SNOW OR SLEET 29.32 INCHES. WIND SOUTH 11 TO 16 KNOTS.[7]

Five minutes later the *George 1* issued its final report, via Aviation Radioman First Class Wendell K. Hendersin:

TRACK REPORT NUMBER 7. TRUE COURSE 180 DEGREES. GROUND SPEED 118 KNOTS AIR SPEED 130 KNOTS. DRIFT ZERO DEGREES.

By this time Kearns had just seen land. He estimated it to be about twelve miles off the port bow. With the fog pressuring them more closely now, Kearns altered course from 180 degrees, due south, to 160 degrees, more southeasterly, placing the point of land to his right so he could watch it from out his starboard windscreen, and leaving pack ice and patches of open water off to port. He also climbed to about one thousand feet as the land approached him diagonally from the starboard bow. He could see a rocky outcrop dead ahead in the distance.[8]

He had taken a bead on it for about a minute when the bottom dropped out of the ceiling and clouds fell on them as they approached land. Robbins, at radar, picked out coastal bergy bits as they approached, but the oblique slanting plain of ice and snow, which sloped smoothly upward toward the southwest, was providing no return signal, therefore no indication of topography beyond the coastline.

This plain of ice, called a névé by explorers, also merged with the low clouds, giving the impression of clear air above the coast. A radio altimeter was reading that the men were still one thousand feet above pack ice, which, at that second, they were—the nearest mountain read more than twenty miles away. Once they crossed land, however, they would be too blind to see how quickly the slope was rising to meet them.

When they crossed the coast, this radio altimeter sent a signal that penetrated the loose snow below. The signal was likely reflected off bedrock and scattered in the layers of ice, giving no information to the airship above.

According to Robbins, at some point just before the crash, he heard LeBlanc over the intercom ask Caldwell if he wanted to pull the plug on the mission, to which Caldwell answered, "It's your ship, Lieutenant." (This meant, "It's your call to make.")

They were trapped in the sky, heading toward God knew what, with no indication of what was in front of them. Visible points of reference had dropped out completely, which was unsettling. This went on for a solid minute. To a man, each held his breath, tried to remain calm, and waited for the weather to clear. Windows continued icing over. Hearts continued to beat.

Kearns's intuition was roiling at this point, and he broke the silence.

"You know, a friend of mine cracked up on a glacier in Greenland last summer flying in soup like this. Let's get the hell out of here."[9]

Frenchy gave him a nod. They agreed to do an about-face retreat to the coast and start down again in clearer air. Kearns dipped the left wing in a shallow banking turn, planning to straighten up on a heading of ninety degrees, then head due north.

But as he turned, the plane was jarred as if by a hard landing.

Lopez screamed, "Pull up! Pull up! Pull up!"

Kearns slammed the throttles forward, Frenchy angled the props for maximum climb, and both men pulled back on the yoke. The *George 1* approached stall speed after a three-second climb in a banking left-hand turn. Leveling out, Kearns looked over at LeBlanc, who had relief written on his Cajun smile. *That* had been close! Whatever they hit, they could now limp back to *Pine Island* and deal with it.

The sound started like a freight train barreling through the fuselage, aft to fore. It felt to Kearns as though someone grabbed him by the seat of the pants and threw him forward like a rag doll. Kearns was popped like a shotgun shell through the disintegrating windshield into a rain of ice, glass, and frigid air. An alarm sounded in his head: *Here I go into the starboard prop.* Three freezing seconds of uncertainty followed.

Hard impact turned things watery blue on a soft layer of snow over a crust of hard-pack. Kearns's head struck something solid as he pitchpoled, cartwheeled, skidded, and somersaulted in an abusive dance down a long, flowing hillside, followed by a sickening metallic thud as the brunt of *George 1* exploded in flames. He was buried headfirst up to his waist in snow.

6   DAY 1 ON THE ICE

"We're all screwed up, Robbie. All screwed up."
–Aviation Machinist's Mate Second Class William G. Warr

LATITUDE 71 DEGREES 33 MINUTES SOUTH, LONGITUDE 98 DE-
GREES 45 MINUTES WEST, DECEMBER 30, 1946, 7:04 A.M.   Bill's
head rang like a hell's dinner bell inflected with the sound of chimes
and the imagined laughter of little children.

That sound was actually the tinny echo of his involuntary moans
and screams; they sounded as if they were reverberating to him down
a long sewer pipe. Just as he realized he himself was making these horrific cries, his vision went purple, gray, and then black again, and he
was facedown in the snow.

His brain had been starting, sputtering, and stalling like an old
Ford for God knew how many minutes. He'd wake up with a bloodied
mouth and a nose sluiced with snow, wipe the gore away, and start
moving around again, giving it another try. Then he'd find he had

passed out again for an unknown period and was a little colder than the last time, slowly freezing to death in a battle for consciousness.

Through this slow and painful reawakening, he asked himself over and over, "Am I the last one left alive?" It was this question that propelled him as he moved his legs through soft snow toward the top of the slope to the wreck. He couldn't really see it at first, but he could hear it, crackling and burning. He could also smell it.

As he caught his breath, sickening bolts and tingles surged through his chest where his cracked ribs bowed inward against his lungs. The pain from vomiting was clarifying. Everything came up to the wafting, sickening smell of aviation fumes pooling around him from above. The fumes cleared as the frigid wind attacked his ice-smeared face. Peripheral vision was gone. The top of the hill was bordered in gray.

When his eyes cleared just enough, he could see that his beloved seaplane was now a soufflé of crumpled metal, flames, and smoke. The *George 1* had blown apart and fallen in three distinct chunks: the combined waist and tail section was there at the top of the hill, and everything forward of the massive wing had broken off and was in flames just over the rise.

Both engines had come off in the explosion, and they had sawed the *George 1* in half through the after portion of the flight deck. He passed the smoldering remains of one of the engines off to his side as ice and snow sluiced down his freezing cheeks with congealing tears. The thought of it all ached. He gulped in the air and willed himself forward, stumbling like a punch-drunk fighter.

Kearns spied two figures silhouetted by rising flames, moving around the aircraft at the low summit. Who were they? The soft snow was deep. Every step was labored. Yards from the wreck Bill went facedown again and lost consciousness for a second or two. Then he scrambled to his feet and kept moving.*

---

*In his account "Antarctic Mayday," and in interviews, Robbins maintains that Kearns had not been blown that far away from the wreck. However, Kearns recalls wafting in

The figures he saw were Robbins and Warr. They seemed in miraculously good shape. They were stunned, bruised, and battered, but fit, strong, and busy searching for other survivors. Kearns acknowledged the men with a breathless nod. Warr, too, had tears in his eyes. Robbins was hunched down, tending to someone lying prone on the ice—someone who was dressed like Fred Williams, but at the same time it wasn't Williams, not at all. It couldn't be. It would take hours to make a man look so horrible, to fake it out like the work of some Hollywood movie technician. His chest and part of his face seemed to have been flayed open by the propeller or other flying debris.

"Robbie, Robbie, Robbie?" the young man asked, through shivers and tears of his own.

Robbins had laid a piece of aluminum deck plating, about seven feet long and two feet wide, down beside him as a windbreak, and then draped him with a parachute.

"It's okay. It's going to be okay," Robbins said.

"We don't know where Captain Caldwell is," Warr said to Kearns.

An eerie moaning came from the crackling cinders of the plane's cockpit. It turned to a high-pitched scream as LeBlanc, still inside, still strapped in, awoke in pooling flames beneath his feet and hands.

"Get me out of here!"

Kearns scrambled inside the twisted remains of the flight deck through the gaping hole where it had been shorn free of the rest of the aircraft. LeBlanc was hanging sideways to his right. His hands and feet were dangling in burning aviation fuel. The flames were licking at his face as he weakly flailed at them, trying to put them out in searing delirium. Kearns tried to get his right arm around LeBlanc to unfasten the snap but couldn't—his shattered right limb hung useless at his side. But he knew he had been followed inside the aircraft.

---

and out of consciousness several times as he climbed the hill. The two accounts can be reconciled since Robbins could have seen him after Kearns had collapsed briefly just a few feet from the wreck.

"Robbie, give me a hand!"

Robbins braced Kearns so he could use his left hand to unfasten the snap. LeBlanc came free in a heap and was partially doused by fuel. Kearns slipped and fell, and Warr and Robbins grabbed hold of LeBlanc and began pulling him. Kearns found his feet again, grabbed hold of LeBlanc with his left hand, and assisted the rest of the way, dragging him into the snow. There was a ring of flame they had to negotiate in order to escape the smoking and melting tunnel. Once free, the men began beating the flames out on LeBlanc's legs, hands, and feet with gloved hands cupping snow.

LeBlanc lay unconscious for a moment, smoldering. He appeared horribly burned. His face, charred and blackened, began swelling up almost immediately. The flight deck was completely gone now. It was burning brightly in a fire that melted the surrounding snow, so that the deck began to sink down into the surface of the hill. A stiff, rising breeze fanned the flames, sending crystals of snow everywhere in blinding little clouds.

As the men finished covering LeBlanc with a parachute that either Warr or Robbins had recovered from the wreckage, the blizzard enveloped the crash site, complete with stinging, wind-driven snow. Kearns looked toward what remained of the waist and tail section and was thankful to see another survivor, McCarty, who sat in a heap between the ripped hole in the plane and one of the engines. A rivulet of drying blood bordered the left side of his vacant gaze.

The waist compartment seemed like as logical a port in this storm as any. There was some shelter there, Kearns thought. He nodded to it. Warr and Robbins were obviously on his wavelength, already preparing to move in that direction.

The men moved LeBlanc up slope toward the after portion of the *George 1*. They ducked and carried him through the shallow opening. It seemed to Kearns that the cold had bitten them deeply in the short distance between the cockpit and the tail section. They fell in a heap for a moment and caught their breath.

A wounded moan told the men LeBlanc was still among the living as they panted and took stock of their situation.

McCarty was coming around too. He pulled himself back inside the waist section and sat, unaware of the huge gash in his scalp, which was bleeding freely.

Warr asked McCarty if he was all right, if he could stand up, and if he was hurt. But the big aviation photographer stared at him wide-eyed and limp, his face lit with surprise and astonishment. He was unable to make a sound.[1]

Robbins and Warr went back outside to check on Williams. He was protected from the wind, but it was obvious that he wasn't going to live much longer. Robbins tried to shake off the horrific images that only he and Warr were privy to up to this moment.

When the crash occurred, Robbins had been bounced around pretty well, but he was amazed to discover that he wasn't really injured. Warr had been thrown clear. At the instant the explosion occurred, Warr had been sitting, and Williams had been standing behind him at the flight engineer's post. Warr had just missed the propellers and had been blown backwards and downslope in the opposite direction from Kearns, outdistancing him by as much as one hundred feet, according to Robbins. But he wasn't seriously injured, and he never lost consciousness.

Warr had scrambled back to the airplane in tears, dreading, as Kearns did, the possibility that he was the only survivor. He found Robbins genuflecting on one knee and holding his head.

"Robbie, we're all screwed up." Warr said. "All screwed up!"[2]

Robbins rose, and the men began searching for others. First came Lopez, apparently kneeling with his back to the men. Robbins reached for him.

"Don't. His head is gone," Warr warned.

A few yards away he discovered Hendersin, who had been cut in half by the propellers. Robbins turned his face from his crewman. Nothing he could do.

Then, of course, they found Williams. There he lay in the snow. Massive wounds had shattered his face and ribs, and his back was broken. If they moved him at all, it might kill him instantly, the men decided. He was also on the leeward side of the tail section, and, thankfully, for now the wind was out of the south, and he was somewhat warm from the fire of the flight deck, which was at its peak.

Robbins bent down and explained that he was not going to leave him. He was going to make Williams as comfortable as possible and find the captain. They were going to look after him. The young Tennessee native seemed to understand, but the pain and confusion must have been horrific, Kearns recalled.

Meanwhile, McCarty was still trying to sort out what had happened, who he was, and how he had wound up in this situation.

"Mac, you're bleeding," Kearns said, looking over to the cameraman for an instant, then back to LeBlanc.

"Mac! You're bleeding."

No effect whatsoever. LeBlanc began moaning in pain. Kearns covered the burns on LeBlanc's face with snow scraped from a hole in the fuselage aft of the starboard waist hatch. Then he leaned back against a bulkhead and passed out for a minute, or ten.

Meanwhile, McCarty was coming around. According to his own account, it had been a terrifying reawakening. He must have seen Kearns there with his head tilted back and his eyes closed, cradling his right arm in obvious pain. There was someone else he knew, draped in a parachute tucked behind him near what remained of the gangway to the tail tunnel section. But where was everybody else?

Were they down somewhere? Yes, obviously they were down somewhere. The plane was in pieces. But where? Not on the ice, not at sea, certainly. For weeks the steady droning and rolling movement of the ship had been so constant, and now, with it gone, solid, stationary earth gave an unmistakably different and unwelcome feeling. A hollow fear crept up inside him like ice water in his veins. The only solid ground they had been near was to be found on Antarctica. They were down on the godforsaken continent itself. They had crashed! It would be an hour more before he fit it all together.

He had been napping, half-asleep and listening to chatter over the intercom, and he remembered Kearns saying, "Let's get the hell out of here."

The explosion had thrown him through the gangway that led between the tunnel and the waist sections. His head had scraped something solid—likely the steel rim on the gangway—as he fell with the plane.

The jagged scar was so deep that when Kearns inspected it, he could see bare skull. The red canyon ran from McCarty's hairline above his left eye all the way back to his cowlick—the most vicious hair-parting job any barber could imagine. But McCarty's keen photographic mind remained intact. He automatically tallied the crushing odds against rescue, and perhaps he knew the score better than anyone. He was trained to operate the trimetrogons and was very good at his job. He knew, photographically, what every minute and second of latitude and longitude translated into in terms of unconquerable space. Better than anyone else, he could look down at a blanket of white and gain a true sense of scale by a mere speck on it, knowing only the altitude above it. Now they had all become part of a speck on that blanket. Would anyone else ever be able to see them? Given his words and actions soon after the crash, he must have doubted it.

He crawled to the hole in the severed fuselage and stared out into the growing blizzard, searching for more answers.

ABOARD *PINE ISLAND*, BELLINGSHAUSEN SEA, 7:30 A.M. Commander Schwartz and Captain Dufek stood on the bridge and weighed their options.

The *George 1* had not been heard from for slightly more than an hour. Schwartz immediately alerted the ship's radio crew to search for all frequencies that might be coming from the airplane. The destroyer *Brownson*, located some two hundred miles to the west, was notified to also be on alert for signals from the *George 1*.

Since the aircraft had reported bad weather near the coast, the possibility that their signals were being blocked could not be discounted.

Ball, whose plane returned to *Pine Island* about an hour and a half after *George 1* took off, and also Howell were questioned by Dufek and Schwartz. The last reported position of the plane placed them on course and on mission, at or near latitude 71 degrees 22 minutes south, longitude 99 degrees 30 minutes west, due north of Thurston.

Both Ball's and Howell's crews had photographed patches of open water in the area, and these could have accommodated the *George 1* if she had been forced down by the weather. So there was reason not to assume the worst just yet.

The men decided not to attempt anything other than broadcasting on all frequencies to the *George 1*, trying to reestablish contact. There was also a slim chance that the plane had merely lost all radio capabilities and would return to the ship on schedule.

Schwartz and Dufek would wait by the clock and by the numbers until the fuel supply of the *George 1* ran out before contacting Admiral Cruzen and the Central Group of the task force.

CRASH SITE, 8 A.M.   When Kearns woke again, he had to reassemble the events of the crash in his mind.

Winds outside the shell of the waist section were howling, and, strangely, there, crouched before him, was Capt. Henry H. Caldwell shivering in his ripped pants while searching through gear recovered from the snow by Robbins and Warr. The ass end of the flight-suit pants had been torn out. It is terrible that physics can render a man ass-exposed a little more than a thousand miles from the South Pole, but that's precisely what had happened. Although he didn't know it, they came to the conclusion that in the explosion Captain Caldwell had been blown backward on impact, then perhaps shot through the thick Plexiglas dome of the observation station like a dud mortar round, or pulled out the side of the disintegrating plane through a jagged breach in the hull. Either scenario explained his injuries and the fact that his pants had been ripped by metal or by exploding, jagged Plexiglas as he was blown out of the airplane. It would explain his chipped and smashed teeth and the gash on his nose, which was also broken. His right ankle was cracked, as were vertebrae in his neck, although he didn't know how severely at that moment.[3] At the time, his neck was growing stiff.

The men found the captain wandering around in the snow in this condition, bleary-eyed and dazed by a head banging and the onset of hypothermia. For a long moment he stood at the perimeter of the wreck site as though studying it, staring into the flames before regaining his senses and coming inside to stave off the cold.

For all that, Caldwell seemed in good condition to Bill and was now working furiously to find something—anything—to wear. He eventually found a spare pair of pants in the emergency supplies. It was a curious turn of events.

Kearns shifted forward in pain and had a feeling that the right quarter of his upper body was disconnected from his left half. Apart from muscle, connective tissue, and his shoulder blade, he was correct. His shoulder socket was dislocated, three of his ribs and his collarbone were cracked, and his right arm was broken in at least three places.

Kearns looked over and saw McCarty writing something on a pad he kept in his flight suit. It was a good-bye letter to his wife, Gloria, Kearns discovered.

When the knowledge of where they were and what had happened finally sunk in, it had come crashing down on Owen McCarty in a huge wave of depression. His despair was so complete, he began to cry to himself. Through sniffles and tears he muttered to himself that he couldn't find his wedding ring. It had either been ripped off his hand, which was jammed and sprained, or he had taken it off for some reason, and now it was gone. He couldn't remember exactly what had happened.

"Now don't you worry, Mac. Don't you worry about a thing," LeBlanc told him. "They'll come and get us out of this mess."[4]

Despite swelling burn wounds all over his face, he had been aware of what was going on around him, and he was giving moral support to McCarty. Bill checked LeBlanc again and wondered how he managed to maintain consciousness, as messed up as he was. Williams was just outside the opening to the fuselage, moaning and asking for Robbins. The men didn't discuss Williams immediately.

Quickly, the healthier men, Warr and Robbins, grabbed what they could, and, working together, they moved through the after portion of the waist section and through the slanted gangway into the tunnel. Temperatures were plummeting. The walls of the fuselage were bitingly cold. The cold seemed to burn and seep through the metal, through the flight suit, and into the skin; it was worse than it had been when they were flying at one hundred knots at one thousand feet. Teeth were chattering nonstop through dusty plumes of exhalation. Everyone sensed that the building storm could spell the death of someone else in the group if they didn't pull together and snuggle in close to conserve heat.

Robbins uncovered three eiderdown sleeping bags from the snow—a welcome surprise. He also covered the exposed ends of the fuselage shell in parachute cloth, to retain some of the heat that they would need to survive through the storm. Kearns and LeBlanc, who apparently were injured the worst, apart from Williams, were each given sleeping bags.

McCarty was given the third by the captain to distract him from his letter writing. Caldwell quietly suggested that McCarty convert his good-bye letter into a diary, a daily log. The captain assured Mc-

Carty that he would do the same. Maybe they could even compare notes as they went along.

"Your plane commander's right, Chief. They're going to come get us out of this," Caldwell said matter-of-factly. And for now that was the end of the discussion about what had happened and where they were.

The men secured themselves in the tunnel section. LeBlanc was closest to the gangway leading to the waist section, followed by Kearns, McCarty, Caldwell, Warr, and Robbins.

Time passed through the fury of the storm. Kearns woke to hear Robbins, now outside the shell of the plane, muttering softly through the wind to Williams, who was crying. Robbins brought the chill of the outside air back into the tunnel with him, balled into the heat pile, and shivered.

But Williams could still be heard calling, "Robbie? Robbie? Help me, Robbie."[5]

The men huddled together inside, but after about a half hour of this, it became almost too much to bear.

Kearns and Robbins kept looking to Caldwell for answers. They never said a word, but their eyes spoke volumes: What are we going to do about him? Can't you see he's dying? Tell us what to do.

Without even knowing it the men had performed what medical professionals and battlefield medics call triage. *Webster's* defines it as "the assignment of degrees of urgency, to decide the order of treatment of wounds, illnesses, etc."

Theoretically, the combatant wounded the worst should receive treatment before those with lesser wounds. That is, up to the point of diminishing returns. Sometimes, especially in a battlefield situation, the wounds are so grave that to attempt treatment is to deny care and sustenance to others who might yet live. Brutally speaking, the man is lost—a casualty before he stops breathing, sometimes before he's even lost consciousness, as was the tragic case with Fred Williams.

Then it becomes an issue of mercy. By now everyone but LeBlanc had looked at the young Tennessee man, and all had the same reaction. There was no way that he was going to live. To move him would be to kill him, so Robbins had tried to make him as comfortable as possible where he lay.

Now they looked for further advice. Kearns tried to remember what had become of the flare gun and his own service revolver in all of this mess, but for the life of him he couldn't; all the while he knew he would never have the guts to end Williams's pain and uncertainty.

"Just give him some kind words, Robbie. That's all you can do for him. Just go give him some kind words," Caldwell said.[6]

Robbins went out in the snow to tend to him again, and then went out a third and a fourth time, risking his own life from the loss of critical body heat during the worst of an Antarctic blizzard.

With all the heart he could muster, Jim Robbins had listened to his cries and tried to offer meaningful encouragement, but at some point even Williams must have seen through it and realized it was over.

No matter what they did at this point, they were being cruel to Fred Williams. If Kearns found his pistol, went outside, and ended what he saw as misery masked as mercy, he was being cruel. If they all let Williams endure in pain and terror for another hour or so, were they being equally or more cruel?

It was a heavy hand fate dealt them all. Especially tricked by the cards was Frederick Warren Williams, who had volunteered at the last minute. He was a young guy from sunny Tennessee who in the space of five hours had managed to ingratiate himself to the tightly knit crew with his courage, ambition, and, finally, a demonstration of superhuman strength and will that kept him alive far longer than expected.

Kearns swallowed his tears, slumped back down next to LeBlanc, and listened, willing the snow and wind to drown out the sounds. No one spoke, but all commiserated silently with the crewman through the thin aluminum skin of the *George 1*.

His cries subsided slowly, growing weaker and calmer. About two and half hours after the crash, Robbins crawled outside again and found that Fred Williams was gone. At the end he had drifted off to sleep, enveloped by the mercifully numbing Antarctic cold.

ABOARD *PINE ISLAND,* 12:45 P.M.   The Mariner *George 1*'s mission flight time had just elapsed.

There was foul weather rolling toward the *Pine Island* and no sign of the missing plane. Men from the remaining flight teams, helicopter jockeys, and the remainder of the crew stood out on deck and milled in the freezing Antarctic snows around the hangar, waiting like stood-up bridegrooms at the altar and scanning the horizon as another spate of gloomy, bad weather began rolling in.

Finally Captain Dufek and Commander Schwartz issued the following message to Task Force 68 commander Rear Adm. Richard Cruzen aboard *Mount Olympus:*

PLANE NUMBER ONE CW AND VOICE CALL GEORGE ONE CAPTAIN CALD-WELL AND FLIGHT CREW THREE OVERDUE SINCE 301945Z (ZULU) X, AC-CORDING TO RESCUE DOCTRINE HAVE MADE PREPARATIONS FOR SEARCH AND RESCUE AS FOLLOWS X PLANE NUMBER TWO STANDING BY FOR FLIGHT AS SOON AS WEATHER PERMITS X PREPARATIONS UNDERWAY TO ASSEMBLE SPARE PBM.[7]

Schwartz considered the option of moving the ship closer toward the continent, but after lengthy discussions with the task-group commander, he decided that this would not be a good idea.

If *George 1* had indeed been forced down and had damaged her radio and perhaps even her radar, and she managed to take to the air again, the natural inclination for her pilot would be to return to the very spot where he had left his mother ship.

The weather was horrible. They were "socked in" with high winds,

the associated uncontrollable swell, and snow flurries. After talking
with Flight Crews 1 and 2, Dufek and Schwartz came up with the following scenarios, described here in their own words:

We reasoned that:

1. The plane encountered bad flying weather and chose to land in the
   open water along the coast and wait for the weather to improve.

2. The plane attempted to climb over the weather, iced up, went out
   of control and crashed.

3. The plane, flying over the continent, began icing, the ceiling kept
   lowering, and the plane was forced to land on the névé. The occu-
   pants in this case could very well be alive, and the radio under-
   standably damaged beyond use.[8]

The first case would of course be the best, but it seemed unlikely.
Hope for that scenario also invited the fear that the men were now exposed, down in an open lake of ice with waves kicking up chunks and
bergs all around them. In the words of Task Group 68.3 leader
George Dufek himself, "We refused to even consider the second case,
and pinned all our hopes on the third."

In retrospect, their hopes turned out to be very close to what had
actually happened.

Nevertheless, Admiral Cruzen issued the following terse reply to
the Eastern Task Group soon after he received word on the *George 1:*

NEGATIVE REPORTS MAY BE DISCONTINUED. I HAVE EVERY CONFIDENCE
IN YOUR ABILITY TO HANDLE THE SITUATION. WE JOIN YOU IN HOPING
FOR A FAVORABLE OUTCOME.[9]

A message like this could seem brutal and heartless. But at that moment Cruzen had more on his plate than he bargained for.

The crew of the *George 1. Back row, standing, left to right:* Chief PhoM Owen McCarty, photographer; Lt. (jg) Bill Kearns, co-pilot; Lt. (jg) Ralph "Frenchy" LeBlanc, pilot and plane commander; Ens. Maxwell Albert Lopez, navigator; ARM 1st Class Wendell Keith Hendersin, radioman. *Front row left to right:* Captain Henry Howard Caldwell (inset), skipper of the USS *Pine Island,* on board as an observer; AMM 1st Class John D. Dickens, crew chief; AMM 2nd Class William G. Warr, flight engineer and second crew chief; James Haskin "Robbie" Robbins, radarman and second radioman; AMM 1st Class Frederick Warren Williams (inset). Dickens was unable to join the crew and was replaced in the flight by Williams, who died in the crash, along with Lopez and Hendersin. Their bodies remain buried at the crash site. OFFICIAL U.S. NAVY PHOTO, COURTESY OF THE RALPH LEBLANC FAMILY COLLECTION

USS *Pine Island* (AV-12) from above, taken by a flying Mariner. The *Pine Island* is the seaplane tender that brought the crews to the Antarctic and whose crew diligently searched for the missing men. OFFICIAL U.S. NAVY PHOTO COURTESY OF THE RALPH LEBLANC FAMILY COLLECTION

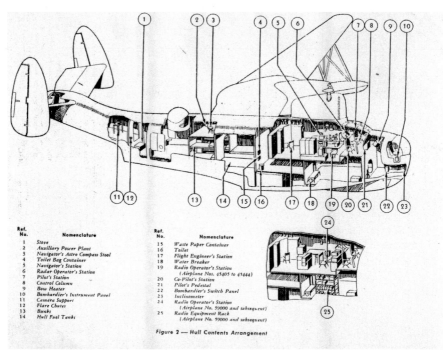

Ref. No.	Nomenclature
1	Stove
2	Auxiliary Power Plant
3	Navigator's Astro Compass Stool
4	Toilet Bag Container
5	Navigator's Station
6	Radar Operator's Station
7	Pilot's Station
8	Control Column
9	Bow Heater
10	Bombardier's Instrument Panel
11	Camera Support
12	Flare Chutes
13	Bunks
14	Hull Fuel Tanks

Ref. No.	Nomenclature
15	Waste Paper Container
16	Toilet
17	Flight Engineer's Station
18	Water Breaker
19	Radio Operator's Station (Airplane Nos. 45405 to 45444)
20	Co-Pilot's Station
21	Pilot's Pedestal
22	Bombardier's Switch Panel
23	Inclinometer
24	Radio Operator's Station (Airplane No. 59000 and subsequent)
25	Radio Equipment Rack (Airplane No. 59000 and subsequent)

Figure 2 — Hull Contents Arrangement

A diagram of the Martin "Ventura" PBM-5 (BUNO's 50900 and later). This is the make of plane that the photographers were using to map the Antarctic. COURTESY OF THE NATIONAL MUSEUM OF NAVAL AVIATION IN PENSACOLA, FLORIDA

George 1 lowered away for her last two flights. OFFICIAL U.S. NAVY PHOTO COURTESY OF THE RALPH LEBLANC FAMILY COLLECTION

George 1 taking off for last flight. Local 0230 December 30, 1946, near Peter I Island. OFFICIAL U.S. NAVY PHOTO COURTESY OF THE JOHN D. DICKENS FAMILY COLLECTION

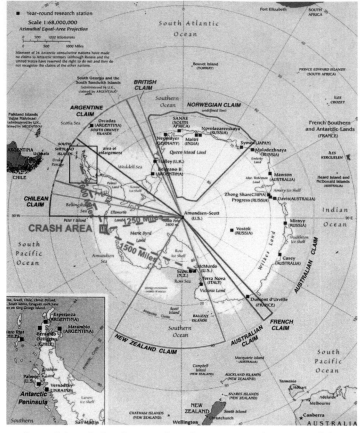

Antarctica and the relative distances from known areas of interest and the crash site.

The bull's-eye is the site of the crash. The *Pine Island* was anchored 350 miles to the north. Thirteen days later, a rescue seaplane from *Pine Island* landed in the area marked "Open Water on Dec. 30, 1946." Survivors then had to walk, drag themselves, and sometimes crawl the distance between the crash site and the rescue seaplane.

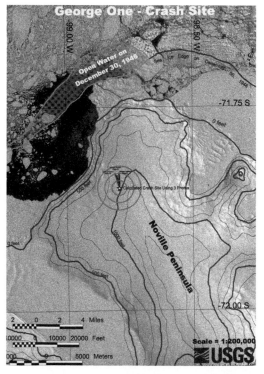

71-30 S 98-45 W 11:11 a.m. Jan. 11, 1947
Crash site as seen from overhead by Crew Two aboard G2. The names of the dead men were painted in yellow primer on the wing. Caldwell is seen with his hand in the air. To his right is Kearns and to his left, near the crumpled tail, is McCarty. Robbins and Warr can be seen carrying LeBlanc to a sled, between Caldwell and the wing section. The men had lived in the waist section during the worst of the blizzard that took them out of the sky. Kearns and a burned and nearly dying LeBlanc remained in the fuselage while others, to give LeBlanc more room, moved into tents on the snowfield over the week.
OFFICIAL U. S. NAVY PHOTO COURTESY OF THE KEARNS FAMILY COLLECTION

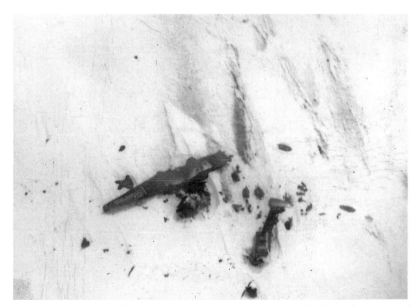

Crash site looking nearly straight down. Note the parachute flap flying loose away from the hole in the tail section. Much of the work, the tent flaps, the tents themselves, one erected as a workshop, the life raft filled with flammable debris as well as numerous incarnations of the antennae to a broken radio that never transmitted, was the result of the furious labor of ARM2 "Robbie" Robbins. OFFICIAL U.S. NAVY PHOTO COURTESY OF THE JOHN D. DICKENS FAMILY COLLECTION

George 1 and entire debris field. Shot could have been taken from *G3*, as lighting has changed and there is a clear departure trail (left side of photo) leading from wreck site to the north. The area of the debris field shows something of the violence of the explosion. OFFICIAL U.S. NAVY PHOTO COURTESY OF THE RALPH LEBLANC FAMILY COLLECTION

Rare oblique shot of the wreck taken from *G2* while the survivors continue to wave and rejoice at being found. Caldwell is on the wing. OFFICIAL U.S. NAVY PHOTO COURTESY OF THE JOHN D. DICKENS FAMILY COLLECTION

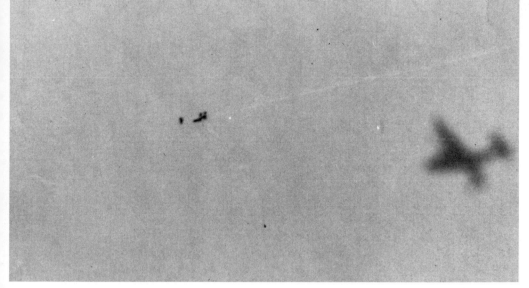

Crew Three walking, at times, crawling, more than ten miles to safety guided from overhead by the Mariner *George 2*, reflected in shadow. Robbins and Warr are towing the sled bearing LeBlanc and supplies. Kearns, McCarty, and Caldwell guide the sled as needed. Antarctica wasn't finished with them yet. Their trek had just begun. They faced crevices, fog, cold, and a thin ice shelf for more than twelve hours before they would reach the place where their rescue seaplane, *George 3*, awaited them. OFFICIAL U.S. NAVY PHOTO COURTESY OF THE KEARNS FAMILY COLLECTION

Kearns and Caldwell exiting the *G3* together. The gaze seems to say it all: "We're going to live. We are definitely going to live." OFFICIAL U.S. NAVY PHOTO COURTESY OF THE KEARNS FAMILY COLLECTION

Pine Island briefing photo shot, January 12, 1947. Seated left to right: Robbins, Kearns, Caldwell, Warr, McCarty speaking with an officer whose back is to the camera. Behind them are the combined flight crews of the eastern task group. Caldwell is speaking; Howell standing to his immediate left. OFFICIAL U.S. NAVY PHOTO COURTESY OF THE KEARNS FAMILY COLLECTION

McCarty, Robbins, Warr, and Kearns in Washington National Airport, February 21, 1947.
OFFICIAL U.S. NAVY PHOTO COURTESY OF THE KEARNS FAMILY COLLECTION

7

DAY 2

TUESDAY, DECEMBER 31, 1946   By the end of business this day, President Harry S. Truman would declare an official conclusion to World War II and to hostile relations between the United States and her former foes. Japan and Germany were welcomed back into the fold of world nations enjoying a spirit of goodwill and benevolence.[1]

The previous week's foreign policy gaffes regarding American intentions in Antarctica could be forgiven for the time being because of Truman's reassuring holiday words of peace. On Friday, Truman and Undersecretary of State Dean Acheson had been called liars by the British in an article posted in the *New York Times*. The British were convinced that the United States was on a land grab, perhaps even a uranium-mining expedition, in territory that arguably had been pioneered, and thus was owned, by Great Britain.[2]

Twenty-nine-year-old navy veteran John F. Kennedy had just completed his first month as an elected official, although he hadn't been sworn in yet. During his November campaign, the U.S. representative-elect from the Eleventh Congressional District of Massachusetts had gotten a lot of political mileage out of his *PT-109* experience, and it had helped him get elected.

New Year's Eve brought thoughts of peace, not only in the White House, where Truman was finishing his proclamation, and in Massachusetts, where voters were snug in their warm homes, staving off winter with eggnog, turkey, and pie, but across the Pacific Ocean as well.

By the close of 1946 the Japanese had ratified a new constitution, which included this hopeful line: "We desire to occupy an honored place in an international society, striving for the preservation of peace, and the banishment of tyranny and slavery, oppression and intolerance for all time from the earth."[3]

And as the world said good-bye to 1946, an invention called the electronic numerical integrator and computer, weighing in at thirty tons and capable of 100,000 computations per second, enjoyed its first year of existence. The huge device filled a whole lab at the University of Pennsylvania, while its inventors, John W. Mauchley and Presper Eckert, tinkered with and perfected it.[4]

It would be more than a decade before the world would see the first artificial satellite launched into space. *Sputnik* would herald the introduction of an age that would combine the powers of satellite mapping and computer-enhanced imaging, rendering photographic images of Antarctica in a matter of minutes, without the need for heroic, death-defying flights to the pole.

CRASH SITE, AROUND 5 P.M.   Throughout much of the last day of 1946, six brokenhearted men slept inside the wrecked fuselage of the Martin PBM-5 while the changes, arguments, and football games taking place in the middle latitudes seemed as far away to them as rescue.

As the winds gusted and blew granulated snow against the sides of the air shell, the men snored, or moaned in pain. Those who had the middle of the heat pile swapped places with those on the outskirts of it, nearest the frigid Antarctic winds.

At some point during what passed for nighttime—a blizzard-filled twilight—LeBlanc fought in delirium to get out of his sleeping bag.

He kept insisting to Kearns, and everyone, that he had to get down to sick bay and see Doc Williamson. McCarty cursed aloud.

"Damn it, Frenchy, can't you see where we are?" Kearns heard this. Robbins, who didn't recall the remark, may have slept through it.[5]

As best he could, Kearns tended to the burned man with a treatment of sulfa medication to fend off infection, and he assured him that everything would be fine. LeBlanc drifted off to merciful sleep again.

At one point Caldwell slithered out of the waist section of the fuselage to retrieve another sleeping bag from the snow.

"That's great, Captain. Now you can be warm too," said McCarty.

Caldwell replied, "It's not so great when you consider where it came from. It had blood all over it."[6]

This remark served to admonish McCarty to watch his own temper when dealing with LeBlanc, and also reminded all of them how serious this was. They weren't on a camping trip. Soon McCarty's wounded pride was nursed by well-deserved sleep. And so it went for hours on end.

During the lapses in snoring, there were moments of frightening silence, as though all the men had just died at once. Kearns was startled awake at one point not by a noise, but by soundlessness.

The blizzard subsided in lengthening pulses of frightening dead calm, during which nothing but the snores of the men could be heard. After those fell in sync, and before they hit their programmed moment of recycling, there was an absolute dearth of sound that made Kearns suspect that some brain injury from the crash had rendered him deaf.

But soon the whisper of snow crystals brushing other snow crystals could be heard, followed by the hissing of flying snow echoing against the hull from the winds outside. The fierce blasts from the south would come rushing down the mountain pass above them, causing the snow to crescendo again until the aluminum airframe was rattling. Dying away after fifteen or twenty minutes, followed by the withering snores, dead silence resounded as harshly as gunfire all over again. The process would start anew. It happened so often, Kearns thought that surely they were being buried slowly in a blanket of snow.

It was during one of these extreme silences that Kearns awoke to find LeBlanc leaning over the gangway and digging his hand down into the snow through a hole in the fuselage. Frenchy had yet to open his eyes. He looked like a blind mummy conjured out of a Boris Karloff movie.

Kearns crawled out through the waist section to answer nature's call. It was quiet again. The mountainside was covered in a chilly fog. He didn't want to look out into the snowfield just yet anyway. To his right, just around the corner on the leeward side of the airframe, was the body of Fred Williams. Lopez was somewhere off to the south in the snow, and near him Hendersin lay dead as well.

The engine stood a few yards away in front of their little hovel. He didn't want to look at it, nor at the forlorn, bent propeller sticking up into the air—another reminder of the deaths of the three men.

Bill's right arm was completely useless. It hung at his side like a crooked stick dangling in a sack of meat. The extreme cold exacerbated the pain he felt in his other bones. When he stood up like this, the pain in his cracked ribs made him dizzy.

He'd tried to remember the last thing Lopez had said to him, but he couldn't. He'd seen him the other day in the chow line and joked about something with him, hadn't he? Lopez had flashed his trademark grin with some wry bit of jest to go with a smart-aleck remark. Without too much effort, Lopez, if he had lived, might have found some source of amusement in their present condition—some basis for a cutting phrase that summed it all up, perfectly and succinctly.

Kearns didn't want to see the body or even be near it. He didn't want to remember Lopez that way. Because that . . . over there off to the side . . . that wasn't Val Lopez.

Kearns didn't know Williams, but he seemed like a nice-enough young guy. Robbie and Dickens knew him. Bill didn't want to think of how they were going to handle this burial detail. That was going to be a tough pill to swallow. He was almost utterly numb for the moment. It was as though he had stepped through a door into a nightmare, and this was it: the smell of death and aviation fuel, all this crumpled metal, gasoline, and oil-saturated snow—all of this mess, which he had helped to create. It gnawed at him, and he had a feeling it would go on doing so until the day he died. There was also the very real possibility that none of them would make it out of here alive. Maybe none of them would survive, he thought, and that would be an even tougher pill.

When he sat back down inside the ship next to his comrades, Robbins and Warr were stirring. The young men were preparing to go back outside and begin scrounging for anything they could find that would be of use.

How long had they slept? No one knew precisely. Some of the men had forgotten to wind their watches at takeoff. But Robbins said it was around 5 P.M. He had wound his watch just before takeoff, and it was still functioning beautifully. He thought he might check what remained of an onboard clock in the center of the cockpit to determine whether his watch was correct. If it was, this meant the men had slept the better part of a day and a half.

Now hunger was creeping into the equation, replacing lethargy and depression. Robbins guessed from the look of the wreck that in the impact the flight deck had been shorn free of the lower portion of the forward section, which not only contained racks of Hendersin's precious radios, but batteries and the galley stuff as well. If he was correct, then perhaps none of this stuff was burned. That meant food. It would involve some digging, but it was well worth the effort.

The captain agreed with Robbins.

"See to it. Good idea!"

Soon he and Warr were donning extra clothing and heading out into the fog, wanting to do their job before the next blizzard rolled through. They found the emergency supply cache. They also found the "Gibson Girl" emergency transmitter and its box-kite antennae. When the weather cleared enough to launch a box-kite antenna, the men could begin transmitting on five hundred kilocycles, using a hand crank to power the signal.

The device looked similar to a coffee grinder, with the exception of a pair of curved handles that allowed some purchase against the tough crank on top if you held the device between your knees. There was also a Morse code key that allowed you to send specific messages. When one cranked the handle without coding a message, the device automatically generated a universal distress signal. At sea that signal carried fifteen miles, just over the horizon. But Robbins said that perhaps, with the creative addition of some batteries, if any could be recovered, and with the antenna, they could boost that distance considerably.

The rest of this cache included a life raft, without paddles for now since they had flown off into the snow in the crash, some fishing gear, alpenstocks, and crampon attachments to be worn over the flight boots. There were 350 cans of emergency flight rations, including canned heat for cooking, Spam, and pemmican in tall paper cones. Robbins said those could be used to make a stew of sorts if he found something to cook on.

When the items had been inventoried, Caldwell asked Kearns where they were, or where he thought they were. Robbins and Warr went off to search the wreck again. Kearns said they were right on course when they became snow-blind, which would put them some-where around Cape Dart.

But from the start Caldwell figured differently.[7] He gravely spread one of the navigation charts over his knees and, using a pencil, began drawing on the chart the changes in course and direction detailed by Kearns and LeBlanc in flight.

Caldwell thought it was entirely possible that they had been blown off course and had crashed far east of Cape Dart, perhaps even as far as the Fletcher Islands. It was a theory he obviously had been nursing throughout the night. Caldwell had been following their flight through the intercom, checking their coordinates during the flight as he sat in the observation bubble.

Kearns was in too much pain to argue with his captain. He merely tried to point out how futile it was to go by the charts, which were as "bare as a baby's ass" when it came to any topographic features, and which were obviously inaccurate when it came to depicting the coast-line in reference to lines of latitude and longitude. The best thing they had going for them was the fact that they had sent back accurate coor-dinates to the *Pine Island*.

The captain wasn't satisfied with this.

"Well, wherever we ended up, Skipper, that cloud sure had a lot of rocks in it," Kearns said. "That cloud sure was full of rocks. . . ." The area was supposed to be clear airspace.[8]

Caldwell asked what was the matter, and Kearns replied that he thought his arm was smashed up pretty badly. Caldwell came over and appraised the young lieutenant's arm, lifting it slightly until a grimace became a moan.

Caldwell said that Kearns's self-diagnosis was more than "a fair as-sessment." The arm looked pretty bad. It was obviously broken. Cald-well also said that it was important to keep it stationary in order not to damage it further. In this weather the swelling and lack of circulation could kill the limb if Kearns exacerbated his injury.

Captain Caldwell helped Kearns take off his flight scarf and make it into a sling so that the arm hung against him, crooked at about a 30-degree angle. It felt better afterwards.

While McCarty and LeBlanc slept, the lieutenant and the Annapolis graduate continued to debate their position. Caldwell pressed Kearns about Mr. Lopez's skills as a navigator. Kearns said while it was true that Ensign Lopez was considered a novice when it came to flying missions, his work in Greenland during Nanook had, according to other pilots, been outstanding. He thought Val was a top-drawer navigator, and he personally had supervised Lopez's work prior to the crash. This also did not immediately impress the skipper.

Kearns said that every 15 minutes the crew sent back a message on continuous wave frequency, detailing speed and heading and conditions. Every 30 minutes another coded message was sent back to the *Pine Island*, giving their true position. They had radioed back not 15 minutes prior to the crash, giving speed, heading, and conditions, and about 30 minutes prior they had given their position.

That meant that when the *Pine Island* went to look for them, they had a starting point that was 30 minutes old. But vectoring in true ground speed along the heading of 180 degrees before trouble began narrowed down the search area.

Caldwell pressed for more details on search patterns. He asked how much area would be covered per search flight, given optimum conditions.

Kearns said that it was somewhere between eighteen and twenty thousand square miles with good weather. Caldwell asked if the last coded message back to *Pine Island* was sent immediately before the crash, and Kearns said no, it had been about ten minutes earlier.

For the moment the exact location of the wreck would remain in doubt. If Caldwell had any further reservations about Kearns's fix on where they were, he didn't immediately voice them.

Kearns could detect something, though—perhaps a hint of blame, was it?—in the captain's tone. It certainly irked Caldwell that they had gone down. Kearns realized that as a good naval officer he could hardly seem pleased that the plane had crashed, but for the life of him he couldn't think of one single thing he could have done to prevent it once the events began cascading for the worse. There was no hint coming from his instruments to tell him where or when he would impact. There was only a vague feeling that they had to escape the cloud bank they found themselves trapped in, and he did the best he could to do just that, taking it stepwise, coolly repeating the turns in reverse, to make it back out to the coast and search for better weather.

Who knows—if he hadn't said, "Let's get the hell out of here" and turned around when he did, all of them might be dead by now. When they became trapped in total whiteout, even his polarizing lenses didn't help resolve what had been clear air and what had been the icy surface of the névé. Frenchy hadn't seen it coming either, and many considered him to be one of the finest pilots and PBM commanders in the navy.

He offered no excuses or apologies to Caldwell, however. He thought Caldwell would consider them an admission of guilt, and he certainly didn't feel guilty. There was no question it was remorse that he was dealing with at the moment. Perhaps they should have avoided the coast altogether, he admitted to himself. Perhaps they should have returned to the ship immediately. Perhaps . . .

Caldwell instinctively picked up on Kearns's doubts and fears about his own performance and modified his fatherly tone gradually from one of interrogatives and admonitions to one of renewed confidence in his lieutenant.

If this was an act, it certainly didn't show. He asked Kearns what he thought Commander Howell would do now. They discussed their predetermined search patterns that were used in the case of a downed aircraft. Kearns felt certain that when they came hunting for them, they would use a standard ladder search pattern. The outside legs of the ladder would be flown 10 miles apart and perhaps 100 miles long, then the rungs would be filled in at 10-mile intervals until chunks of the area in question could be blocked off the map as they were searched.

They had a few variations of the same theme, to be sure. But every pattern would maximize the potential to cover every spot beneath the search area from above at least twice. They knew that clear days over the continent would not always coincide with clear days over the *Pine Island*, which was located 300 miles to the north.

Caldwell said that the seaplane tender had plowed about as far southward through the ice pack as she could go, and without an ice-breaker to bring her farther down, they risked the entire crew if they were to proceed farther southward.

Which still left about 300 miles to cross, one way. The Sikorsky helicopter on the forward flight deck only had a range of about 400 miles, round trip. It would be useless as a rescue plane and would con-tinue to serve only as a spotter, finding the leads in the ice pack to af-ford the seaplane tender closer access to the continent.

The men knew that without *George 1*, there was only one remain-ing operational PBM. The *George 3*, which had donated a few parts for the wing pontoon assembly, would have to be fully restored. Caldwell imagined that the crew was working on that right now but that it would still take about two days to fix and test *George 3* thoroughly enough for a mission.

They would want to search in tandem, staggering their flights to overlap by an hour or so at takeoff and landing.

"How long do you think it will be before someone is actually out looking for us, Skipper?" Kearns asked Caldwell.

"It all depends on the weather, Lieutenant. Without that—without its being favorable both here and there—they can't come looking for us at all."

Caldwell added that to push the limits of flight in poor conditions would only invite another seaplane crash. And while George Dufek was a brave and generous officer, not to mention a fellow academy man, he certainly wasn't about to let another crash take place. It might take two weeks to find a window, or that window might come the day after tomorrow. There was just no way to tell.

Soon McCarty, lying near LeBlanc, could be heard stirring. He was smiling about something—Kearns couldn't see what until Robbins and Warr arrived again, sheltered in the warmth of the fuselage. Robbins informed Kearns that the chief had found his wedding ring. He was so happy about it, he dug out three or four cigars he had been secreting in his flight suit and gave them to Captain Caldwell. The burly skipper took one, returned the rest to McCarty, and told him they should be saved for later use. Then the captain began to make a poultice out of the one he kept. He needed it to cover his chipped and broken teeth.

Robbins and Warr had been busy. As Robbins suspected, the upper portion of the flight deck had burned, but the lower portion had come apart in the explosion prior to hitting the ground, scattering most of the food into the snow near the airplane. All the men had to do was dig around for it. Some of it hadn't frozen completely yet, perhaps owing to the heat from the fire's dying embers.

The upshot of this great news was that on the very last day of 1946, they would each receive an apricot and a half swimming in freezing apricot juice. Robbins also uncovered two one-gallon tubs of peanut butter.

"Robbie, that wasn't part of our rations. Where did you come up with that?" Kearns asked.

Warr explained through shivers that Robbins was not only a pack rat but an expert thief. He had been given the task of outfitting the three PBMs before their flights with basic food supplies and other necessities. He made sure that they were all stocked and then some. A parachute bag accompanied him on just about every trip to the ship's mess. When no one was looking, Robbins and his appetite "liberated" anything and everything not nailed down; thus the huge tubs of peanut butter. For the first time since the crash, everyone had a reason to chuckle.

The men smiled and wished each other happy New Year after passing around two cans of semifrozen apricots. LeBlanc slept on unaware.

Kearns tried to wake Frenchy so that he could take some of the juice, but he wouldn't stir. Bill concluded that the thing his Cajun plane commander needed most at this point was rest.

Outside, the weather was turning worse again. Kearns tried to sleep, but the pain in his shoulder and his ribs kept him awake. He began mentally replaying every second leading up to the crash, trying to find the keyhole that would have allowed them to escape unharmed.

Time and again, the only thing that worked in this scenario was "naval aviation's most ancient and honored maneuver," retreat. They should have turned around before reaching the bad weather, no matter what Izzy or Caldwell or anyone else might have said when they got back on board the ship. They should have turned around.

8

DAY 3

All the king's horses and all the king's men
Couldn't put Humpty together again.

–nursery rhyme

CRASH SITE, WEDNESDAY, JANUARY 1, 1947, 7:00 A.M.   By the morning of the third day on the ice, Frenchy LeBlanc hadn't moved in more than twelve hours—not a good sign. Kearns checked LeBlanc's breathing. The steady rising and falling of his chest were normal, though a little "rattly" from his having lain around all this time.

Bill tried to wake LeBlanc but got no response. Both McCarty and Kearns had scooped up handfuls of ice and applied these to his lips during the night. He slurped thankfully on these meager offerings. Now he wasn't moving at all. Kearns had applied a small amount of the sulfa medication powder that had been stored in the emergency supplies to some of the more vicious burns. But the chances of infection here were not that high. Kearns remembered from some of the material supplied during the onboard lectures that Antarctica was an

93

incredibly clean environment. There were scarcely any bacteria present in the snow or within the water that melted from it since there was no food source for them. There hadn't been for millions of years.

Still, the angry burns on Frenchy's face needed protection from the harsh cold to prevent frostbite. Kearns had given himself over completely to the role of nurse to LeBlanc. In his mind he just wasn't going to let Frenchy die. The man had a fighting chance, and Bill meant to maximize it.

Caldwell had even commented on it before the men turned in. Robbins and Warr would do the scrounging this day, and Kearns would look after LeBlanc, as he had been doing since the plane went down. Something about the way Caldwell said it—something to the effect of, "Lieutenant, you keep taking care of our plane commander, will you?"—made it a standing order upon which all their lives depended.

Kearns had an idea. He opened one of the tubs of peanut butter that Robbins found. The top two inches of the tub contained nothing but peanut oil. Using part of a scarf to at least protect the wounds from the cold, he spread the oil over Frenchy's burns.

Kearns then asked to see McCarty's scalp wound. He spread some of the sulfa powder on this, and McCarty covered the dried gash with his flight cap, which sealed it from the cold.

McCarty slipped into depression again. As Kearns looked over LeBlanc, McCarty skewed into a downbeat ramble about their current status. Like all of them, he had been calculating just where they were and where they weren't in relation to rescue chances.

The *Pine Island* was more than three hundred miles away. There was only one working PBM on *Pine Island*, and the weather outside was miserable, so that even if Ball or Howell could fly over, they probably wouldn't see the wreck. The Central Group of the task force hadn't even reached the continent yet. They were more than one thousand miles to the west-northwest.

McCarty also said he was damned hungry. Kearns tried to put a good spin on it. A healthy appetite meant he was recovering. But Mc-Carty said he certainly didn't feel as if that was the case. His left leg was so swelled that he could barely move it.

Kearns gave up. He couldn't tell whether McCarty was merely complaining about genuine aches and pains or whether the remarks were meant as an indictment, since Kearns had been at the helm when the plane crashed.

Having listened to enough of this, Kearns blurted, "Jesus Christ, Mac. Give it a rest, will ya?" But McCarty kept on.

He thought their prospects looked grim. He thought they would probably die here. The Gibson Girl transmitter had a huge dent in it, for one thing. Anyone with half a clue could see the thing was out of commission. There was no one out looking for them, apparently. They were coming up on three days after the accident, and not a sound had been heard letting them know someone was circling over the clouds and fog.

There wasn't enough food to last the winter, and they hadn't seen the worst of the weather yet.

"One guy, he says to me before we left, 'Mac, it's been nice knowing ya.' Man, I wonder what that guy's thinking now."

Kearns tried to distract McCarty from his maudlin ramblings. He remembered telling McCarty, "This plane sticks out like a sore thumb. It's blue as all hell, and made of metal. It gives off a nice radar reflection. They are going to find us." But it didn't do much good. At that moment Kearns remembered that for some reason McCarty felt that fate had targeted him for extinction. Everything hurt. Things were uncomfortable, and his leg was immobile, swelled up like a Mississippi watermelon.

Later, Robbins, Warr, and Caldwell returned. The three were shivering uncontrollably, but their spirits were obviously high. Robbins and Warr described how they scouted out the snowfield for usable goods and were digging in the snow like badgers with their flight mitts. They found a kerosene stove. They were wondering how they were going to use this since they couldn't find the kerosene, when they found that two of the wing tanks had survived the crash scorched but intact, and full of fuel. Robbins managed to open one of the valves and stick a rag in it. He would siphon off fuel for the Coleman stove later with a section of a hose if he found one suitable for his purposes.

They also found a pressure cooker, a frying pan, and about four loaves of bread to go with all that peanut butter.

They discussed the condition of the wreck itself, as Kearns later recalled. The tail and waist sections were about twenty yards south of the forward portion, which was just a few feet from the wing. The wing was laid out in one piece, with the starboard tip hanging about three or four feet off the ground. Nearby, dug down into the snow, were the remains of the starboard engine.

It was a quiet moment. Caldwell sat down beside Kearns and told him what he observed from the snowfield as he leaned back on the fuselage. In that age-old language of pilots, Caldwell's hands did some of the talking. It looked as though Kearns had clipped the snow ridge to the west. The ridge tended generally west and south. They had landed on the face of it. Given ten or fifteen more feet of airspace, he would have cleared it. The engines sawed into the plane; the wing came off, flipped, and spun. The forward compartment split in half, smashed into the ground, and also spun out on its side, and it looked like the rearward section—the tail and the waist—may have impacted end on and flipped over forward, with McCarty inside.

The cause of the explosion was simple enough. The impact of the initial bump put a hole in the hull tank. Engine exhaust and a few sparks lit the trailing aviation fuel in midair. The fire consumed the spilling "avgas" up to the hole in the tank as the plane rose, and Kearns knew the rest of it.

The delivery was deadpan, but it helped. Caldwell, who said he gained his impressions from looking at all the debris in the snowfield, was essentially stating, one pilot to another, what Kearns already knew: it could have happened to anyone caught in a whiteout. They had been ten or fifteen feet shy of a safe return to the ship.

"Good God," Kearns sighed.

"Try to get some rest, Lieutenant. We're going to make it out of this."

But Kearns's mind continued ruminating on where the other guys had been and what allowed one guy to live and sealed the fate of another. What Caldwell had basically said was that all three men had been killed by the unforgiving arc of the propellers. These had broken free and bitten through the fuselage just forward of the auxiliary power unit, a generator stored behind the flight engineer's panel on its own platform. Only the cold prevented the plane from erupting in an instantaneous explosion. Low temperatures had also saved some of the supplies from being consumed in flames.

In checking what remained of the cockpit, Robbins and Warr came to the realization that LeBlanc probably had a serious concussion in addition to his burns. The throttle column had a considerable kink in it from where Frenchy's head had slammed it on impact. Robbins said that Kearns was lucky that he had been blown out through the windshield. If he had been strapped to his seat, he would have been torn to pieces in the blast. Nothing remained of the copilot's station; where it had been, there was now a huge hole in the flight deck.

Caldwell said that given the fact they had recovered utensils, canned-heat, and stoves, it looked like eating during their "stay on the ice" would not be out of the question, which was great news to everyone. Kearns looked at McCarty and gave him a sly wink as if to say, "Ya see Mac? See?"

However, they would try to stretch out their food supply by rationing the meals to twice a day. In the mornings something would be provided for each man to get him going. The heavy meal would be in the late afternoon or early evening. They could only go out into the blizzard for thirty minutes at a stretch, so, to conserve heat and mark the time, they would stay inside when the weather was down on them. With any luck they would only be here for a few days, he said.[1]

By 8:30 A.M. everyone but Frenchy had been given one can of hot spinach soup, courtesy of Robbins, who had seen to it. The canned heat was in short supply, but it would suffice until they got the stoves working. The Sterno product, a gel made with methyl alcohol, had a low ignition point. Robbins poked holes in the top of a can and with a quick light, voilà, a makeshift stove was born.

Caldwell said that one of the two droppable wing tanks, containing between 150 and 250 gallons of high-octane aviation gas, could really prove a saving grace to them all. The tanks were located in the wing nacelles and connected to the remaining tanks through a hose in the wing. The one they could reach was intact and full. The hull tanks, although armor plated, had burned, which was why the middle section of the plane no longer existed.

Soon thoughts turned to Frenchy again. He hadn't moved since falling asleep last night, and with the crash site fogbound, temperatures were still so low that it hurt to move around. Kearns later guessed that temperatures hovered somewhere around ten degrees below zero outside, and just ten or fifteen above inside: frostbite weather. He remembered the onboard lectures that were conducted after setting off from Balboa. They had been warned that if they found themselves trapped on the ice for any length of time, they should keep stamping their feet and doing other little things to increase circulation and prevent frostbite, which killed the extremities first. Frenchy couldn't do any of these things.

Circulation to the fingertips, tips of the ears, and toes was reduced to conserve heat. This was the body's natural response to the assault by the cold. The remaining fluid in these areas would ice up, further reducing circulation.

When Kearns could, he continued to rub LeBlanc's legs, but he knew this was totally inadequate. Each movement brought moans of pain as the wounds on his face, hands, and back chaffed against his flight suit. He hadn't opened his eyes yet, and McCarty wondered aloud whether LeBlanc was blind from his burns.

"There's no way to tell until he tries opening his eyes," Kearns said.

"Your eyes don't look so hot either, Bill," McCarty added. It was true: the head-banging had caused the whites of Kearns's eyes to fill up with blood. He was a mess.

"Get a load of Robbie over there. His left eye looks worse than mine, I'll bet," Kearns said, and sure enough, it had swelled shut.

Robbins was busy getting the canned heat going again. He looked over at his more senior crewmen and smiled. He knew they were talking about him, but he had no clue what they were saying. He also was oblivious to the fact that one of his eyes looked as though it had been welded shut.

Kearns and McCarty smiled.

"He's tough. He can take it," Kearns said.

When the spinach soup was ready, Kearns and McCarty tried to get LeBlanc to sit up and take some, but he wasn't interested at first. It took some coaxing.

LeBlanc blearily leaned up through moans and groped the air in front of him for his hot cup. Through cracked and blistered lips beneath eyelids glistening with angry burns, he managed to take in some of the broth. Then he asked for water.

Kearns didn't want to give him any more handfuls of snow, which was all that he seemed to want. It caused more harm in the form of frostbite to the lips and tongue than it was worth in fighting off dehydration. Kearns remembered that he had expended more effort getting it down than it had been worth. And after drinking enough of it, you suffered wicked, debilitating cramps.

It took about ten handfuls of snow, melted, to equal one cup of water. Robbins and Warr soon located three four-gallon jugs of water, but they were frozen solid. It would take some time over a hot flame before these began to thaw.

So a cup of water was prepared for LeBlanc, using the snow and the canned heat. Kearns noted that a thin skin of ice formed on the surface of the water within ten minutes. LeBlanc had drifted off to sleep again, but Kearns and McCarty finally coaxed him to sit up and take a drink.

The cracks in his lips bled quite a bit after every sip. It was silly to think he'd be taking solid food anytime soon.

Looking down at his friend, Kearns was amazed that he had lived this long. Indeed, when he took stock of Frenchy's condition following the crash, it seemed as though he were already gone. Kearns tried not to think about what the burns had done to his sunny friend. He had no idea how the doctors would ever repair that handsome face.

He silently recalled a nursery rhyme that seemed cruel but apropos: *"And all the king's horses and all the king's men / Couldn't put Humpty together again."*

Food and drink tended to brighten LeBlanc for a while, but that surge in energy also made him feel pain more acutely. Kearns and Robbins talked about available pain medication. Morphine had been stored in the emergency kit that was lashed to the bulkhead behind the cockpit; it was burned up with whatever bandages had been inside it.

No one had the slightest idea what all that sulfa medication was doing to LeBlanc. Other than Robbins, who had been an Eagle Scout, no one had any survival training. The only formal first aid education Kearns possessed came from what he remembered of the onboard lectures about frostbite and the use of the foul-weather gear. That was about it. They would have to use common sense and a consensus to keep their buddy alive.

Kearns shook his head. Was it even worth it? Were any of them going to live? For a long time Kearns lay back against the bulkhead between the ribs of the fuselage, unable to move much. He envied the healthy men their mobility. They seemed a blur of motion, dragging things in from the snow, heading out again. It gave them purpose.

At 5 P.M. Robbins opened the parachute flap and entered their little shelter with fixings for dinner—cans of spinach soup warmed over canned heat. The meal was rounded off by a dollop of peanut butter on a slice of bread, sluiced down with a cup of water. Frenchy slept on without stirring.[2]

Afterwards, Caldwell, Warr, and Robbins managed to rig the box-kite antenna despite high winds. Then all they could do was hope for the best. The kite sailed aloft into the clearing twilight.

Robbins took a turn cranking on the grinder. A switch on the device allowed it to be set either on automatic, in which case it broadcast a standard SOS, or on manual, which allowed the operator to code in a message. The dent on the box was troubling, but a small diode indicated that at the very least the antenna had picked up the current, so there was hope that the message was being transmitted. Kearns drifted off to sleep with the sound of the device churning in his ears.

9

A LITTLE KNOWLEDGE
IS DANGEROUS, FEAR
IS CONTAGIOUS
DAY 4

CRASH SITE, THURSDAY, JANUARY 2, 1947, 3 A.M.   Kearns woke from a sound sleep to the shotgun silence again.

Beside him Frenchy was stirring fitfully. Kearns knew it was going to get worse. That was the pattern. Any minute now, LeBlanc was going to try to get up and go see Doc Williamson. Bill would have to practically wrestle him to the floor to prevent him from tearing open his wounds. But this time LeBlanc dreamed on peacefully with the pleasant memory of *Pine Island*.

"She's a helluva ship, she is. One helluva ship."

In his mind LeBlanc was back aboard ship. He had said these exact words sometime en route to Panama, weeks ago—this after walking her stem to stern, giving her a thorough once-over, and telling Kearns he thoroughly approved of the big seaplane tender and what she was capable of under power.

Even in delirium LeBlanc was a positive influence; he had good thoughts about things and was keeping a bright perspective.

Kearns looked over at the Gibson Girl through the dim light of the gangway. The rustle of the parachute over the opening told the story: the breeze was rising again. A spoke of light knifed into the fuselage through the rustling parachute cover, bouncing off the accumulated snow, momentarily lighting up that portion of the waist compartment, and illuminating the Gibson Girl as if she were the Holy Grail itself. The fine snow was like diamond dust, reflecting light in brilliant little coronas.

Kearns knew it was a trick. The Gibson Girl was no holy relic. It certainly wasn't capable of any miracles. She had her dents, her scratches, lending a used and abused quality to her girlish figure and letting a guy know she would prove unreliable when it came right down to it.

The fine, powdery Antarctic snow worked its way into everything the way sand worked itself into your bathing suit at the beach. The beach. Hell, any beach in Jersey would be better than this freeze-dried meat locker. Better still, Melbourne Beach, Florida. Yes, that would be nice about now—a little cottage on a sandy strip of road, the rustle of Australian pines in the breeze, and the smell of palmettos after a rain shower.

Bill thought about the people he had left behind back in the States: his sisters Joan and Rosemary. He thought of a lonely young woman in Melbourne, and his last date back in the States with the lovely and blonde Mary Murphy. He wondered if he would see her again. Would he see any of them? What would his father think of their current situation? He'd probably expect young Bill to buck up and find a way to maximize the situation—to make the best of it.

Explorer Robert Falcon Scott's account of his famous polar misadventure— of how he and his men died just eleven miles from an unseen supply depot after losing the race to Amundsen—was widely known. Scott's lack of sled dogs and his inadequate provisions were starkly similar to the *George 1* crew's current situation.

Kearns and his crewmates, like Scott, were sheltered, and they had food just now, but the moment would also come when they would find themselves totally without provisions, and then they would be in precisely the same predicament. Then what? The obvious conclusion was that they would be forced to devour the bodies of their dead comrades. Then what? They would be forced to devour each other as they perished one after the other.

Either that or they could all write a nice note for the families and just give up. Somewhere around in all this mess there was a Colt service revolver with a full clip in it. There was also a shotgun from the emergency cache with a broken stock. Robbins and McCarty had found it in the snow sometime last night, along with six twelve-gauge shells to go with it. Would five shots sound the end to Crew 3? Who would go first? Who would go last?

Bill and his dad were fans of Antarctic and Arctic adventures. They had even had a discussion about Scott before Bill went off to boarding school.

"Dad, what would you do?"

"Well, Bill, I wouldn't sit there and die. I don't think I could be that resigned to it. I'd have to try something, to do something."

Yes, to do something. To make some attempt, even if meant dashing your brains against the wall of futility. Well, at least you would leave a mark on it, so that when your carcass was found, someone, somewhere, would know you gave a rip about life. You hadn't just given up.

Something in the way Captain Caldwell had been behaving these past two days was just so damned admirable that it made you smile. He was not only going to keep on moving forward as a man, he was also going to use the exact same tone of voice, with nods to formality and procedure, that he would have used if he were safely on the bridge of the *Pine Island.* He was going to stow all his personal fears no matter how bleak this situation got. He would be Capt. Henry Howard Caldwell right up to the last moment of his life, right here in front of his men, even if they all were to freeze to death in a few days, or a few hours.

In so doing he was going to teach them all how to behave as sailors, but to what end, why? So that they could carry the lesson into the afterlife, should God himself ask them to serve as standing officers in his navy? *Exactly*, thought Kearns. On the outside chance that happened, precisely right.

Kearns had heard Caldwell cite the renowned British admiral Horatio Nelson just yesterday afternoon with a great beaming grin on his broken face. He had been standing there in ripped pants, a huge gash on his nose, with his hair jutting at furious angles and a two-day beard—a parody of himself in every way. And his education, the fact that he was still an officer through and through, was bursting through the seams of his ragtag appearance.

"As in Nelson's day, boys: 'Every man to his duty. Every man to his duty.' "

All cynical thoughts aside, this act, if it was one, warmed Kearns's heart and brought a smile to his lips as well. It was ludicrous, and marvelously doomed—and just about the most heroic display of courage and manhood he had ever witnessed.

Caldwell was saying, "Yes, let's get on with it. Let's behave in the best tradition of the navy. So we can say when it's all over that this huge mother never got the best of us."

Well, it was a comforting thought that someone was going to set the tone properly. But could a man, who was, after all, just a man, made of yearning flesh and blood, carry it all the way through to the end? Could Caldwell guide them through the time when fanged hatred would flare over a mere crust of bread? Kearns certainly hoped so, because if not, things around here were going to get messy, depressing, and nasty. And he didn't need that.

If he was going to die, along with the rest of them, he wanted things to go smoothly, without a ton of emotional blubbering and babylike whining. Conversely, he certainly didn't want to be in the middle of it if and when all the crewmen turned on each other like some Donner Party family reunion. With broken ribs and a shattered right arm, he was a defenseless combatant and might just be blamed for their predicament when it came down to assigning the proverbial shit end of the stick.

Kearns tried to calm his spinning mind. Certainly there was no need to begin thinking like this just yet. They had enough food to last them awhile, maybe a month. They all had every reason to suspect the Gibson Girl would send a signal. The ship would begin looking for them just as soon as the weather cleared. Long before this little expedition turned into another Donner Party, they would be rescued.

Kearns had never been particularly religious, but the image of a sweet, benevolent Christ, opening his arms and forgiving all his sins, like an umpire calling him safe at home plate, was definitely welcome and needed now.

He could think of the words to the Rosary, but after awhile the mantra lost meaning. He didn't have a Rosary on hand to begin with, and, no offense to the Holy Mother, the prayer seemed poignantly depressing under the circumstances.

"... *now and at the hour of our death, Amen.*"

He searched his religious repertoire for the lines to the Catholic creed, scarcely getting beyond, *"We believe in one God, maker of heaven and earth"* before the horrible images of the last two days stopped him in his mental tracks, forcing him to return to the top again and again. About the only words he could remember from a litany of Sundays came from the Sermon on the Mount. The phrase was attributed to Christ himself.

"Do unto others as you would have them do unto you."

Yes, that worked. In his mind he repeated the words over and over; whatever their significance or pertinence, they would have to suffice as his petition to the Creator for now. He might have been mumbling them as well, but it didn't matter: someone else inside the hull was praying also—praying through tears.

It might have been Warr or McCarty. Heck, it could have been anyone, but whoever it was, there was commiseration and fellowship there. And what was it the man said? *"Wherever two or more gather in my name, there too shall I be."* Kearns kept on until his eyes grew weary from staring above into the darkness, seeking the visage of Christ himself calling them to his awaiting arms, where he held the crew in one hand and the *Pine Island* in the other, slowly merging them as the smile on his face grew.

He was making the image up in his mind as he prayed, but it didn't matter—lapsed Catholics had to make do with what they had. It gave him the idea that he should continue to minister aid to LeBlanc, redoubling his efforts to keep his friend and pilot alive.

He felt that God had spoken to him indirectly, saying that through helping each other the crew helped themselves individually and would survive. He would try to live up to the challenge, if it could be called that, or the bargain that he had just signed with God. Satisfied that he had been heard, Bill Kearns drifted off to sleep as the wind strengthened from the south again.

ABOARD *PINE ISLAND*, 7 A.M.   Without the slightest whimper of a radio signal to support their wildest hopes, the men of the *Pine Island* seemed to know that their shipmates—at least some of them—were alive and in trouble.

Both flight crews were prepared to search for the missing men of the *George 1* with the remaining functional aircraft, *George 2*. They would have fought each other for space aboard ship. Fortunately, the order of rotation placed Howell's crew on alert and Ball's crew on standby, eliminating the need for a tussle over seating.

Early on New Year's Day a thick, soupy fog had descended upon the *Pine Island*, covering the area in low temperatures and low expectations. Despite everything, flight quarters were sounded. The men lowered *George 2* over the side and prepared her for flight. Though the water near the ship was glassy and calm, fog hemmed them in throughout the day.

Dufek and Schwartz decided it would be unwise to risk another crew: on takeoff the plane might smash against the side of an unseen iceberg, or detonate after having its hull ripped open by a jagged chunk lying just beneath the waterline like a submerged mine.

So the PBM was secured to the stern, floating free and aft with a three-hundred-foot rope, waiting for the fog to clear.[1]

The following day, *Pine Island's* radio room and the hangar were jammed with personnel eager to do their jobs and begin searching for their crewmates. From the bridge to the ship's laundry, through all her passageways, everyone, everywhere, felt a sense of urgency that can only be explained as arising from genuine intuition.

But just after 7 A.M. the crews gathered on deck and looked aft in horror: somehow during the night the airplane had swung free of the mooring boats into the side of the *Pine Island*, damaging a wingtip-deicing boot and an aileron. She had to be hoisted back aboard for repairs.

Now neither PBM was functional. The *George 3* sat on the stern with her wings stowed in the hangar and her wing pontoon assembly in pieces. The *George 2*, with its damaged wingtip, was also going nowhere fast. Pilots and crews stalked back to the ready room in disgust, chomping cigarettes and splashing more hot coffee into cups with curses on their lips. Every available machinist was needed now in the rush to get both planes operational before the weather cleared again.

Aviation Machinist's Mate First Class J. D. Dickens would work round the clock on as many shifts as he could endure. With a sense of dread in his heart, Dickens couldn't stop wondering whether or not the fact that he had not been aboard *George 1* played a part in whatever had happened.[2]

In less than forty-eight hours, windows in hardware stores and barbershops all over middle Georgia would display a cutout newsprint photo of Crew 3—including Dickens—lifted from front pages from Atlanta to Macon. The headlines wouldn't deviate too far from the central theme: THOMASTON BOY AMONG FLIERS LOST AND FEARED DEAD ON BYRD EXPEDITION.

These of course would have to be corrected, but only days later when Dickens was able to wire word home and make up for the heartrending news given to his parents and his wife.

CRASH SITE, 8 A.M. The subdued daily routine began again. The last of the canned heat was put to use warming breakfast, which consisted of five apricot halves per man and a cup of water.

Kearns cleared what he thought were tears from his eyes to find that the blood pooled in the whites was slowly seeping out onto his eyelids like the red tears of some miraculous religious icon. He continued to fight the effects of the cold, which rendered him immobile. He couldn't imagine how he had been able to move around so much just after the crash. Now every movement was pure hell and pain.

Everyone was lifted in spirit, though, by the weather, which was clearing for the first time since the crash. Robbins had been out early to check the box-kite antenna. Patches of blue scooted by through a background of rolling gray as winds from the south pushed the last of the fog banks out to sea.

By 10 A.M. Caldwell, Warr, and Robbins, joined now by a recovering McCarty, scrounged to find their polarizing lenses to combat the blazing glare of the Antarctic.

As the sun warmed the area, Caldwell organized the men into a burial detail. McCarty buried Williams near the plane, placing a small flag at his head in a shallow grave near where he died. Caldwell, Robbins, and Warr collected Lopez and Hendersin and buried them also in shallow graves side by side out in the open névé. Meanwhile, Kearns tended to LeBlanc, who was cogent for the moment.

LeBlanc asked Kearns if he had any idea where they were. Bill said he thought that they were on the northern tip of Cape Dart, but that Caldwell might have other opinions. LeBlanc advised Kearns to stick to his guns if he felt strongly about it. Kearns, of all people, knew best where they had come down.

Following the burials, Robbins collected aviation gas to fire up the two stoves they had found. When these were lit, the men began collecting buckets of snow. The idea was to fill the two five-gallon breakers of water. The job seemed endless; snow amazingly did not boil down to much water at all. Bucket after bucket was added to a slowly accumulating pot. Robbins and Warr fought through the morning to gather snow that seemed to evaporate into the pot.

"Ice works better," Kearns said weakly after watching Robbins's slow progress. "Ice. Find ice where you can."

There was a ledge of ice on the wing, and soon Robbins and Warr were breaking this up and carting it back to the stoves. But there was a limited amount of it, and soon they were back at it, scooping up buckets of snow, careful to avoid the divots of yellow snow where they could be seen. By consensus the men agreed to "do their business" downslope of the plane every morning, to avoid confusion hereafter.

Sometime just before noon Kearns clambered out to watch the men working. By now the sun had cleared all fog away from the crash site, and he squirmed back inside the wreckage until he had uncovered his polarizing lenses. Kearns then sat for a moment leaning against the outside of the airplane. The immensity of this place, her blazing glare and glory, were astounding.

They were situated near the end of a long peninsula, on the spine of a snow slope that rose to their southwest toward the tips of three or four mountains in the distance. There was really no way to judge how far away these features were. Besides the absence of sound, Antarctic landforms also had an absence of scale—nothing familiar like trees or buildings by which to reference distances.

The overall hillside sloped downward to the north toward a field of broken sea ice in the blue. There were patches of open water visible just beyond the pack. Over the eastern slope there appeared to be two nunatak-spiked islands sheltered in a protective bay. They were coated with solid ice. In the absence of wind, it was possible to hear massive icebergs periodically smashing into each other in the north, clinking against floe ice as they were carried into each other by the rolling swell. Kearns could listen to the jibes and gripes of Robbins and Warr as they searched through more piles of wreckage, downslope and to the east by more than one hundred yards.

Other than that, the silence felt like mufflers over his ears. It seemed to have weight and viscosity.

Caldwell came by and looked down at his pensive young officer.

"Lieutenant, how are you feeling?"

"This is flying weather, Skipper."

But Caldwell didn't want to raise expectations about immediate rescue just yet. He cautioned Kearns not to boost hopes too high with the younger men. The *Pine Island*'s crew would likely try to get both planes in the air on a perfect day, and they all could see that the thick fog bank they had just suffered was making its way to the north and east, directly toward the *Pine Island*'s last position. About all they could do here was hunker in, prepare for a fight with the elements, crank on the radio, and wait.

"They'll be coming for us. We just have to be here in good shape, and be ready for them when they do."

"What else is on your mind, Lieutenant?"

"Captain, I think we ought to do something special for Robbins and Warr."

"What do you mean?"

"Well, look at them. I feel ashamed that I can't get around. They're doing everything, especially Robbie, sir. We'd be in pretty tough shape right now without him. There should be something, some award or medal. He should know . . ."

Caldwell waved him off. He said Robbins would learn soon enough how invaluable the men considered him. Additionally, Caldwell said he would recommend all three of them, Kearns, Robbins, and Warr, for the Navy Marine Corps Medal. He said it so matter-of-factly, Kearns couldn't believe what he had heard.

"Why, sir? I can't do anything. I can't even move."

Caldwell said that the way the three of them braved the burning fuselage to save Mr. LeBlanc was beyond the call of duty. It was precisely the kind of act for which the medal was intended. Implicit in that heroic act had been the message that all of them—LeBlanc included—had to survive.

Until that point the rescue hadn't entered Kearns's mind. He couldn't speak other than to manage a grateful, "Yes, sir. Thank you."

Caldwell walked over to the airplane wing and lifted himself up on it with surprising agility. Kearns watched him go and listened. The wing would serve in the minds of the young men as the "captain's quarterdeck," the place from which he would direct scrounging efforts. Caldwell immediately recognized it as a place from which he could also search the sky for rescue planes.

When Kearns reentered the fuselage, LeBlanc was awake. He opened his eyes and sighed. "Some fix we're in, Bill," with a charred half smile.

But he could see. His eyes weren't damaged, although one of his eyelids was torn free with crusty burn wounds.

LeBlanc wanted Kearns to take a look at his feet. With great pains Bill removed LeBlanc's foul-weather galoshes and then his leather shoes. He had not worn his regular navy boots. A true "brown shoe" aviator, LeBlanc sometimes complained that the heavy-duty boots gave him less dexterity with the foot controls.[3] But they had been very tight and not much good against the cold. Robbins commented on this earlier as well. It made him mad that Frenchy had done this—the shoes were far too flimsy, he said. His feet were essentially dressed like those of a businessman going down to the bus station in a rain shower.

A pungent odor hit the air immediately. The skin was clammy to the touch, puffy, and gray. The feet were frostbitten. This was not good.

"How are they, Bill?"

He lied at first and said they were fine, but LeBlanc knew better.

"Fine? I can't feel 'em anymore."

"Well, to be honest they're not that great, Frenchy. We'll just have to keep an eye on them," Kearns said.

Kearns decided he would inventory the rest of LeBlanc's body. He discovered that the burns on his back, face, and hands were bad. He was losing weight. The places on his body that weren't black from burns were sallow gray.

But LeBlanc said he was hungry—another first to go along with the fact that he had opened his eyes.

Soon Robbins had heated a can of milk with one of the stoves, and he added a small pad of butter and sugar to make buttermilk. Kearns gently lifted LeBlanc's head as Robbins poured the life-giving mixture down LeBlanc's throat.

NORFOLK, VIRGINIA, 12:48 P.M.   Rear Adm. Richard E. Byrd stood on the bridge of the *Philippine Sea* with her commander, Capt. Delbert Cornwell, as the great ship backed away from the navy yard docks on her maiden operational voyage. In five days or so she would be through the locks at the Panama Canal, finally heading for Antarctic waters.

On her decks were the six R4D aircraft—the brunt of the Central Group's efforts to unlock the mysteries of the Antarctic continent. Byrd had escaped the glaring lights of the press; the first word regarding the loss of the *George 1* would reach stateside news bureaus in less than twelve hours. The navy had managed to convince the press corps aboard *Mount Olympus* not to send word of the downed aircraft back to their media outlets in the States until families could be notified. By the time the news of the downed and missing *George 1* was all over front pages everywhere, Byrd would be more than one hundred miles off North Carolina's Outer Banks, unavailable for comment.[4]

10

ABOARD SHIPS
DAY 5

"Oh, Mother of God, we'll be here all year!"

–Rear Adm. Richard H. Cruzen

ABOARD THE ICEBREAKER *NORTHWIND*, FRIDAY, JANUARY 3, 1947, AROUND 10 A.M.   Fred Sparks, a news correspondent reporting for both the *Boston Globe* and *Collier's Magazine* during the operation, must have been psychic.

As Central Task Group 68.1 slugged through pack ice twelve hundred miles to the west of *Pine Island*, Sparks was tailing after the operational commander of the entire task force, Rear Adm. Richard Cruzen. Wiry and balding, Cruzen was a hard-nosed all-navy veteran of Arctic and Antarctic expeditions. He was tough-minded, practical, and, it was said, not overly fond of reporters and politicians. Sparks obviously had hounded the cigarette-puffing rear admiral for the chat, and he had relented. It should be noted that during this time even Byrd's top science adviser, Dr. Paul Siple, was having trouble communicating with Cruzen.[1] The interview was thus a testimony to Sparks's diligent hounding.

As he sat in a wardroom grilling Cruzen about the fate of the nine men feared dead, Sparks was armed with questions that can only be described as prescient. He and all the other news correspondents had agreed to hold off reporting the story for a day or two, to give the navy enough time to notify next of kin. But Sparks fired his questions as though he were going to issue a radio report immediately, with pinpoint accuracy.

But the admiral, and the more than two thousand other men in the Central Group of four ships and one submarine, had their own survival problems to deal with.

Like any good reporter Sparks was keenly focused in on his story, but a larger one was taking place right under his feet, crashing against the bow, vibrating the ship's bulkheads like a gigantic pod of rabid whales bent on sending the crew to their deaths.

Everyone was in danger. The farther the Central Group steamed into this garden of ice, the more it became apparent that they all could get stuck here, permanently. Yet millions of dollars had been invested in getting Operation Highjump this far, so the danger was going to continue until the mission was accomplished—until this group broke free to the open waters of the Ross Sea and steamed into the Bay of Whales.

The admiral withheld the extent of the danger from the reporter. Obviously the idea was to break it to him slowly over several days. Let him get the message as he watched the action unfold. The immediate truth in one good lump would have sent shivers down the young man's spine. He might have ceased asking questions related to *George 1* and begun asking about his own survival. Sparks's journalistic "what if" checklist would have been a mile long, and Cruzen didn't have the time.

The ice pack blocking the way to the Ross Sea was far worse than even the reports of the Norwegian fishing trawlers familiar with these waters had painted it.

It was unyielding ice—huge tabular chunks capped with snow, some of which were twenty feet thick on top and fifty feet thick below the waterline. The chunks made up a patchwork of white over violet cracks; they stretched into the gray-white horizon like broken puzzle pieces, each five times the size of a football field or larger. It was dawning on the admiral that all this ice could do far more than just hamper the operation—it could actually kill his men.

This perception rings true from the detailed account Sparks would eventually write the following June for *Collier's*. But at that moment Sparks was working on his daily piece for the *Globe*, concentrating on the *George 1*.

As the U.S. Coast Guard icebreaker pushed forward, pressure ridges, formed by hockey rinks cleaved in two, would rise up and batter the bow, sending bolt-shearing thuds and sickening scrapes through the ship again and again. Steel rivets began to "weep" with seawater. So, weary of the reports, Cruzen squawked, "Weeping rivets be damned, we're pushing ahead," over TBS (Turner Broadcasting System) radio.[2]

Daily, Cruzen had the daunting task of launching off the deck of the *Northwind* in a Sikorsky to locate cracks, fissures, and patches of open water that would afford the Central Group a little more yardage. The *Northwind's* six-thousand-ton double hull would run blocker at eight knots through this mess, and the other ships would follow in her wake.

But then eight knots became five, became four, became negative yardage, while the *Northwind* turned around repeatedly to free the *Mount Olympus* or another ship and keep the ice away from vulnerable propellers. And what if *Northwind's* bows began to leak from all this abuse?

What if Capt. Charles W. "Tommy" Thomas cut things too close in all this turnaround and mashed one of the more fragile ships with his icebreaker?

It was anyone's guess how many times he had uttered the exasperated phrase, "Go get her, Tommy!" in the last two days.

While the men of the *George 1* were licking their wounds from their crash, the entire Central Group began fighting for their lives along the 180th meridian east. The ice was winning for the moment, and Cruzen, decked in a duck-billed fishing cap, inhaling cigarette upon cigarette while not swearing to the rafters, obviously knew it.

The *Sennet* was slowly tearing herself to pieces, delaying the perilous passage of all ships through the growing pack ice.

The *Sennet* had to be towed free of crushing ice floes repeatedly, and things were only getting worse. The fear was that *Sennet* would eventually see her bow pushed in, trapping and killing the eighty-five-man crew in the freezing water. When a meeting was convened to discuss abandoning her part in the mission, her commander, Capt. Joseph B. Icenhower, put up a great roar, as did his cocky crew of submariners, all of whom wanted to be a part of the historic journey to Antarctica and have their names permanently etched in naval annals as the first submarine crew to accomplish this outlandish feat.

Nevertheless, a day after Cruzen finished with the reporter, Sparks, he directed Captain Thomas and the *Northwind* to tow the *Sennet* and their skipper, Icy Joe, out of the ice pack completely—a dangerous trek to the open waters near Scott Island, where *Sennet* would then serve as a weather station. Three times the steel tow wire frayed and snapped, threatening to sever arms and legs in its whip as they hauled her away.

That detour also included a dramatic race to return, just as the entire Central Group became hopelessly trapped in the crushing pack ice, like Shakleton's ill-fated *Endurance*.

To trim time getting back to the fleet, Cruzen decided to leave Icy Joe and the *Sennet* not quite out of the woods, but near enough to safety. Later he would return to pull the ship to safety again. It was a call based on the number of lives at stake on either end of this freezing corridor within the ice.

The omens were getting progressively worse. At one point the men of the Central Group spotted a giant fulmar taking flight off the port bow of the *Northwind*. In old naval parlance the bird is called everything in English from "stink pot" to worse. Chilean fishermen refer to it as *gallinazo marino*, meaning sea vulture, which is precisely what it is despite its outsized petrel appearance. It is known to subsist on whale carcasses and baby penguin chicks and is a sometime attacker of floating sailors who haven't been finished off yet by the cold water.[3]

In addition, a strange pinball game of wandering icebergs began soon after the *Northwind* departed with *Sennet* in tow. Underwater currents and winds conspired to move the malevolent bergs around like huge chess pieces, tormenting the mariners with feints and near misses. Then the icebergs seemed to take aim at the ships, which were locked in a temporary safe harbor, just as the admiral and the *Northwind* returned.[4] Cruzen also had the burning worry that his steel hulls were more at risk than Shackleton's wooden *Endurance* had been, because chilled, brittle steel cracks, weeps, and sinks far faster than flexible oak.

At the height of this ice fight, two ships, the *Mount Olympus* and the *Merrick*, reported life-threatening leaks below decks and bergs bearing down on them. *Northwind* arrived just in time to save the day. Dr. Siple deployed teams to test the pack ice and find out whether it would hold the weight of the men and supplies if the crews were forced to abandoned ships. The answer was no.

While in some places the ice could temporarily support the weight of the men and even that of tents, its variable thickness would cause it to roll and crack when longer swells came through from the north. Shackleton's men had to play this chess game for weeks on end, constantly positioning and relocating their tents on floe ice, trying to catch catnaps between moments of terror, and wondering where the next fissure would open with the rolling swell, perhaps swallowing them whole. A repeat of that predicament would court disaster when played out with two thousand men, even though they had supplies for a few days. *Northwind* must not be trapped or become disabled.

The *Currituck*, the seaplane tender of the Western Group, had already reached the waters of the Balleny Islands, about eight hundred miles to the west, followed by two support ships, *Henderson*, a destroyer, and the tanker *Cacapon*. However, they had managed to send two of their PBMs over to aid in the search for clear leads through the ice, which was a godsend, not only for the logistics, but also for the boost in morale the great blue birds engendered.[5]

The Eastern Group was focused entirely on finding the *George 1*, although their efforts were hemmed in by bad weather.

For a while Cruzen surely felt as trapped as Caldwell did, only he had hundreds of sailors looking to him for reassurance, not just five. He had major weight bearing down on him—the bleak notion that by the time Byrd showed up, there could well be a graveyard of dead sailors amid all this ice, added to the men lost from the *George 1* crash.

He must have asked himself what Byrd and navy secretary James Forrestal would say to that news. How would that play out in the media? What would potential enemies think about the U.S. armed forces' state of readiness if the navy couldn't complete this hell-or-high-water act that had been touted for months?

For the moment, and as the gravity of it all descended on him like a lead elephant, he had a dozen reporters within this armada of ships, biting around the edges on this ice issue like nipping dogs, and asking him questions about the fate of the *George 1*.

At that moment of contrived calm, while he tolerated the questions from another scribe, this postwar U.S. Navy must have seemed a very strange animal indeed to Admiral Cruzen. A day earlier, before he gave his interview to Sparks, Cruzen had transferred the command flag from the *Mount Olympus* to the *Northwind* to oversee the operation from the icebreaker's vanguard perspective.

Here was Sparks trailing after him like any good reporter should, asking about the *George 1* again.

In his dramatic narrative for the *Globe*,[6] Sparks faithfully set down the details of his interview with Cruzen, noting the tension in the man's face and other details that enhanced the telling.

> The Rear Admiral is very deliberate: that is his nature. He crushes a cigarette in a butt-filled tray and lights another.
>
> "Not a single break in the weather. We've got two more planes on the *Pine Island*. We'd keep them out searching all the time if we could. We finally got one off today but after a few minutes the weather closed in and it came back." [Actually, the plane never did get off, due to a damaged wingtip.]
>
> Suddenly the ship—the Coast Guard icebreaker *Northwind*—vibrates like an automobile crossing a rough gravel road. The Admiral gets up, looks out of a porthole and says, "I don't like that sound. The ice is not as soft as I had hoped."
>
> He returns to the table and says, "Here's the way I figure it. If the plane landed in open water, they've got a 50-50 chance. If they came down on solid icepack it's better than 50-50. But if they sank in the water or rammed a mountain, and we know there are mountains all about, it's all over."
>
> "Just what was the last message received from the plane, Admiral?"
>
> The Admiral puts down his tortoise shell glasses, leafs through a stack of onion skinned papers, pulls out a pink one and reads:
>
> " 'There is a very low ceiling. Objects not visible at two miles. Snow and sleet. Sky completely overcast.' "

Sparks further related that the admiral thought the airship had likely been forced down by bad weather shortly thereafter. Cruzen told the reporter that the *Pine Island* continued sending hourly weather reports on the chance that the seaplane was merely down temporarily, awaiting a weather change. They might be stuck with a damaged radio that was receiving signals but could no longer transmit.

The ship was also sending out long-wave "beam signals" that might allow the seaplane to home in on the *Pine Island* if they were coming back through bad weather.

But by now both men probably knew this was a false hope.

Just then Lt. Jack Cornish, helicopter pilot, burst in and told the admiral the helicopter was ready for another mission over the pack ice. Sparks recorded the intrusion in his news story.

> "Now one more thing admiral, one more thing before you go. If they're on water or icepack they can be rescued by plane or ship . . . but if they're spotted on land, what then?"
>
> "They've got enough supplies for 30 days and we'll keep them supplied by air."
>
> The Admiral starts to don his foul-weather flying gear and takes another look out of the porthole at the pack ice.
>
> "If the men are spotted on a mountainside we'll put a dog team in the rescue plane."
>
> "And if they're on land and someone is hurt, then what, Admiral?"
>
> "We'll parachute doctors and medical stuff to them," he replies.

Sparks faithfully records the admiral leaving the room, descending a ladder, and hopping aboard a helicopter, its rotors primed and whirring in anticipation of another trip over the white expanse of ice beneath a gray, sullen sky. With as much detail and drama as the reporter lent to the story, we can even imagine Sparks watching the admiral leave—Cruzen glancing back through the helicopter's windshield as he straps in swearing under his breath about reporters who never let up. The helicopter lifted off the fantail of the *Northwind* and retreated into the sky.

Later, after ninety-six hours of vigilant duty, followed by a brief nap, Cruzen would learn that his son, Nathaniel, had died in a tragic hunting accident back in the States at the very moment he was fighting on three fronts to save the lives of men attached to Operation Highjump.[7]

181 COMMONWEALTH AVENUE, BOSTON, MASSACHUSETTS, NOON   The reporters were camped out in front of his two-story walk-up before he got to the steps. Apparently they had been waiting there in the cold, anticipating his return home for lunch.

William H. Kearns, Sr., had been given the news by office mates at the U.S. Maritime Administration who had heard the first radio dispatches. "A Boston maritime engineer's son is among nine fliers missing at the South Pole."

Kearns let the men into his home. He wasn't despondent, just a little surprised and anxious for a greater level of detail than he had received thus far. He got a lot of the information from the reporter and the cameraman as he unlocked the door. A Western Union telegram had been sent, but it had arrived at an old address for William Junior, at the home of his godmother, Ms. Kathryn Murray, schoolteacher at Lawrence High. The men had searched there too. She had informed them where to find the elder Kearns.

William Senior spoke with the newshounds from the Boston daily paper, telling them that he thought there was every reason to remain optimistic. Bill had spent more than a year working in the jungles of Panama before going off to war, the elder Kearns said. He helped train young fliers from Chile and other Latin American nations at Corpus Christi before volunteering to learn how to fly PBMs in the Arctic, where he performed with distinction as one of the youngest pilots to fly the Northwest Passage Route.

He spread on a table a chart detailing Antarctica; Bill's crossing, and the progress of the *Pine Island* from the time the ship left Norfolk, were sketched in red marker. The photographer snapped a shot of the senior Kearns, his pen positioned just of shore of Thurston on the chart.

Later, William contacted the Boston offices of Rep. John W. McCormack about the address mix-up that kept him from receiving word immediately. He asked the congressman for some assistance. McCormack requested that the navy department contact him personally should they hear anything regarding his constituent's son. The following day McCormack forwarded a telegram he received from then vice admiral Louis Denfeld, chief of navy personnel, telling McCormack and Kearns that everything possible was being done to find all the missing fliers.

In the Newport, Rhode Island, home of CPO Maximo Lopez, another quiet vigil began with the first Western Union notifications, which were followed by the newspaper reporters and photographers. Mrs. Lopez and her fourteen-year-old son, Richard, were told of the plane's disappearance.[8]

The waiting also began all over the nation. Denfeld sent personal telegrams to each of the families, acknowledging their concern and reassuring them that the navy was hunting for the fliers. News bureaus everywhere were picking up the story.

CRASH SITE, 11 A.M.   Kearns crawled out of the black and blue hulk of the airplane to find that the outside air temperature was actually warmer than the inside—above freezing, possibly even approaching thirty-five degrees. After what they had been through, it felt like a day at the beach.

Robbins had been working all morning on an idea to get some of the radios functioning again. They had found that some of the gear was salvageable. However, he needed to find the batteries, which were on the racks below the flight deck. They could be very deep in the snow.

Kearns sat down next to Robbins on the airplane wing and listened to the young Californian chatter away. God, how he envied the man's energy.

In addition to his efforts at marshalling the ice-melting—which he all but gave up on because once you filled the four-and-a-half-gallon breaker with water that you labored so hard to melt from snow, the low evening temperatures turned it to ice all over again—Robbins and Warr had also strung a wire from the tail section to a high point on the wing. The box kite had blown off in the breeze last night, but they needed something more permanent now anyway. He rigged the kite so that anyone could sit inside the after portion of the *George 1* and, protected from the elements, crank away on the Gibson Girl, and, if the damned thing was working at all, it would transmit about as far as it could be expected to transmit, whether there was wind to hold a box kite up or not.

Caldwell and McCarty said with reserved confidence that perhaps today they would see a seaplane searching for them; meanwhile, the men busied themselves laying pieces of the fuselage and radar reflectors all over the snowfield strategically, in a spider's web of metal so that an approaching plane sending out a radar wave in a long pulse would pick up a strong reflection. The crosshairs of his target of course centered on the wreck.

Robbins lay back on the warming airplane wing and relaxed for a moment.

The weather was astoundingly beautiful. There was so much light blasting off the icy névé that it felt, at least to the eyes, like they were sitting on the sun. The air was dry, and, for the moment, there wasn't the least breath of wind. Kearns recalled how the construction crews would sit around like this in Panama just after lunch, staring off into the jungle with the sound of cicadas and canopy larks providing background music to their weary daydreams.

The only relief from the present glare came from the icebergs bobbing in the distance, surrounded by patches of royal blue and a light, bright blue where the ice was thin. In the distance it was CAVU all the way out to sea, which meant the men on the *Pine Island* could probably send up a plane.

Robbins was quiet and reflective for the first time since Kearns had met him. He stared out to sea at the tabular white bergs and chunks of ice playing bumper cars in the bay in the distance.

Kearns suspected that Robbins was thinking about his family or loved ones. Perhaps he was remembering a girl, or even delving into the great mysteries of the universe. Why had fate spared them? To what end?

"What are you thinking about, Robbie?"

"Enough scotch to go with all that ice."

It hurt terribly to laugh, but a loud, booming bellow sounded out across the névé just the same. Caldwell, Warr, and McCarty lifted their heads from their chores. Robbins turned to Kearns with an innocent and surprised smile. He hadn't meant to be funny. It just seemed so obvious. Hadn't everyone been pondering the same thought all morning long?

Kearns realized that was pure Jim Robbins. Even in his wildest fantasies he was dealing with the tangible, the here and now. Kearns tilted his head and looked out across the ice, viewing everything now from a different perspective—from a Jim Robbins perspective.

"It would take about that much, wouldn't it?"

"To what?"

"Well, if they don't find us, I'd rather drown in scotch than the alternative, wouldn't you?"

"Now no one ever got out of a fix thinking like that, Lieutenant. C'mon now, captain's right. They'll find us."

"You're right, Robbie. You're right."

Soon McCarty wandered up to the men. He had found an additional sleeping bag and three two-man pup tents. McCarty said that if the weather held, and the plane didn't come today, the tents could be used. It felt warm enough when the wind was off them. If the wind came up, they could always crawl back inside the tail section.

Robbins said that one of the tents could be used as a shield for him as he worked on the radio gear. Warr and Robbins decided immediately that they would bunk together. McCarty asked the captain if he could bunk with him, and Caldwell said yes. The men got to work laying out the tents and setting up the stakes.

With break time over, Kearns shuffled on back to the tail section. LeBlanc was very thirsty. Bill spent the better part of an hour with LeBlanc, helping him to take water and the buttermilk concoction that Robbins had come up with.

Bill told Frenchy that he was going to remove his shoes again to increase the circulation in his feet. Every movement was sheer agony for the pilot. The feet were now very gray and puffy.

"Still bad?" Frenchy managed.

"We'll look after you, Frenchy. Just try and relax," Bill replied.

LeBlanc said he didn't mind lying here all this time, it was just that there wasn't any music. If he could hear some music, it would make things tolerable.

"It's just so damned quiet, Bill." LeBlanc said. "You sure my ears aren't gone bad?"

"No. It's quiet here, real quiet."

Kearns thought about it. If the silence was deafening to him, a young guy who had spent a lot of time alone as a child and had whiled those hours away reading adventure stories, what must that same silence be like for LeBlanc? The guy carried a whirlwind of conversation wherever he went. If there wasn't a conversation in a room, he would start one, or tell a joke. If the joke that someone else had started was particularly lame, LeBlanc would laugh at it anyway.

———

ABOARD USS *BROWNSON*, 4:00 P.M.   According to operation reports Comdr. Harry Gimber had been ordered to serve as a weather station for the Eastern Task Group some 200 miles west of *Pine Island*. He would be their outpost, letting air operations know when a window of opportunity was approaching.

But once it was evident that there would be a significant delay repairing the planes, Gimber sprang into action. Without the aid of an icebreaker to pave the way for him, Gimber steamed into the ice pack, cutting his own path with the ship's thin-skinned bow as he went. He and his hearty crew would wager their very lives in order to provide the *Pine Island* with a contingency plan should it prove impossible to get the PBMs into the air.

The idea was to provide a stopover point for helicopter flights en route to the continent by building a temporary wooden platform for a single Sikorsky to land on. If he could get the *Brownson* within 150 miles of Thurston, this would enable a helicopter to take off from *Pine Island*, land on his deck and refuel, then take off again for Antarctica.

Nothing in the mission report of Task Group 68.3 shows that Gimber was specifically ordered into the ice pack. And nowhere does the report show that Captain Dufek ordered him not to proceed, either.

Gimber was acting on his own, with the wholehearted support of his crew. Strangely enough, there wasn't a shred of evidence to indicate that the risk was warranted as Gimber set out toward his mark. At the very least, the gallant gesture put the pressure back on *Pine Island*.

CRASH SITE, 9:30 P.M.   The twilight sun was playing some amazing tricks on the eyes. With the sun lower on the horizon, the field of blazing white from earlier in the day became a cool blue. The strip of open water to their north was converted into a stripe of violet surrounding the icebergs, which gleamed brilliantly in the slanting sun.

There still wasn't the least breath of wind, and it appeared as though there were no clouds to seaward either.

Caldwell and Robbins took turns hand-cranking on the Gibson Girl following the evening meal, for which Robbins pulled out all the stops.

Robbins made a tasty stew with a healthy portion of their last fresh vegetables. For the meat he added the men's first taste of the pemmican, so that they would become accustomed to the flavor. Caldwell said they might have to eat it soon as a survival staple, so they might as well get used to it.

Someone asked Robbins how he became such an expert cook, and he said it was because he was frequently tapped for cooking duties during Nanook. He had learned to make do so well, the crew referred to him as Cook. A lump of sugar, a stick of butter, a can of milk, some onions, and there was no end to what you could accomplish.

With the bitter, dry air cooling their nighttime world, they were all grateful for the pot of stew. After grinding on the Gibson Girl, Caldwell slumped back down next to the fuselage and pondered things while Robbins took a spin.

He seemed to be lost in thought, his mind balancing everything from LeBlanc's condition to the daily rations and how long they would hold out, on down to the last thing Robbins had said.

But something seemed amiss. Something was wrong. Kearns sensed what Caldwell was thinking. They had done everything and then some. They had followed the procedure of rational beings who wanted to be rescued. They had found shelter, conserved their food; they had tried to make themselves more visible. They had all prayed for good weather, and here that favorable weather was, holding for the better part of two days. They had maximized every factor in their favor without receiving the slightest reward from fate.

With all this open sky above them, it seemed inconceivable that they hadn't seen an airplane today searching for them off to the north.

They hadn't even heard one. When Robbins sat down again, Caldwell brushed the clouds of doubt from his brow, got up, and began cranking on the transmitter again. Then he stopped dead.

His face said it all to Bill. Was it better to be quiet and listen for a while? Or was it better to be active and generate a signal? Slowly he began collecting his coat and other gear in preparation for bedding down. Warr and McCarty followed him out into the twilight.

Kearns helped LeBlanc take some of the life-giving stew as Robbins cleaned up after the evening meal. Kearns settled in beside his friend and Robbins wandered off to his tent, and it wasn't long before Kearns could hear Robbins and Warr talking about what they were going to be doing when they got back stateside. High on that list were their favorite foods.

A groan could be heard from McCarty as their ideal desserts grew, dollop by caramel and chocolate dollop, until they reached the priceless cherry, floating in its own pool of chocolate syrup.

Surrounded by all this ice, all they could think about was ice cream. Of course, they began to covet its powdery white essence. They had been looking at it all day, and like Robbins regarding the brash and growlers in the distance and thinking immediately of a nice stiff drink, a young kid who had viewed that field of white all day long naturally thought of chocolate syrup, powdered sugar, and other confections to go along with it.

The field of snow became something to eat. It was the same thing men endured when marooned at sea: one of life's cruel ironies. "All this water, and none to drink."

It was no wonder that Robbins kept coming up with all these creative ideas involving peanut butter, snow cones, and sugar.

There were also the mathematics and mechanics of shivering at work. Your body had to shiver to generate heat. In so doing, it consumed every last shred of energy brought to it from food. Fat stores went first. Then, if a body did not find a way to replace the lost energy in the form of increased food, it began to consume itself. Even the energy to keep moving or shiver would soon be hard to find.

Caldwell mentioned something about this earlier; he had read some of the survival material supplied and come away with the impression that the human body, apart from its unquenchable thirst at the South Pole, was also in a life-and-death caloric race as long as it remained exposed to low temperatures. This while telling the men it was okay to eat a "dollop or two," of peanut butter and some of the candies they had found amid emergency supplies. That was what it was there for—little bursts of energy that kept the fires going. There was no point saving it for a later time when a body was so done in; it wouldn't do the slightest bit of good anyway.

"A roaring fire is easier to sustain with kindling than with a spark," he said.

He said the human body burned more than four thousand and some odd calories per day while engaged in strenuous work like hiking or scrounging around an icy hillside. But it could also burn an equal amount in the act of shivering. Compound the situation by adding cold temperatures on top of work that had to be done for the sake of salvation, and what happens? If the body did not ingest at least two thousand or more calories per day, the race was over. No approach will subvert the brute equation. Eventually, without calories to stoke internal fires, there will come a time when you will be irretrievable, even if someone does find you.

Kearns could see analogous math in some of his flight-training manuals. If your angle of approach was too steep and too fast, there was a point along the glide slope at which even full throttle wasn't going to save you from impact. All you could do was watch as it happened. If you sat and thought long enough, you could plot it out.

Witness Robert Falcon Scott and his men, too weary to continue after hundreds of miles of trekking, resigning themselves to death eleven miles from a supply depot. This was one of the reasons Scott and his party simply could not go on: their bodies had lost the race by the time they reached their final resting place. Then, hemmed in by cold, they simply went to sleep, having at least chosen their ground, if not the calm, dignified method of their passing.

Kearns looked over at LeBlanc and wondered where his plane commander was on his own personal glide slope. How close was he to that point of no return? The man who needed food the most had eaten the least.

It was a very good sign that everyone else still possessed healthy appetites. Even better, they maintained a sense of humor. But something in one glance Kearns had seen, one glimmer of doubt in his captain's eye, made him wonder.

Kearns vowed to be more energetic the following day and add more to the communal pot of energy. Like Caldwell he would smother any fears he had and put a good face on things for the sake of the group. If that meant spending more time outside the airplane, he would explain it to Frenchy. He of all people would understand.

And something else was taking over. This entire situation, this tiptoeing around and being afraid of death, was really beginning to piss him off.

If death were another guy he could chat with, Kearns was beginning to feel like he would grab hold of him and beat the living shit out of him, then stick a rusty oyster fork in his eye for good measure.

Deep down in his bones, he began to tell himself he would buck the odds. *God damn it all, I am just not going to die here. I flat refuse.*

11

SKUAS
DAY 6

CRASH SITE, SATURDAY, JANUARY 4, 1947, 6:00 A.M. The dag-
gers of angry noise, punctuated with scratchy ululations, cut into Bill's
dreams of warmth, girls, turkey, roast beef, pizza, and beer. It was a
sound the like of which Kearns had never heard, carrying all the qual-
ities of a seagull's cry at twice the volume, without any of the customary seabird grace, and it was dragging him back to reality, back to
Antarctica.

Kearns looked out through the porthole in the tail section. Had he
imagined the hellacious noise? Nope. Sure enough, there they were,
circling and wheeling directly overhead—perhaps eight of the massive, dirty gray, speckled birds with six-foot wingspans.[1]

One after the other they swooped in and landed around the fuselage. Men clambered out of their respective hovels for a glance at the

inbound and web-footed squadron and wordlessly regarded these new arrivals.

It was written on their sardonic smiles in the freezing dawn. Here was yet more ironic betrayal. They had all been praying throughout the night for deliverance from above, and this, apparently, was His answer for the moment—all He could muster just now.

And they were unpleasant, arrogant birds, strutting around, badgering through pieces of the wreck like park raccoons. Ignoring the men, the birds made threatening, belligerent motions toward one another, which were accompanied by feints and jabs with their huge razor beaks. Others sat preening and crying insolently at nothing. They were all hungry, and not happy about it.

One of the birds walked less than ten feet from Kearns, cocked his head to the side, and began screaming at him as though Kearns were blocking his way, and how dare he? Kearns weakly flung a leg at the flying mutt just to get by him. It fluffed its wings, gave the human a wide berth, but thrust its head out toward his flight boot all the same.

Hunched over like the bell-tower freak, Kearns stumbled over to the rest of the crew.

"What are they, Lieutenant?" Warr asked.

"Skuas," said Kearns. "I read about these guys. They're like a combination of seagulls and vultures."

"What do they want?"

"What the hell do you think?" Robbins said with a smile. "They want us."

Sure enough, their actions and belligerence said it all. They seemed completely without fear of the men, who might have been bums at a bus stop for all they cared. They were obviously waiting for something to happen like a pack of muggers waits for one among their number to make the first move on an unsuspecting passerby.

One of the creatures sauntered over to a patch of furrowed snow to the south of the wreck and began pecking the icy mound. He was followed by another, and then a third sullen seabird waddled in their direction.

"Hey, damn it all, isn't that where—?"

Before anyone had time to think—*where Lopez and Hendersin are buried?*, McCarty was limp-running downhill toward the battered port engine, with Robbins trailing behind.

The men hastily dug in the snow until they found the shotgun. Caldwell or someone else had buried it there for safekeeping. Cold hands seated a cartridge, and Robbins came back up the hill armed and ready to defend his dead comrades.

"Better not shoot that damned thing; it's likely to blow your head off," Kearns warned. But Robbins ignored him. No one had even test-fired it, and since it had no stock, who knew what else was wrong with it? It might just explode.

The men gathered behind Robbins, at a safe distance, to watch him as he raised the gun with one hand like Aaron Burr at his duel with Alexander Hamilton. Robbins turned his face away, narrowed his eyes, and fired.

After a deafening bang the shotgun jumped in his hand, kicked back against his shoulder, and fell to the ground. The echo seemed to ricochet off icebergs in the distance and return up the sloping field of ice.

The birds stopped digging near the shallow graves of the dead men and regarded their assailant with mocking calm.

Robbins took another shell from McCarty, took steady aim with both hands, and fired. The shot peppered the ice near one of the birds, prompting the animal to swivel its head and preen its tail feathers.

By this time the others were laughing and cheering. Robbins shook the sting from his hands and recovered the weapon from the ice.

"That damned thing hurts. But I hit the son of a gun. You saw that. I hit him!"

"Maybe you just grazed him, Robbie."

By now, Robbins was not only concerned for his deceased

crewmates—his mind had leapt forward in time. He had a vision of the crew huddled around a stew pot simmering with the good smells of greasy skua meat, heavily seasoned with onions, peppers, salt, and sugar, wafting into their shivering faces.

On the third shot, he didn't hesitate or flinch. Clearly the group of pellets hit the target somewhere, chipping away a small portion of the animal's plumage. But the impact was far from fatal.

It didn't even hamper the bird's flying capabilities as the squadron casually took to the air and circled away from the wreck of the *George 1* in search of quarry elsewhere.

"I can't believe that. Did you see that? I hit him. I hit the son of a bitch, and he just looked at me!"

Their spirits brightened a bit as they prepared the daily morning meal. Robbins told them men what he would have cooked for them if he had been able to bring one of the big birds down. He and Kearns debated whether they were true Antarctic skuas or some other type of gull. It was eerie the way shots seemed to bounce off them.

Whether the birds had some type of iron plating or whether Robbins's aim with a stockless shotgun needed improving, one thing had been settled: the shotgun was useful for making noise and not for much else.

"It's about as good as a one-legged man at an ass kicking. And it's dangerous," Kearns said. He didn't want to see any gun at this point. A firearm only served to remind him of what fate might have in store for them all.

The air seemed very cold this morning, with a hint of moisture in it. Caldwell wondered if that didn't mean they were in for more bad weather.

Everyday when the weather was good, Caldwell was approached at least once by someone and asked, "Do you think they'll be coming for us today, sir?" He had heard it again this morning, and he had to confess that he had no idea.[2]

The trip outside had been painfully tiring for Kearns. He had wanted to make a better showing of it, but with his bum arm, the dizziness, and his ribs, he knew he was going to be much more useful tending to LeBlanc. The pain of stepping outside for that mere fifteen minutes was descending on him in waves. That had been unwise. He would finish the day inside again.

The plane commander was more cogent than he had been at any other time since the crash. He had asked the men, "What's all that commotion?" when they came inside for the daily ration and dispensation of duties. When Robbins told Frenchy about the birds, a smile beamed through his cracked lips.

"Don't you worry. We'll be back eatin' steaks on *Pine Island* in no time."

Robbins conjured up his buttermilk broth for LeBlanc, and Kearns gave it to him.

Later in the afternoon, Warr and Robbins were able to recover more useful items from the plane's former galley. They found plastic plates, stainless utensils, a bag of flour, cans of milk, a spilled pound of sugar, and another container of powdered sulfa medication for LeBlanc.

Recovering the sugar had been an interesting chore, according to Robbins. When they discovered a pile of it, it had been barely distinguishable from the powdery snow around it. Robbins found the edges of the broken sack by tasting and sifting. Then began the laborious process of deciphering and sorting the sugar from snow, entirely by taste. Not one to shrink from a challenge, for the sake of his shipmates, he went to it a handful at a time, despite the ridiculousness of the job.

Around 4 P.M. Warr uncovered a handheld mirror.

"Hey fellas, get a look at this!"

They all stopped what they were doing to take a look at themselves in the mirror. Grown men, giddy at the marvel like some tribe of

Amazon Indians, gaped at their own reflections. Beards, cuts, and bruises covered weathered tans and sunburns. White crow's-feet and raccoon eyes were apparent where squints and polarizing lenses had protected the men from the Antarctic glare. In less than a week Caldwell had gone from a gentleman's gentleman to a Scottish oysterman with a gash on his nose and broken teeth. He didn't stare too long at his own discomforting visage.

Robbins noticed for the first time that his right eye was nearly swelled shut from bruising sustained in the crash. Less tan than the others, Kearns looked like he had been on the losing end of a New Bedford brawl. The whites of his eyes were runny with blood.

Someone joked that they all were in open defiance of Atlantic fleet regulations, which strictly prohibited beards—Schwartz would have a fit! Kearns said they should go right on openly defying the "regs." The men agreed. They would not shave, if only to hasten their salvation by those anxious to prosecute them for disobeying standing orders.[3]

It was ridiculous to think they would find anything to shave with in the first place. Discussion of this no-shaving rule was part of the chatter designed to keep them from falling into introspection, and for the moment they did not do so.

By 7 P.M. they were all huddled in the tail section as a cold, dense fog rolled in from the sea.

Just after dinner Caldwell directed Robbins to cease grinding on the Gibson Girl since no signal would make it through the approaching bad weather. It was a particularly dense, thick gray bank of clouds, which made Kearns think of an approaching tidal bore. It covered and consumed what had been a cheery white and blue afternoon. First the majestic ice cliffs dreaming in the Bellingshausen Sea were covered; then the flat fields of broken sea ice before them were overrun by the billowy clouds.

The dense mass pooled at the ledge where the sea ice and the land ice joined. Gathering steam, fog ascended the foot of the hill to meet them like a tide. It was miles deep.

The men retreated inside the tail section and chatted into the evening as the temperature plummeted. Soon the air was cold enough again to freeze water in a cup inside ten minutes. This was a problem for LeBlanc, who would get a couple of sips then drift off to sleep, only to reawaken and find his badly needed water was now rock solid.

The men bundled up and huddled together for an hour or more, talking about what they were missing back aboard *Pine Island:* a scalding hot shower for starters, followed by clean clothes and food, but not necessarily in that order. How did Shakleton and his men survive months of this on end? It was anyone's guess.

By 9:30 P.M. the twilight had returned, along with a little heat. Warr and Robbins began their evening ritual.

They never ran out of steam or spirit. Presently they were arguing about their latest game of checkers. More often they could be heard musing and telling sea stories.

These consisted of everything from lurid, stranger-than-fiction tales about screwups they had witnessed to jokes they had heard on board.

At one point Robbins told the tale of how Commander Schwartz had sent a subordinate into the common latrine located amidships to find Jim Robbins. Something Robbins had eaten in Panama or elsewhere had not agreed with him, so there he sat, well past 10:15 P.M., the hour of lights-out.

Suddenly a flashlight shot through the darkness, finding Robbins coiled at his business above the *Pine Island*'s communal bench.

"He says, 'Robbins, what are you doing in here at this hour?'"

"I said, 'What the hell do you think I'm doing, sir?'"

After the laughter subsided, the winds calmed, and the men drifted off to sleep. In all, it had been a good day, one of gathering strength.

12 FORMAL BURIAL SERVICE FOR LOPEZ, HENDERSIN, AND WILLIAMS DAY 7

CRASH SITE, SUNDAY, JANUARY 5, 1947, 9:00 A.M. The shuffling of feet in the snow and the rattle of an unseen hand banging on the fuselage were cut by Caldwell's steady baritone growl.

No one had asked him for encouragement at this time of day. He was just offering it like reveille—a wake-up call that went out to the entire camp. They had slept long enough, even by the navy's Sunday standards.

"Cheer up boys, cheer up. Don't get discouraged. Don't get down. C'mon now."

No one had wakened on his own, even though the sunshine was so powerfully bright it all but made noise. There didn't appear to be any weather to seaward either, which meant the *Pine Island* could send a plane out today . . . if it felt so inclined.

Caldwell had a more immediate request than preparing for rescue, which might not come anyway the way things were going. There was an unpleasant detail he had to see to.

"I think we need to do a little bit better by our crewmen, boys. It's time we gave them a proper burial," meaning, the skuas may have been chased off for a day or two, but they'd be back. This was a question of duty, whether the crew was stranded or not. Caldwell assured the men that once it was over, they would feel better about it.[1]

Soon hands were busy digging in the powdery snow, excavating a pit beneath the starboard wingtip. The starboard wing was chosen because it seemed a natural place, elevated slightly above the surface of the icy hillside.

Warr, McCarty, Caldwell, and Robbins moved the bodies from where they were in the shallow makeshift graves to the pit in the snow scoured beneath the wing. Robbins also gathered into a pile all the flagpoles and metal canisters with the leaflets that claimed territory for the United States. He and Caldwell decided that when the men were recovered, the metal canisters and flagpoles would provide a decent return signal for a magnetometer in the event the wreck site was buried deep in snowdrift.

In the tradition governing the burial of fallen Antarctic explorers, the bodies were oriented with their heads pointing toward the south.

Caldwell included a handwritten note in the grave, detailing how the men had died, the mission they were on, and the rest of it, in the event that someone stumbled on the wreck site before the United States could return. An American flag was added to the grave.

Kearns, still fighting vertigo and extreme pain, wandered out with Quasimodo grace to take part in the proceedings.

When heads were bared, Caldwell bowed at the appropriate moment and began the time-honored naval service.

"Into the deep we commend the souls of our departed shipmates, Ens. Maxwell Lopez, radioman Wendell Hendersin, and machinist mate Fred Williams. . . ." It was all he could muster in one breath. The pause was dramatic, but it also stemmed from an obvious problem he was having with the service. In Kearns's recollection, Caldwell's face betrayed the fact that he really didn't know what to make of this situation.

The traditional Naval Burial Service wasn't really appropriate. They weren't burying the men at sea, but everyone knew that's where these three would eventually go, along with all this ice on the hill, if they were just left here. It was hard to know precisely what to say. His big barrel chest heaved once, and he continued with a tremor in his voice.

Caldwell improvised appropriately, commenting to the effect that the men died bravely in the service of their country, discharging their duty to the utmost of their ability, and in so doing, they continued the finest traditions of the U.S. Navy. He didn't use the official language of the Naval Burial Service. He trailed off slightly at the end, but he had said enough given their current situation.

The quiet that followed was so deep that the men could hear ice calving off the bergs to the north, soughing off into the sea. Three minutes of dead silence followed as each man looked down into the shallow grave. It seemed to Kearns as though every member of the surviving crew was not only saying good-bye but was also seeing a part of himself in that grave with Lopez, Hendersin, and Williams.

Bill was wondering why he had been spared. Why was he standing at the edge of the pit, and why had they found themselves in it? Where was the fairness in that?

Not that he wasn't glad to be alive; he was. But why did his friends have to die so horribly? What had any of them done to deserve this? *Not a thing*, he thought. *Just like during the war,* "it happens," he told himself. It would have to do for an explanation until later in life, if he survived. Then he could piece the events together and try to make sense of them.

Kearns wandered back to the fuselage with the sound of snow filling that grave forever ringing in his ears. The men worked without a word, and soon they all were wandering toward the waist compartment, their backs bowed like those of a football team crushed by loss.

Gone were the jokes. Gone were thoughts of skuas and snow cones seasoned with sugar and peanut butter. The only thought remaining in Kearns's mind was a question: would anyone else be joining Lopez, Williams, and Hendersin in that cairn of snow?

Caldwell obviously hadn't conducted this special service to make them more serious about their situation, but that was the effect. He merely wanted to make sure the dead men were properly seen to, that they weren't left there as easy targets for predators.

It was his duty to provide a burial, as unpleasant as this duty was. But the proceedings had a chilling effect on morale, an unintended downside.

Kearns made a conscious effort now to keep a lid on his fear. Marine corps trainers at Corpus Christi preached that fear was a virulent and contagious thing. It had to be smothered like grease fire to prevent it from spreading.

At that moment he wasn't worried at all about Robbins. The kid was absolutely indestructible. Warr was quiet. He did not speak his thoughts and sort of grafted himself to Robbins like a twin. No, Kearns was worried about McCarty, who had seemed silent for a couple of days now. He seemed as though he were about ready to pop open in a fountain of tears, and that burial service, necessary though it was, just might have done the trick.

As the day wore on, the contagious fear was more palpable. Men averted their eyes from one another, finished sentences for each other in grunts and in "yeah," "right," and "uh-huh." After a morning like that, there wasn't much a guy could do to pretend the fear wasn't there and wouldn't be a factor. Kearns couldn't remember when or if anyone broke the silence with anything that resembled a decent conversation.

The morning meal, consisting of four apricot halves, spam, and sugar washed down with water, was consumed with minimal gusto.

Caldwell remained out on his quarterdeck listening to and watching the sky for two hours.

The day dragged on, with the men lounging in their tents or puttering listlessly around the wreck site.

LeBlanc needed more water than the men could provide, and soon he was seen digging absently into the snow for mouthfuls through a hole in the fuselage. No one tried to stop him.

ABOARD *PINE ISLAND,* 10A.M.   Flight quarters were finally sounded after two days of nonstop efforts at preparing the *George 2* and the *George 3.*

Commander Schwartz reported to Captain Dufek that the problems with flight operations were not likely to improve drastically. The weather wasn't cooperating.

Fog and snow blanketed the area, records show. Still, Dufek did not want to move from their current location, a few miles north of Peter I Island. Obviously, he felt they were thoroughly under the jurisdiction of Murphy's Law, and he didn't want to invite further prosecution under it by wandering the seas in search of better launching grounds. Even at this point in the game, a week after losing contact, the idea that the *George 1* could be made airworthy and would return to the *Pine Island* must have seemed far-fetched. Nevertheless, the superstitious old sailor living within the skin of George Dufek wasn't prepared to risk moving location.

In the early afternoon, holes of blue could be seen peaking through the clouds and fog banks. It was an encouraging sign.

Both PBMs were lowered over the side. Minutes after they touched the water, the conditions worsened again. A rolling swell began building from the stern quarter. As fog engulfed the area, the flight department found itself in a race to get the planes back aboard ship before the swells damaged the aircraft.

George 3 made it back aboard in fine shape, but as the men were setting the hook on the *George 2*, a foul-weather pendant became snagged in the rigging and smashed into the leading edge of the wing, denting it and punching four holes into the hull, the largest of which was about a foot long.[2]

One can only imagine the blistering, paint-peeling curses that flowed freely from the lips of the air crewmen and boat operators. The level of frustration must have been sufficient to render a man weak with rage, unable to even curl a fist. None of them had slept much in the past two days. They had finally gotten their act together with both aircraft, and now this.

Yet *George 3* was airworthy and ready for flight for the first time since Panama. Seas calmed temptingly after 2 P.M., and *George 3* was reeled over the side again. Each man working on every position, from the crane to the support boats, must have felt like it was the bottom of the ninth inning and he had been called to bat with two outs and bases loaded.

With cautious hopes rising, Howell and his crew boarded for a test flight, which proved that the blue Mariner was in perfect working order. The men landed her and sidled up to the side of the vessel to begin fueling. Fingers and toes all over *Pine Island* remained crossed as the arming crane extended out toward the flying boat, lines were attached, and fuel began flowing.

At precisely 7 P.M., Howell and his crew lifted off from the Bellingshausen Sea, circled the ship, and headed south toward the continent. The first search flight since *George 1* vanished was airborne.

CRASH SITE, 7 P.M.   For dinner everyone received a healthy portion of beef stew. It helped to ease the pain. The crew used their last fresh vegetables in making it. Each man also received a slice of bread with a dollop of peanut butter on top and half a dill pickle.

In his diary McCarty noted that Caldwell wordlessly turned in early. McCarty tried to cheer the captain up later by engaging him in a game of checkers, using wafers and candies as playing pieces. But Caldwell's heart obviously wasn't in it: the naval academy football standout lost to the cameraman without putting up a fight.

By 9 P.M. Caldwell was asleep for what McCarty thought was the first time since the crash. McCarty was likely staring into the dark space of that drab tent as thick clouds and fog rolled in from the sea. A seriously dehydrated and delirious Frenchy LeBlanc began moaning in pain again.

"Honestly, Bill, I've got to go down and see the doc."

"You can't, Frenchy, he's very busy right now."

"No you don't understand. I hear something Bill. There's a plane coming," LeBlanc said.

"Okay Frenchy, try and relax. Take it easy. We'll look for it."

LATITUDE 71 DEGREES 22 MINUTES SOUTH, LONGITUDE 98 DE-GREES 41 MINUTES WEST   Roughly at that moment, Howell and his crew just passed the *George 1*'s last reported position and began their search pattern.

Everything south of the coastline near Cape Dart was covered in thick overcast. Low ceiling and low visibility made it impossible to penetrate airspace over the coast. So Howell and company took the opportunity to cover more than ten thousand square miles of pack ice, looking for any sign of the *George 1*. It took nine hours. Even so, with the low angle of the sun being blocked by clouds, they couldn't be sure that they hadn't missed something. Low on fuel and facing worsening weather, Crew 1 was ordered to return to the *Pine Island*. At one point during the evening flight, Howell and his crew had passed within fifteen miles of the crash site. The drone from his engines was met by sleeping ears, or never made it over the fogbound horizon.

Either LeBlanc had dreamed the sound of the engines at precisely that moment, or he somehow had known Howell and his crew were close. Later in life, Kearns recalled the incident and marveled. There hadn't been a sound. Not even Caldwell, who never seemed to rest, and who was sharpening his listening skills to a razor's edge, heard a thing.

13   MURPHY'S LAW
DAY 8

"Anything that can go wrong, will go wrong."

–Murphy the Optimist

CRASH SITE, MONDAY, JANUARY 6, 1947, 9:00 A.M. Captain Caldwell started keeping that diary he had promised he would maintain right alongside McCarty's.

Pine Island's report on their part in Operation Highjump faithfully copied his assessment of how things were as the crew started their eighth day on the ice. He was not pleased with the weather.

> The sky is down on us today. The ice and snow background merge into the fog and overcast without distinction. This is not flying weather. The breeze is from WNW blowing the fog in from the sea and over us. For breakfast we had half a slice of bread covered thick with peanut butter. We ground the emergency radio like mad for a full half hour and then for the most part, just sat around and talked.[1]

McCarty noted in his own log:

> I got two pieces of decking out of the waist compartment. The captain and I put them under our tent so that we'd have a straight surface to sleep on and not get a round kink in our back from the snow under us melting.[2]

Kearns passed out from exhaustion from listening to LeBlanc and trying to keep him calm throughout the night. He spoke to McCarty briefly, letting him know his concerns about LeBlanc's delirium. He asked McCarty if he or anyone else had any ideas about administering the sulfadiazine medication. Was he giving LeBlanc too much, and was this dehydrating the pilot? No one seemed to know.

For about three hours Kearns finally dropped off to sleep, despite the oppressive smell building up inside the waist compartment. Frenchy LeBlanc's body was dying bit by bit, and now the odor of death permeated the waist section completely.

The other guys didn't know what it was like to sit beside your best friend for twenty-four hours a day and watch him die. It wasn't pleasant for either of them—especially for the guy who was doing the dying.

LeBlanc would wake up periodically and ask, "Hey Bill, how am I doing? How do I look?" and Kearns felt like a damned-to-hell liar every time he replied, "Fine, Frenchy. Just fine."

To be sure, the other guys got glimpses of it in bits and snatches. They probably understood why Kearns seemed glum and down just now. He couldn't put a mask on it. He couldn't pretend to be "up" with the weather like it was, so he said, "To hell with it," and rested.

The remainder of the men congregated at the opening to the waist compartment, framed in a field of white as everything—all distinguishing land characteristics—blended into nothing.

Caldwell, whose spirits were rising somewhat, listened as the men discussed what they would do when they got home.

According to an account in McCarty's log, Robbins coveted a "long white convertible" second only to rescue. He wanted to drive around the country in a long white ragtop. It would naturally be a Cadillac, or the like.

He grew up in San Diego, joined the navy because of his dad. He had figured that would be the quickest way to see the world and get back at the Japanese for starting all the fuss with Pearl Harbor. He had a girlfriend named Dale who lived in the D.C. area. He called her Dolly Dale, because she really was one. He would drive to see her in his new car, and wasn't she impressed!

Speaking of girls, Warr had a sweetheart from Reading, Pennsylvania, named Jean Zwoyer. She was a schoolteacher, loved her job, and was good at it because she adored kids.

Once he got started talking about her, he couldn't stop. He had been quiet since the crash, but now the words flowed like honey in summer. The way Warr spoke, the men began to think they knew her too. Apparently, next to the word *sweetheart* in *Webster's* was a picture of the pretty schoolteacher named Jean. She had a voice like an angel's, he said.

McCarty said the greatest thing in the world would be for the entire crew of survivors, including Captain Caldwell, to drive to Warr's wedding in Robbie's long white car. There couldn't be anything better than that.

They let the thought sit in the still, foggy air for a while as they gazed out into nothing.

Soon Robbins spoke about more-immediate issues. He'd found two radio receivers earlier in the day, but he didn't know if either was any good. And the batteries he had located were cracked and semiuseless. He would try to rig one of the receivers so that they could at least know what the *Pine Island* was up to and plan accordingly.

The truth was, they were all getting more than a little nervous. Was the *Pine Island* looking for them in the wrong place?

Caldwell said some of those paint cans they found a day or two ago should be put to use now. They needed to paint the names of the dead on the wings, so that when the first rescue plane came by, the messages to anxious family members could be relayed immediately.

ABOARD *PINE ISLAND*   Ens. Robert Howard Jones of Connecticut, navigator of *George 2*, wrote a letter home in the morning hours of January 6.[3] We can imagine him sitting in the dimly lit quarters during the fogbound morning, his eyes watery red from exhaustion. Apparently repairs had been made to the *George 2* as in his letter he notes that the plane had been floating alongside the *Pine Island* in preparation for a flight, waiting for weather to change.

Dear Mom, Dad, and Ray:

In two weeks another Mail Call will be made. So I'm starting now so I won't have to rush at the last minute. I should have several letters to you by that time.

I've been terribly busy because of this other plane that is missing. It disappeared a week ago . . . and as yet no trace has been found as to its fate. My three buddies were on board as well as the captain of the ship. He was a wonderful man and well liked by everyone. I had known the two other men from Banana River and had just made the acquaintance of "Frenchy" LeBlanc in Norfolk. They were swell guys and I miss them very much. I haven't been able to sleep until I was exhausted.

Besides worrying about them, I am wondering how you feel. . . .

Jones went on to say that he attempted to send them a telegram by way of a town doctor in Norwich, but was told no telegram traffic would be permitted for the moment. Ever the conscientious son, he thought it better to send the telegram through a third party than have it arrive through Western Union carrier. He said it might have proven too much of a shock for his mother's worried and ailing heart.

Aside from the fact that even the most caring and conscientious members of *Pine Island*'s aviation department were thinking of the men of the *George 1* in the past tense, Jones's letter to his family mirrored the level of frustration felt aboard ship.

> . . . *I have been working pretty hard all week trying to get the plane in shape. I can't do much about maintenance but I help the crew out by getting in there and doing whatever they tell me to. They have all been slaving away pretty hard. We are up all hours putting the plane over the side. I was up all night last night. The plane was out on the water with two boats tied alongside it. We had to keep it away from the side of the ship and all the ice floating around here. . . .*
>
> *I have never seen so much ice in all my life. . . .*
>
> *Love, Howard.*

That afternoon, Jones's logbook recorded a one-and-a-half-hour flight called "tender operations." This was most likely the test flight, intended to make sure the *George 2* was in working order. Such flights remained in the vicinity of *Pine Island*, taking the opportunity not only to test all systems but also to make crucial weather observations.

In his log Jones faithfully noted that the flight officers and five passengers were aboard. By now crews were itching to get however much air time over the continent they needed in order to find their missing comrades. Surprisingly, and perhaps under strict orders by Schwartz and Dufek, the anecdotal and historic records include few references to the usual bets and competitions that can arise in situations like this.

Men could have made book on whether Howell's crew would be first to find the *George 1* or whether it would be Ball's plane. There is no mention of such bets being placed. There's no mention of even a sense of competition arising between the crews. It may have had to do with the fact that one of Crew 3's senior members, who had been left behind aboard *Pine Island,* was an accomplished boxer.

And as the days dragged on, J. D. "Dick" Dickens began to sense the impending complete loss of all his friends. Normally gregarious and outgoing, the scrappy Georgian grew introspective. The officers aboard ship trained the men to choose their words carefully, partly because of the impact glib or crass remarks might have on fellow crew members who were close to the men of *George 1,* but mostly because of how the remarks would make them feel later, when and if they discovered that no one had survived.

At 11:30 A.M. Lieutenant Commander Howell and his crew, including copilot Lt. Dale Mincer and navigator Ens. Martin Eugene Litz, took to the sky aboard *George 3* and headed for Antarctica.

The men were turned back by blizzards and buffeting winds after a negative search. The *George 3* was hauled in and secured aboard *Pine Island* shortly before 9 P.M.

14

SALVO
DAY 9

CRASH SITE, TUESDAY, JANUARY 7, 1947 Caldwell's spirits dipped close to their lowest point. His diary included this terse notation: "There is no flying on such a day as this so we have very little to look forward to. Such days drag on interminably."[1]

Though he was feeling down, he wasn't letting it show to the men. There's almost a sense of offhanded amusement in McCarty's account of his hardy tent mate. For example: "Today the captain discovered that he had a broken nose."[2]

For his own part, McCarty described dizzy spells, headaches, and a swelled right leg that plagued him much of the time.

Kearns again spent the entire day with LeBlanc, who slept on unaware of anything.

It was on days like this, he recalled, that fear was something so close and thick that you could slice it with a knife. Fog covered every-thing, reminding them all of the whiteout that had gotten them here in the first place.

"You didn't dare stray very far from the waist compartment or the tents in the fear that you'd be swallowed by it," Kearns later recalled.

They could do nothing but sit there in their tents and play games and talk. Every so often Kearns could hear either Warr or Robbins bellow out.

"I'm putting you through war college, buddy." (This meant, "I am taking you to school.")

"No, I'm putting *you* through war college."

They were like kids playing with a new toy at Christmas.

The game was called Salvo. Milton Bradley later perfected it and named it Battleship, but navy men had been playing it for years.

A barrier—a piece of cardboard or such—was used as a divider. Opponents drew a standard matrix, using numbers and letters on a sheet of paper, then penciled in a set number and the desired positions of various ships on their concealed page. Then they took turns calling out positions of impact for each "salvo." Chits of paper and old radio forms were used for the seemingly endless game, which always commenced around midmorning and took up much of the day.

The game could get as elaborate as the two players desired. For in-stance, players could assign a minimum of four hits for a carrier, three hits for a battleship, or two hits for a cruiser and then try to deduce how many and what type of ships remained on their opponent's sea surface and their positions. Robbins and Warr, making their game fairly sophisticated, whiled away downtime hours in this fashion, staving off their uncertainty in play.

Hearing them, Kearns despondently wondered whether a similar technique was being used by the *Pine Island*'s flight teams to find them just now. He couldn't understand why there had been no sign of them.

The odds were about the same when you looked at them. In fact, if each square inch on a piece of paper corresponded to a designation between *A* through *J* down the side, cross-referenced with numbers one through ten across the top, Robbins and Warr had infinitely better odds of scoring a direct hit on their first random salvo than the men of *Pine Island* had of finding them all on their first search flight, or on their a second, or even on their third.

Rigged poker, a tilted roulette wheel, a game of craps in a dank Brooklyn alley—these all seemed to hold better odds than those favoring immediate salvation. Kearns leaned back and slept away the rest of the afternoon.

ABOARD *PINE ISLAND,* NOON   The *Canisteo* and the *Brownson* both were called back to a rendezvous point with the command ship of the Eastern Group. They sidled up to *Pine Island* for what records referred to as "a routine transfer of supplies," which was completed in about two or three hours.

Soon afterwards, the ships stood off, with *Canisteo* remaining nearby and *Brownson* renewing its efforts to find a lead through the ice southward. Flight quarters were sounded in the early afternoon, because the weather appeared to be clearing. But within a few hours both planes were called back due to worsening conditions.

By this time Dufek and Schwartz decided that, with both seaplanes in commission, and while swells were minimal, leaving one of the PBMs tethered to the stern of the ship represented a head start against inclement weather. They would do this whenever possible. They risked incurring further damage to the ship or the airplane; nevertheless, they held fast to their belief that the risk was warranted.

In light of their track record, the decision made sense. It seemed that when they began hoisting a vessel over the side, things were usually fine. Only when the hull of the seaplane kissed the sea surface did Mr. Murphy make his presence known with his miserable swells, squalls, and cloud banks gathering in the distance. If they were lucky, leaving one plane dragging aft of the ship meant they would eventually get one off the water.[3]

CRASH SITE, 7 P.M.   Just before dinner the sky over the crash site began clearing for the first time in two days.

Grabbing a pair of binoculars, Caldwell searched for any hint that the flight crews had been seeking them out. He spotted something in the distance that appeared to be a plume of black smoke extending from a point of land at the edge of the ice shelf. The men considered all the options, from a stranded whaling party to flairs dropped by rescuers, until they had a chance to focus in on the mirage with steadied hands.

It was just a massive crack in the sea ice that showed up black against the all-white background under cloudy skies. It jutted northward from the peninsula, flaring outward into the slushy brash and bergy bits in the distance.[4]

But the clearing fog at least provided a needed jolt to morale.

Soon afterwards, Robbins threw open the tent covering in preparation for the evening meal.

"Hiya Robbie. How's it going?"

"Okay, Bill. How you fellas doing?"

"Not bad. Not bad ay-tall," LeBlanc rasped through a chalky throat.

This was now part of their routine, this silly banter. Bill started it because of the way Robbins tended to brighten the room when he walked in. You knew food was coming along with Robbins's jokes, chatter, and overall good spirit. So Kearns began the routine as a way to say thanks. It grew sillier as the days dragged on—they chatted as if they were two guys crossing paths at the downtown lunch car after a half day of work. LeBlanc joined in whenever he could. It was the high point of the afternoon.

Soon Warr, Caldwell, and the others joined in, making light mockery of their situation. No, they weren't trapped in Antarctica: this was just business as usual.

During the meal Robbins said that he had all but completely cannibalized one of two radio receivers found in the snow, to make the second usable. The only problem was, he still could not draw enough power from the batteries, which were damaged. He estimated they could drag sixteen volts, but they needed twenty-four. The *George 1*'s onboard generator, the "putt-putt," had been located but was damaged beyond repair, as he and Warr had discovered after many bitter, swearing hours of trying to fix it.[5]

As an alternative, Robbins and Warr would begin collecting all disposable flashlight batteries in the camp to see if they could be put to use to gain the required voltage.

That way they could at least listen for signals from *Pine Island* that would help them figure out where the hell the ship was and what it was doing. It didn't seem to make sense that they were taking so long to send out a rescue party. All the men felt that they had been vigilant enough to at least hear or catch a glimpse of an airplane, and they had passed some days of excellent weather that obviously extended well out to sea.

Caldwell mused about their predicament with McCarty. He said that if the *George 1* had been correctly on course as had been relayed to the *Pine Island* during their last radio transmissions, there should be every reason to expect a flyover during the first sign of good weather. However, if they had been blown off course, as he suspected, then the delay in seeing a search plane made frightening sense and could mean they were never coming.

Again he and Kearns and McCarty went round and round on this issue. By now a little tired of this doubt, Kearns remained steadfast in his defense of Lopez's work at the navigation table. They were near Cape Dart, he said. Caldwell had plans for creating a sundial of sorts, the next day of good weather, to see if he could get a better fix on their exact latitude and longitude through knowing the time of day.

But without the known values for inclination given in the navigation table—which, for the moment, was nowhere to be found—the project wouldn't bear much fruit.

In the meantime Caldwell and McCarty resolved to walk to the snow ridge to the south of the wreck site at the first opportunity. From that high vantage point perhaps they could better make out the shape of the cape to their north. Comparing this with the charts, they would make the determination whether they were indeed near Cape Dart, or whether, as Caldwell suggested, they had drifted to Fletcher Isle.

Kearns knew that at this point there was no swaying his captain, who was now completely supported in his assessment by McCarty. It more than angered him. In Caldwell's case he couldn't really argue. Aside from the fact that Caldwell was a qualified flight officer who outranked him the way a cardinal outranks an altar boy, Caldwell, at the very least, had been following transmissions and discussions during the flight. He must have misunderstood something someone said just prior to the crash and come away with his own conclusion. Wrong though it was, it had at least an arguable basis in fact.

But Kearns brooked no argument on the matter from McCarty, who, in Kearns's opinion, was obviously playing yes-man to his captain.

McCarty may have been a good judge of distances and topography because of his photographic work, but he knew not a damned thing about flying a plane and little more about navigation. How McCarty could have pinpointed anything when he had been asleep during the last moments of the flight was a mystery that defied logic. He said as much to McCarty, letting it all spill into Caldwell's ear as well.[6]

McCarty stood his ground, and the discussion became heated, with Caldwell trying to calm ruffled feathers. Warr and Robbins stayed out of it, and Frenchy LeBlanc slept through the whole thing.

Kearns reined in his temper and his tongue as best he could, praying with all his might that the men would not send the *Pine Island* the wrong position if they managed to get a transmitter working. But he could not convince Caldwell to take his word for it. That part of it stung. It was a vote of no confidence from his captain, and it obviously put some of the blame for the crash on his judgment.

The captain believed strongly they were on Fletcher Isle, and not anywhere near Cape Dart.

In his record of the account, McCarty noted, "Lieutenant Kearns insists it's Cape Dart." But he also admitted they were "just groping" for answers and didn't really know where they were.

15

SPIRITS DROP
DAYS 10, 11, AND 12

Day 10

CRASH SITE, WEDNESDAY, JANUARY 8   Caldwell's diary entry:

The weather is still down on us. It is completely overcast with a light snow. The air is *light* from the NW and visibility is 500 yards. We have put in our morning 30 minutes on the emergency radio. It does moral good just to hear the grinder turning. We had our usual breakfast of a half a slice of bread covered with peanut butter. This won't last much longer as we are now in our last loaf of bread. To date we have feasted on the plane flight rations. They are nearly used up and at that time we will be on pemmican alone. Not a very pleasing outlook.[1]

In fact, he called Kearns to his side and told him that they needed to be found soon; there were only about thirty more days of rations, period. With the Antarctic winter fast approaching, even if they resorted to the unthinkable, eating the deceased crewmen, there would be no way they would survive the long Antarctic night.

In Kearns's mind he was hearing from Caldwell that resorting to the unthinkable wasn't even going to be a consideration for that reason. They wouldn't go out like that. If they weren't located soon, they would have to make alternate arrangements for food. If those failed, well, that was it.

Of the things included in the emergency rations, the shotgun and its remaining shells, a flare gun, if it could be located, some fishing poles and lures, and the two life rafts (sans the paddles, which had yet to be found) could be put into use. But the question was, how effectively? How much time and energy would they have to hunt for fish and penguins? When would that regimen begin?

Obviously, starting such measures was an admission that they were planning for the long Antarctic night. Robbins quietly voiced to Warr his hope that they wouldn't have to do that; McCarty would surely eat them out of house and home when it came down to it. The dent in his head, and the associated depression he crept in and out of, had somehow cranked up his appetite.[2] Robbins had noticed it recently, and so had Kearns.

Caldwell asked Kearns about LeBlanc, who, for the moment, was having a good day. He was cogent, clear minded.

Kearns guessed that the cold, sanitary nature of the continent had a lot to do with staving off the infections that would have killed the pilot by now in warmer latitudes. Nevertheless, LeBlanc was dying of his burns and of frostbite, dehydration, and weight loss. His frostbitten legs and feet had gone from gray to purple. The dark area of flesh was now moving toward his knees. Kearns admitted that he didn't know how to tell his friend his lower legs were a lost cause. His assessment was that LeBlanc would most likely die within a week if they weren't rescued.

Caldwell chose to put a good face on it in his notes, however:

> Kearns and LeBlanc are still improving. Kearns can move his right arm now and he has started sitting outside with the rest of us. He is coming along fast. LeBlanc seems to have passed the delirious stage now. He has full control of his senses and is improving steadily."[3]

Day 11

CRASH SITE, THURSDAY, JANUARY 9, 9 A.M.   It may have been a ploy by Captain Caldwell to quell arguments once and for all about where they were. It may have been an effort to aid the flagging spirits of Chief Photographer's Mate Owen McCarty.

Whatever the motivation, records show that Caldwell took McCarty on their "long walk," during which the men discovered the wonders of Antarctic perspective, not to mention how enfeebled they had become by dehydration and losing the caloric race.

The weather was excellent. The day started cloudy, with "blue holes," as McCarty noted in his personal log, giving way to blaring, headache-causing sunshine.

"Before the Captain and I took our walk, I ground the Gibson Girl, and he sent a message: BROKEN SKIS. 6 ALIVE, CALDWELL, LEBLANC, KEARNS, MCCARTY, WARR, ROBBINS, FLETCHER ISLE."[4]

Robbins said that he had sent the coded message himself, as he was the only crew member fluently versed in Morse code. But certainly Caldwell also had some familiarity with it, being an academy man and pilot.

Whatever the case, once they were on their walk, Caldwell and McCarty quickly discovered they would not get a bird's-eye view of anything to confirm that they were indeed on Fletcher Isle. The shoulder of that ridge, which had seemed "right there" to the south and west of them, was in reality twenty miles away, all uphill.

They must have seemed an odd pair to a passing skua flying over them as they trudged through the soft snow. For one thing Caldwell discovered that not only was his left ankle sprained but bones in his foot had obviously been cracked. The stabbing and grinding pain slowed him as he went. McCarty's right leg had swelled up "like a balloon,"[5] still filled with fluid from being dashed around inside the tail section on impact.

It takes little imagination to see the men sloshing through knee- and hip-deep snow—Caldwell with his emergency-ration pants exposing his purple shins just above his socks and with a nasty gash across his nose beneath his polarizing lenses as he puffs furiously through chipped teeth, and, limping beside him, a stocky, out-of-breath photographer who throws a stiff and swelled right leg through the drifts, one hand nursing his flight cap so that its movement doesn't reopen the nine-inch gash in his scalp.

They came to a halt on the face of the massive snow dune, which was fifty times larger than the Wright Brothers' hill at Kitty Hawk, North Carolina. They turned and faced the wreck site a hundred feet below, less than a half-mile downslope—a few coal shards in a white frying pan of blazing glare. They had labored for half an hour. On a well-aimed toboggan, they could have skidded into camp in less than three minutes.

An exhausted McCarty later wrote: "[H]ow helplessly anchored we are to our wreckage. We are fully at the mercy of the elements and our shipmates' determination to find us."[6]

———

ABOARD *PINE ISLAND,* NOON Wordlessly, the grim-faced flight crew of *George 2* boarded their launch and were hauled back toward ship.

Flight quarters had been sounded at 5:30 A.M., when weather appeared favorable. They had saved time by leaving the ship on standby, tethered to the stern of the *Pine Island.* They had attempted to cheat Mr. Murphy, but once again he had thwarted their best-laid plans.

Their flight had lasted just over half an hour after encountering impenetrable weather to the south soon after takeoff. Ten men, in addition to pilot, copilot, and navigator, had been aboard, as Ensign Jones noted in the logbook.[7] The two or three additional crewmen were pharmacist's mates, trained to administer medicines and triage. Their greater number also meant that additional eyes would be trained out every porthole as they flew. That's how hopeful the flight department was that they'd get a shot at flying over the continent today.

The *Pine Island* spent the remainder of the afternoon taking on fuel from *Canisteo* as the *Brownson,* now miles to the south, pushed dangerously into the pack ice again.

CRASH SITE, 7 P.M. Caldwell's entry in his personal log included the following:

Good day today. Visibility excellent, low broken clouds—much blue today. The only mountains visible to date are off to the west. It is good flying weather here; if only it could be good weather at the ship's position. McCarty and I took a short walk this morning and now we are positive that if we get rescued it will be from this spot. None of us are in condition for any long hike.

LeBlanc is taking a turn for the worse. We really could not endure much good weather such as this without something happening. Our spirits improve with the weather and this condition will continue until it is proved that good weather here will bring us no AID. The wind has picked up to 15–18 knots from the west and we have the emergency radio antenna kite flying. [Robbins and Warr had created a new one with battered pieces of balsa and parachute fabric.] I just finished 30 minutes on the grinder. Our best weather is in the morning. It clouds over and turns definitely much colder after 1700.[8]

Day 12

ABOARD *PINE ISLAND,* FRIDAY, JANUARY 10, 1947   The following notation is included in the *Pine Island*'s report: "On the morning of 10 January, hoping for a break in the jinx of this damnable weather, the PINE ISLAND was moved to the westward, to a position Lat. 66 degrees, 30 minutes S. Long. 104 degrees 30 minutes W."[9]

The change took most of the day and represented a one-hundred-mile westward jog.

CRASH SITE, 9 A.M.   Caldwell wrote:

What a day! I was the first one up and didn't say a word when asked the state of the weather. It was completely overcast, almost; off to the south horizon I saw a very thin rift of blue. I kept watching this blue, called all the others, and within two hours the SE wind had driven off all the clouds and we had CAVU.

For breakfast we used our last bit of bread with peanut butter. We used the emergency radio and tapped out signals. . . .

Robbins and Warr took a hike south and the result was additional information that pointed to our being on the north end of Fletcher Island.[10]

For the remainder of the day, five men, excluding LeBlanc, who was still semiconscious in the back of the tail section, "just sat around and enthused at all this good weather," according to Caldwell's diary.

Kearns later looked after Frenchy. He seemed to have a ravenous appetite for snow. In a semiconscious haze he would dip his hand through the hole in the fuselage and bring scoop after scoop to his lips. Kearns was through trying to warn him of the dangers of frostbite.

He couldn't wait for the water to be boiled then cooled. He just went after the snow. McCarty's head wound was beginning to fester as well.

As Warr and Robbins continued their never-ending game of Salvo, McCarty recorded his prayers to God that the weather would hold: "If God will let us have two or three days of good weather, we feel our troubles will be over."

ABOARD *PINE ISLAND,* 6 P.M.   Lt. Comdr. Walt Sessums and Capt. George Dufek took off aboard a Sikorsky helicopter in search of leads into the pack ice. Though they were able to find suitable launching grounds for air operations, they decided that the *Pine Island* would not be moving farther southward into the pack.

Weather was worsening to the extent that air operations would not be possible for the remainder of the day. They landed safely back aboard and secured flight operations.

16 SIX ALIVE! SIX ALIVE! DAY 13

ABOARD *PINE ISLAND,* SATURDAY, JANUARY 11, 1947, 4:30 A.M. Plane commander Lt. James Ball got out of his bunk to the shrill echo barked over the ship's intercom.

"Now hear this. Now hear this. Captain Dufek has issued flight quarters. That is all."

How many times would they listen to these words? The men of *Pine Island* had spent all of their flight time to date searching for *George 1.* Men stumbled in darkened gangways, assembling their gear as word about the good weather topside made the rounds. Reports from both *Canisteo* and the *Brownson* were favorable. Word from the Central Group was also good: the weather had been clear in their vicinity as well. This meant CAVU extended far over the horizon in any given direction. The men were excited at the prospect of good weather and hoped like hell it would hold up.

After a quick breakfast, it was decided that Crew 2 would be first off the water, and several additional pairs of eyes were sent with them. One belonged to Chief Pharmacist's Mate W. A. Long of Monroe, North Carolina.

Also, Chief Photographer's Mate Richard "Dick" Conger, lately of Norfolk, Virginia, had been assigned to fly on Crew 1's flight with Lt. Comdr. John Howell when his plane took off after Ball's.

Conger was an accomplished underwater demolitions man as well as a photographer, according to Kearns. Conger had seen action in the Pacific during the war. He was also a close personal friend of Owen McCarty.

Winds were light, and seas were calm, so fueling of the *George 2* went off rapidly. She was airborne, heading for the continent, by 7:00 A.M. according to the reports.[1] That morning, Ens. Robert Howard Jones, at the helm, got the honor of negotiating his first JATO takeoff. He later noted in his personal log the elation and pride that swelled within him as the takeoff went off without the slightest hitch: "[I]t was a good one!"[2] That was only the beginning. He was entering one of the most exhilarating days of his young life.

CRASH SITE, 8:20 A.M.*   True to McCarty's prayers, it was another gorgeous morning, almost too beautiful in that having two or three days of agreeable weather without the slightest indication they were being sought by their shipmates might be as crushing as an equivalent period of ice fog and wind.

Each man had had five apricot halves seasoned with sugar. They were out of bread. The peanut butter would hold up for a little while

---

*Kearns later recalled looking at his watch and noting that the time was 6:20 A.M. It is impossible that the time of *G2*'s first flyover was thirty minutes before it took off. It is reasonable to conclude that Kearns's watch was on local or Mountain time, while the men on *Pine Island* had set theirs to EST, or that flight logs were recorded afterwards in EST.

longer, but aside from that it would be pemmican stew from here on out.

Robbins said disgustedly that the damned stuff tasted like liverwurst and cheese; he wasn't looking forward to a closer association with pemmican. He was going to miss actual meat, vegetables, and spices. It surely occurred to him that he might be missing these tastes for all eternity.

LeBlanc was awake but quiet. Kearns, watching over the pilot as he munched on peanut butter, was thinking about the wonders of that food. Kearns hadn't much cared for it before this happened, but now, if he ever got out of this mess, he would be its ever-loving devotee. You could fill up on it. At the very least it made you feel like you had eaten a large meal. He snuck a dollop for himself and asked Frenchy if he could coat some of his wounds with peanut oil. LeBlanc declined. Robbins wandered out into the snow somewhere with Warr, searching for more gear to make his radios work. Caldwell was sitting on his quarterdeck staring into the sky while McCarty dozed in his tent.

The sounds weren't really sounds at first, Kearns recalled. They were more like a reverberating pressure on the ears that he recognized from all his time at Corpus Christi and Banana River. Only one thing in the world did that to his ears—props on helicopters and big aircraft flying towards him.

It went *thop-thop-thop*, abating after a few seconds. The sound recycled before resolving into the familiar drone of an airplane.

"Damn it all! That's a plane," he said to LeBlanc as he began scrambling outside the fuselage.

"Airplane! Airplane!" he screamed. "Can you hear that? Can you hear it?"

Caldwell was already pointing, as was McCarty, now out of his tent and waving madly.

"There she is. There she is, lads!"

The PBM was on a standard search pattern, about six miles away heading south and west. It changed course to due south. According to Kearns, the plane looked like it came nearly right over the campsite, but it was very high up—more than two thousand feet. The men screamed, threw their arms in the air, and jumped up and down. One of the men lit two small smoke grenades, but the plane sailed right over the horizon. What they had been waiting for, for two solid weeks, was over in a few brutal seconds. One of the men sank to his knees and covered his face. "They didn't see us. I just can't believe they didn't see us!"*

A slew of curses came from every quarter of the camp, followed by a few seconds of stunned silence. Kearns merely stood there. True, they had anticipated not being seen on the first pass, but it couldn't have hurt more when it happened if he had been kicked in the guts with a rivet welder's boot. He doubled over and sat down in the snow.

As soon as he saw their disappointed reaction, Caldwell began hobbling from man to man, screaming into their faces.

"Kearns, McCarty, Warr! C'mon, boys. Snap out of it."

They had discussed this many times over. The search patterns would have been redundant. If they weren't seen on the first pass, or on a second pass, they should do everything possible to make themselves more visible, up to and including blowing the wing tanks to create a fireball big enough to be seen for miles.

That would be a last resort because they could end up making a bonfire out of their campsite, and if they weren't seen, then, they really would be, in the parlance of the time, "screwed, blued, and tattooed." Kearns asked Caldwell about the logic of destroying the only shelter they had, to which the captain calmly replied, "It won't matter much if we aren't found, Lieutenant."

Days earlier, Robbins had collected cardboard, paper, life jackets, and everything else that would burn into a rubber raft. According to

---

*Kearns doesn't remember who it was, but said that the man was speaking for all of them. Robbins does not remember events this way. According to him, the first flyover resulted in the men being sighted immediately. This discrepancy between the accounts of the last two survivors is dealt with in an addendum to the book.

Kearns, he scrambled about camp again, searching for shotgun shells to provide powder, and anything else he could get his hands on to complete the pyre. Soon all that remained was to soak it with gasoline and light it aflame the next time the bird came over. More flammable material was added to the raft, in the form of 250 pounds of unused film from McCarty's trimetrogons, carried by a limping McCarty himself—his sacrificial offering to the gods. A few more items scrounged from the wreck site were added until the little raft looked like a dumpster from a demolition project. Robbins took as much gasoline as he could carry in a canvas bucket and a five-gallon canister and began dousing everything.

Caldwell sat on his quarterdeck and lit another one of the cigars McCarty had given him, ready to detonate the wing tanks, if it came to that, by lighting a gas-soaked rag stuffed inside the hole used to siphon gas from the tanks. The men waited and watched the sky.

One hour passed without a sound, then another.

ABOARD *GEORGE 2* LATITUDE 71 DEGREES 03 MINUTES SOUTH, LONGITUDE 98 DEGREES 47 WEST, 11:10 A.M.[3] Lt. (jg.) James Ball and his crew were halfway through the third leg of their search.

According to Jones's personal log, they were headed due west at this point. Fifteen minutes previously they had radioed back to the *Pine Island* their standard report in dots and dashes, spelling out their overall assessment:

NO OBSERVATIONS[4]

It was coming up on that time again, and the next message was coded.

Through a window on the port side, W. A. Long had been staring out at the mantle of blinding white under blue for the better part of an hour through his polarizing lenses when he saw what appeared to be a long black sash with a frayed end pointing skyward on the horizon to their south. It rose three hundred feet in the air, fanning out in a long wide tail.

"Hey, fellas! I see something. I got something that looks like smoke over here!"

Seconds later Ball, Goff, and Jones saw it too off the port bow, ten miles away: a column of black smoke.

CRASH SITE, 11:11 A.M. James Robbins looked like the butt of a prank in a Warner Bros. cartoon. His face was smudged greasy with ash, and his hair and eyebrows were singed black. But not even the sun could compete with the smile on his face.

He dropped the life-raft paddle, the end of which had been covered with a gas-soaked rag that McCarty lit with his cigarette lighter. This had been introduced into the cloud of evaporating aviation gas near the raft. He had fought to get it lit as the plane threatened to disappear again, but when it went, the combustion was so great it nearly blasted Robbins from his shoes.

Caldwell came over and, before patting him on the back, looked into his eyes to make sure he was all right.

"Damned good job, son. Damned good job. You won't have to worry about those eyebrows of yours for a while!"[5]

Robbins collected himself and watched as the *George 2* continued on course for two seconds, then three, then four. Finally her left wing took a sharp dip. A shaft of sunlight shot from her fuselage as she turned and dived, the pitch of her engines getting louder and higher as she descended on the wreck site in attack posture. The guys went wild aboard ship and on the ground as the bluish shadow of the airplane grew and raced up the hillside beneath the diving PBM.

Robbins screamed, "Hey! Hey! Hey!" and ran out into the snow, flailing his arms like a child greeting Santa Claus. Warr and Caldwell waved trail-marker flags and bellowed into the sky. Kearns ducked on a reflex as Ball swept less than fifty feet above them, cut to starboard, and climbed in a long flowing arc. Jim Robbins thought that the display of airmanship was one of the most beautiful things he had ever seen. Joy was surging through everybody. The roar from the engines thundered off the icy plain as the plane passed. She came close enough to kick up clouds of hissing snow, billowing loose tent flaps and scattering debris in her wake.

"It's the two. It's the two plane!" someone screamed through the din, noting the big white "2" just beside the star and bars painted on the fuselage.

Through the binoculars Kearns could make out Ball clearly through the port-side windscreen, a huge smile on his face just before he rocked her wings and came around for another close pass. The young Bostonian began to shudder as tears of relief fell from his eyes. Likewise, McCarty sank to his knees, giving thanks in a quick prayer amid the hooting and screaming from Warr, Robbins, and Caldwell.

"You see that, fellas! I told you guys they'd get us out of this mess!"[6]

It was Frenchy. He had crawled out through the tail turret to point at the sky and smile through a crust of burns and scars.

ABOARD *GEORGE 2* In a second of hushed silence following the second pass, men gazed in pure astonishment at the wreck site.

"Five by my count. I count five standing," Goff said quietly, reading the message painted on the wing: "Lopez, Hendersin, Williams DEAD."

Men in the back of the plane whispered in amazement. How could anyone have survived? The *George 1* looked like a hastily gutted fish splayed out on a white cutting board. The pilots noted the positions of the port and starboard engines as they circled for another pass. They guessed that the men had been living for the last two weeks in what remained of the after portion of the airplane and in those flimsy tents between the wing and the tail section.

"Another man alive. One more."

ABOARD THE *PINE ISLAND,* 11:16 A.M. The radiomen had to recheck their Morse and then check it again to make sure they had it right before acknowledging.

MARINER GEORGE ONE BURNT WRECKAGE AND ALIVE MEN AT 71-03 SOUTH 98-74 WEST.[7]

By the time they were sure, they had received another coded transmission from the *George 2.*

FIVE MEN ALIVE BY OUR COUNT.

And then:

LOPEZ HENDERSIN WILLIAMS DEAD, SIX OTHER MEN ALIVE AND ON FEET. PLANE DISINTEGRATED AND BURNED.

Dufek, who had actually run through the gangways of the *PI* screaming the news like a town crier, made his way to the bridge and relayed a message over ship's intercom that the *George 1* had been found, with survivors seen walking around at the crash site—details would follow. A massive cheer erupted throughout the ship. He then began directing the radio department to relay the messages to the Central Group, which was still locked in the final stages of a two-week slugging match to reach the Bay of Whales.

Rear Adm. Richard Cruzen radioed back an encouraging response:

BEST POSSIBLE NEWS.

He and many others had privately considered all the men of the *George 1* beyond hope.

The news was flashed from *Mount Olympus* to communications stations in the Atlantic and Pacific fleets, to the *Philippine Sea*, which was, at that moment, a day out of Panama, and to Secretary of the Navy James Forrestal, and was also relayed to the administration office for Task Force 68 in Washington, D.C.

CRASH SITE, NOON   Caldwell, Robbins, and McCarty had been hand-cranking on the Gibson Girl and sending Morse code like mad banshees, but the plane appeared not to respond to their direct transmissions.

For their part, the men in the plane began sending messages with an Aldus lamp, a red flash for dots and a white flash for dashes. For the moment, the ground wasn't responding to these either.

The *George 2* left the area temporarily, descending the icy slope to the sea, then returning again with its flash transmitter signaling out one of the portholes. Robbins caught some of it and was out in the field with flags, waving his own semaphore signals back to them, but no meaningful communication was occurring.

Then all manner of goodies started falling from the sky, attached to emergency parachutes and trail markers. Apparently the men of *George 2* had seen how lightly clad Caldwell was. A flight suit came down as one of the first items of care.

It was Bob Goff's. Caldwell immediately put it on.

"Hey, fellas, it's still warm!" he shouted up at the *G2* with a wave.

Inside the suit pocket he found a book of Psalms. He swallowed hard, smiled, and remarked to Kearns that the prayer book had been a very nice touch indeed.

ABOARD *GEORGE 2*, 2 P.M. Ball was busy scribbling a message to the men below on a radio transmission form in large blocky text. The problem of communication had to be resolved ASAP. The *George 2* was approaching the middle of its flight range by fuel supply, and they had to decide how they would get them out of here.

Ball's note read:

OPEN WATER 10 MILES TO THE NORTH. IF YOU CAN MAKE IT ON FOOT, JOIN HANDS IN A CIRCLE. IF YOU CANNOT, FORM A STRAIGHT LINE. WE WILL PICK YOU UP.*

This was not standard operating procedure. Ball had invented it, flying, as they say, by the seat of his pants. The note was dropped inside a messenger sandbag, which Robbins retrieved from the snow.

The men gathered around Caldwell to review the note. Caldwell read it aloud, and then everyone remained silent for a moment, thinking about the situation. They had a toboggan-type sled from their emergency supplies. There was no question that LeBlanc would be brought down the hillside on that.

When it came to hiking, the weak link in the chain might have been Kearns, who had just started spending appreciable amounts of time on his feet the previous day. He was going to survive, but he was still a mess. Could he even walk that far?

Kearns looked at the other men, who were sunburned and bearded. Caldwell with his injured left ankle and the gash across the bridge of his nose, McCarty with a swelled leg and his flight cap fused to his head by a festering wound, Robbins with one eye swelled, Warr with his own bumps and bruises, not the least of which was frostbite

---

*When quoted in the December 29, 1979, *Jacksonville Time-Union*, Caldwell read the note directly to the reporter. Both of Ball's handwritten letters were among his keepsakes from the crash.

to his feet and fingertips from all his badgering around in the snow. They were looking to Bill Kearns for an answer. He didn't mean to let them down.

"Let's go," he said, and as he did, they all joined in a circle, remaining like that, huddled hand to hand, hand to shoulder, until Ball's plane rocked its wings overhead, letting them know they had gotten the message loud and clear. It took them about a half hour or so to prepare the sled for transport. Water, ice-climbing crampons, rope, a harness for the sled, alpenstocks—these were all included for the trip.

Robbins collected a compass from what remained of the cockpit and fastened this to the back of the sled so that they could keep an eye on their course. They filled a five-gallon water breaker and strapped it to the sled, then fashioned the harness for towing. LeBlanc was lifted gingerly from the wreck and placed on a sleeping bag strapped to the toboggan, and then he was covered with parachutes. As Warr and Robbins lifted him and were moving him to the sled, Crew 2 photographer's mate First Class. James B. Payne, of Orlando, Florida, presumably since he was assigned to the task, snapped a photograph of the wreck site while Ball, now back at the helm, angled over the site in a banking left-hand turn.

In the shot, according to Robbins, Kearns is seen near the sled with his arms folded. Captain Caldwell is waving his left hand in the air between Kearns and Chief Photographer's Mate Owen McCarty. The grainy figures of Warr and Robbins, again supplying the brunt of the leg and back work, can just be distinguished hauling LeBlanc toward the shadowy figure of the sled. Other items in the shot include the life raft in the upper-left-hand corner. The starboard tail rudder is jutting into the air beside McCarty, and of course there is the wing itself, with the first words of the story written in yellow on her starboard tip.

As Ball angled seaward again, supplies were dropped for the men to follow and use in their march toward rescue. Payne snapped three more shots as the *George 2* circled the crash site from various distances and perspectives. In these shots three outcroppings from the Noville Mountains gave the needed scale-lending perspective to the immensity of Antarctica. It would be nearly sixty years before they would be put to full use.

As they began trudging toward the coast, tethered together by rope like mountaineers, with LeBlanc in tow, the photographer snapped another picture from on high. The men are mere specks on a field of solid white, accompanied by the faint shadow of a Martin PBM overhead.

Ball and crew dropped one more note for the men of the *George 1*. In his large blocky scrawl, he told the men not to lose courage, that Howell had left the *Pine Island* aboard *George 3*. *George 2* was low on fuel.

Less than a mile from the wreck, the men feasted briefly on some of the stores that Ball and company had dropped to them, and with the words, "Let's get this show on the road" from Frenchy LeBlanc, they set off again as Ball and the *G2* disappeared over the horizon. It was just after 4:40 P.M. when all sight and sound of the *G2* vanished in the blue.

17

**RESCUE
DAY 14**

ABOARD *GEORGE 3,* 1:30 P.M.   "Litz, your buddy Lopez is dead,"
Howell flatly informed his navigator as he strapped in.[1]

There had been rumblings among the crew, rumors that some of
the men on *George 1* had not survived.

Shocked, Ensign Litz looked to his pilot for confirmation. Howell
was looking right back at him, judging him for a reaction. He let him
have it right between the eyes. *Had to do it that way,* Litz supposed.
The plane commander wanted to make sure his navigator wasn't going
to break down in the middle of the flight when he was needed the
most. Something written on Howell's face seemed to hold a question:
"Can you handle it?"

Litz nodded and got to work. Lt. Comdr. John D. Howell went
over the checklist with his copilot, Lt. Dale Mincer.

Somewhere below on board, Chief Photographer's Mate Dick Conger also strapped in. Lieutenant Commander Williamson, the ship's medical officer, had been preparing to come on board the flight, but an emergency appendectomy on a crewman prevented him from going. Conger was preparing himself, mentally, to become the first man to parachute down to Antarctica.

Stocked on board with them were numerous extras that could be parachuted down to the helpless survivors. Among these items was a quart bottle of Old Crow whiskey that Dufek had handed to Litz, ordering him to put it aboard the *George 3*.

Litz wasn't sure how the Eastern Task Group commander came by this whiskey. He didn't need to ask. Litz merely carried out orders and handed the bottle to the crewmen before they departed, instructing them that the precious item was to be parachuted for medicinal purposes. It was his impression that the whiskey was a personal message of encouragement between classmates George Dufek and Henry Caldwell, and that it could also be used in a medical emergency.

The *George 3* lifted off at 1:57 P.M.[2]

"ON THE ROAD" WITH CREW 3   At first the going was relatively easy. The men chose the spine of the northward, downward-flowing hill slope, which afforded them shallow snowdrifts and strong grip for their towing.

Robbins strapped himself into the harness and did most of the hauling at first and managed to pull slightly ahead of the group, with the remainder walking behind. Caldwell's program was fifteen minutes' walking followed by five minutes' rest.

When it appeared someone was faltering, he offered them cups of water, a pat on the back, and one word: "Mush."

As they descended along the spine of the hillside, they came to a crest that dipped at a sharper angle toward the sea ice in the distance.

Kearns turned around for a final glimpse of the *George 1*, now nothing more than tiny ash splinters on a background of glistening white. He would later write about the vastness of the place, and wonder how anyone had ever seen them at all. It had been an error to assume that they could be seen from the air—a charred blue airframe with puny yellow letters painted on the wing—amid all that open space.

Immensity itself had swallowed them, and somehow a pair of keen eyes had pierced into all that white and retrieved them. Kearns wanted to thank the first man to set eyes on them, for the sheer impossibility of what he had accomplished.

It seemed as if they had been "on the road" for about on hour when they heard the familiar drone of Howell's PBM.

ABOARD *GEORGE 3*, 5:50 P.M.   Litz had been dead on target with his navigation work. After a few minutes of chatter, it was agreed he had not slipped, not a jot, in his course work, despite the fact that a good friend was dead and he had just gotten the news.

But Howell and the rest of the men soon discovered that the last reported position from *George 2* had been 71 degrees 03 minutes south, 98 degrees 47 minutes west, which was as much as twenty miles seaward of the coast.

Apparently, the men of *George 2* had filed where they were when the wreckage was spotted, not where they were when the wreckage was found. In later years Litz said that a transposition error from the grid system to the lines of latitude and longitude may have been to blame. To his memory, 71-03 south crosses 98-47 west as much as fifty miles seaward of Thurston.

Whatever the case, *G2* and *G3* were in open radio contact just before *G3* landed in the calm waters beside *Pine Island*. The radio contact can be confirmed in Ensign Jones's personal log.

Consequently, *George 3* had to find the wreck site and the men all over again. One can understand this error, given the rush to fly over the crash site and find out if anyone was left alive, forgetting all else temporarily.

George 3 located the pocket of open water about two miles off-shore amid pack ice. It was an oblong bay that seemed to have been made specifically for their purposes, carved into the ice by some merciful warm currents. Fortunately, Ball's radio description of it was so precise that once this lake was located, the mystery was easily resolved.

The *G3* then headed due south and found the wreck site, with Conger snapping photos as they flew inland.

Finally, according to Litz, Aviation Radioman Second Class William Smith said the words everyone was waiting for—"There they are"—picking out the tiny figures trudging below in the merciless glare through a portside window.[3]

Conger made a request over the interphone. He wanted to parachute down to the men to help them pull their burden to the sea.

"Negative, Conger. Stay where you are," Howell replied.

But as the men of *George 3* began tossing out more supplies to the survivors, Howell kept calling back, "Conger, are you still aboard? Are you still back there?"

When interviewed circa 1979 by Antarctic author Lilse Abbott Rose about the crash and rescue of the *George 1* crew, Conger mused that Howell was hinting for him to go ahead and jump; he just couldn't officially okay a request to do something so risky.[4]

Conger opted to stay put, which was a wise decision in light of the fact that no one had ever attempted to parachute over Antarctica before. Conger took off his parachute, perhaps a bit relieved. Courageous though the notion had been, he had never jumped out of a plane before; now Howell was telling him he couldn't do it anyway.

———

ON THE ROAD WITH CREW 3   The shot of whiskey went down Kearns's throat like burning gasoline and rebounded to a small stain on the snow, which was seasoned with apricot chunks.

That had been an interesting experiment. He wiped his lips and smiled sheepishly.

Robbins's shot hit the mark and remained. He took another belt from the bottle and offered it to the others, who waved him off. His eyes glistened with tears of warm appreciation and adrenaline above a beaming grin.

Caldwell cautioned the men not to take any more from the bottle. They might get dehydrated. It was already getting much cooler as a sea breeze ascended the step toward them. Some of the clothing they had shed on the glaring white plain of ice above was now put back on.

A new batch of supplies descended from the waist hatch of the *George 3*. Some of the weighted parachutes and flagpoles penetrated the snowdrifts, swallowed by the deep, soft powder. That wasn't a good sign. It meant the going was about to get more difficult.

Caldwell said that time was of the essence and that some of the stuff the men from the *G3* had dropped would have to remain where it fell.

One of the supply caches landed nearby, and Kearns asked if they could retrieve it. Caldwell agreed, and Robbins and Warr complied. The men opened more of the food rations that had been dropped.

"Now boys, don't gobble this stuff. You'll get sick," Caldwell said as he twisted open a can of Spam with one of the can openers. Before he could contain himself, Capt. Henry Caldwell was digging his fingers into the spongy meat product, wolfing it down like a madman. He did everything but lick the can clean.

The laughter that followed was contagious and welcomed.

"Don't wolf it down, ey, Captain?"

The men watched as the *George 3* lined up on approach to land in the open water four-to-six miles away.

———

ABOARD *GEORGE 3,* 7:20 P.M.   The lake was glassy and calm, less than a mile wide, and ten thousand feet long.

There were several medium-sized bergy bits floating around the edges of this ice lake and many chunks of ice riding just at or below the surface. Men crossed their fingers as Howell threaded the needle between them all, skimming the plane over the surface until it took on the familiar feel of a boat again.

Litz's thought was that if the winds got kicking up, those bergs could come loose from the sides and crash into the *George 3* fairly easily. He noticed a low cloud bank to the north that was going to ground.

Howell and Conger pulled the CO_2 cartridge on the nine-man life raft and stowed paddles, a sled, food supplies, and additional survival gear aboard.

Mincer and Litz were told to stay in touch with *Pine Island* and keep the *George 2* away from the icebergs as Howell and Conger boarded their rubber raft and paddled ashore.

Soon after leaving the ship they noticed a school of blackfish heading directly toward them, pursued by some unseen predators below. Robbins said these were likely emperor penguins engaged in a hunt.

Whatever was chasing them, the foot-long silver-sided fish with midnight blue dorsal stripes slashed and jumped in frenzied shoals toward the raft but were diverted by Conger's panicked, flailing paddle. He was afraid the swift blades of meat might puncture the craft, sending him and Howell into the twenty-eight-degree brine.

Reaching shore, they were met by another problem. The sea ice formed a ledge about five feet high, comprised of jagged shards jutting in all directions.

"Back! Back!" Howell bellowed as their little raft nearly impaled itself on one of the shards. They crept along the edge of this shelf until they found a suitable foothold, an area where the ice cliff was little more than three feet high.

Howell hacked down the shards of ice with an axe until a smooth landing spot was available. Howell and Conger then piled the supplies ashore and set out for the tired men of *George 1*. Only then did Howell notice that he had cut himself, perhaps on the jagged shards of ice. He took off a bloodied glove and grabbed hold of an alpenstock. His bloodied hand fused to the ski pole in a matter of minutes as he worked. He would later have to pry and peel the hand free, injuring it further.

By now both groups of men were fighting through hip-deep snowdrifts. Howell and Conger were on the sea ice, which was covered by a thick blanket of snow. They were heading toward another ledge of ice in the distance; this one was twenty feet high. Beyond it a sloping plain of ice rose sharply to gently rounded foothills five hundred feet above them.

Breaks and crevasses dotted the hillside in menacing little pockets. Howell and Conger moved on. After a while they could see the men of *George 1*, miniscule specks coming downslope. They seemed to creep along so slowly, like wounded ants. There they were, still dragging their sled behind them, a field of danger before them on the slope and below them on the ledge.

Kearns could see the men of the *George 3*, and they also appeared miniscule and immobile. Someone asked why their rescuers weren't moving. Caldwell took a closer look, piercing the distance, and said, "They are. It just doesn't look like it from here."

Conger and Howell stopped for a moment. Howell was nearly snow-blind. He had forgotten his polarizing lenses and now could barely see anything other than a field of white in front of him.

"Commander, where the hell are you taking us, sir?" Conger finally asked when Howell seemed to fall off course. Howell stopped for a moment to wrap his injured hand and admitted he couldn't see the men. The two rescuers had stalled out earlier, adjusting the fold-down runners on the sled. Doing this greatly impeded their progress, but now one of them was virtually blind—not able to see a damned thing in all the glare.[5]

The air temperature plummeted by tens of degrees while they stood there, and the sun began dipping behind the mountainside to their south.

At this point a panicked Bill Kearns watched in disbelief. The far side of the ice lake was now obscured by fog sweeping in toward the *George 3*.

Caldwell had seen it too. Everyone then wordlessly doubled their efforts in a race to reach the edge of the sea ice before they were again cut off from rescue.

The snowdrifts rose to the chest in places. At times bolts of pain from Caldwell's ankle would cause him to stumble or double over. More than once McCarty fell. When the big photographer went down in a heap, the other men were hauled back with him.

He complained bitterly about pains in his legs and his head, and Kearns stifled the urge to give him a good balling out.

Gone was all the humor in their situation. Some of their supplies and even some of their clothing were discarded in an effort to trim off weight and make forward progress, drowning as they were in snow. Each man remembered well the facts that the last time a big fog bank like this moved in, it didn't let up for hours, and that on one occasion during their two-week stay, the fog didn't let up for days.

If they were trapped in the open, they would soon be coveting some of what they had sacrificed for speed. LeBlanc hadn't spoken in some time. His eyes were covered over with a greasy film. That was not a good sign. Was he even alive anymore?

ABOARD *GEORGE 3*   Through a starboard porthole Litz had been watching the fog as well. He wanted to know how deeply it extended to the north. He told Mincer they should take off and survey the fog bank from the air. If they became fogbound and a larger storm behind the fog hit them, the walls within this ice lake could close in on them like a vise, crushing the *George 3*.

But Mincer wouldn't go for it, as Litz recalled. He did not want to do anything that ran contrary to the standing orders of Iron John Howell. Howell said nothing about taking off on any survey flights. He didn't want to be responsible for whatever happened.

"Alright, I'll do it," Litz said. "I'll take the heat."

Within ten minutes they were in the air. Litz, a qualified pilot, guided the *G3* carefully around the lake and above the fog bank. It was deep, but there didn't seem to be any serious weather to the north of it. He landed again, this time much closer to the brightly colored life raft. The men threw canvas sea anchors out of the waist hatches and prepared for the fog, which was now halfway across the lake.

ON THE ROAD WITH THE *G1* CREW   When they negotiated the side of a hill, they came to a broad area before an ice cliff. A few steps out onto this, and Owen McCarty disappeared with a horrified scream, dragging Robbins, then Caldwell, then Warr with him on the lead rope. Everyone dug his heels and elbows into the snow and ice and braced.

Kearns was also tugged to the ground, either by a rope or by one of the falling bodies.

"Help! Help me, guys! Get me the hell out of here!"

Kearns managed a glimpse over the hole in the ice where McCarty hung flailing his arms and legs as he tried to gain a foothold and climb from the deep, slippery crevasse. The rope held at his shoulders. It appeared as though the hole ran down into the dark blue sea itself. If he had fallen, Owen McCarty would have been lost forever. The men hauled him up, and everyone lay flat on the ice while McCarty, with tears of relief in his eyes, collected his breath in gasps.

Obviously, they had strayed out onto a field of crevasses. The men took a good look around now.

Some of these cracks were not very deep. Others, concealed beneath the soft layer of snow, obviously ran all the way down to oblivion. It was like waking up to the fact that you've sleepwalked halfway out into a minefield. Any step could result in a horrible, plummeting death.

The edge of this field of crevasses appeared to be stable. So they carefully picked their way toward it, gingerly clawing the fifty-to-sixty yards over the ridges, with the sled-bound LeBlanc in tow.

By now the cold was numbing their senses so much that Robbins very nearly walked off the edge of this cliff, dragging LeBlanc with him. Caldwell coolly warned him in the nick of time. Robbins stood there and looked over the edge, a sixty-foot drop straight down.

The fog had covered the *George 3* completely and was moving toward the shore of the ice lake. The two figures that could be seen earlier were somewhere amid a field of broken white blocks and huge butter pads of pastel blue. The sun had dipped completely behind the mountains to their south, casting a long azure shadow over everything.

There didn't seem to be a way down to the hard, flat shelf below. They looked to the east and west, and nowhere did the cliff height dip to a level above the sea ice that would afford them passage. They weren't mountaineers, but some of the emergency supplies included mountaineering gear, such as crampon attachments and alpenstocks for digging and testing the ice.

But where to descend? They had to do it soon, or they risked becoming trapped on this ledge of crevasses for hours, perhaps even days. Caldwell, Kearns, and Robbins struck out along the ice cliff to the east, while McCarty and Warr remained behind with LeBlanc. Splitting up was a dangerous ploy but necessary.

The group stumbled along the ledge in the gathering fog. Either Kearns or Robbins* discovered that a part of the cliff had sloughed

---

*Both survivors claim to have seen this feature first. It is likely they saw it simultaneously.

away, providing a perfect incline comprised of three large blocks of ice down to the ice shelf. They hadn't seen it before, and now, miraculously, there it was.

Kearns remained to mark the spot, and the other men went back to collect Warr, LeBlanc, and McCarty. En route, Robbins accidentally dropped his compass. It skittered down a hole in the ice, gone forever with his curses trailing after it, but Caldwell told him not to worry about it. They would beat the fog to safety, he said.

They rejoined Kearns with the other men. Warr and McCarty traversed the snow-covered ramp down to sea level, slowly, using the crampons and alpenstocks. The men up top then belayed LeBlanc downward, using the sled and ropes.

"Fellas, what's going on?" LeBlanc muttered weakly.

No one said a word.

After everyone was safely down on the sea ice, McCarty whispered to Caldwell and the others that it was a good thing LeBlanc's eyes had remained closed during the descent. His heart might not have been able to take the shock if he had seen what they were up to.

Just before the fog obscured everything, Kearns had seen an exposed, rocky outcropping—a nunatak—halfway between the ice cliff and the patch of open water. And sure enough, through holes in the falling curtain of white, they saw it again a few hundred yards away. The group made for it.

Men fell out one by one as they strode up to the side of the frozen black obelisk, sending out powdery plumes of exhaled breath into the darkening twilight. LeBlanc's sled skidded to a stop. Now that the entire area was covered in dense, cold mist, they feared for the well-being of who ever that had been out there trying to get to them. Kearns guessed that it had been Howell and another man. Where were they?

That meant the men of the *George 1* were on their own again. They sat for a while, listening to the reassuring, distant sounds of the *George 3*. Every few minutes someone would start her up and rev the engines.

The fog didn't appear to be lifting, so they decided to begin picking their way to the edge of the sea ice, using the periodic sound of those engines as a guide. The men were on their feet again, preparing to move out, when suddenly they heard the unmistakable flat clap of a .45-caliber service revolver. Then another.

Out of the mists came two lifesaving silhouettes, Conger and Howell. Howell held a pistol in his bandaged hand. Conger reached for his camera to record what he saw, but, struck to the core by the condition of the men, he resisted his photographer's instinct, deciding that his primary role should be that of a shipmate. He offered his shoulder to his pals for support and solace.

In an interview for this book, Howell said the men before him were "bedraggled, bearded, tired, and elated." For a moment, no one said a word. Kearns later wrote, "We got down on our knees and cried like babies."

Conger later wrote an account of their evening clawing over the ice and trying to reach the beleaguered men of *George 1*. These impressions, written for the *Saturday Evening Post*, were an addendum to McCarty's log and became the centerpiece for the May 17, 1947, edition of the magazine. His writing served where his photo skills would not.

There was no laughing, or cheery greetings. The survivors were past that stage. First in line was Lt. Kearns, who looked as if he couldn't believe it. Second was Chief McCarty, a fellow photographer and good friend. I slipped an arm around his shoulder and said a few words. He just let out a sob and said, "I was never so glad to see a photographer in all my life."

Conger added:

I saw quite a bit during the war, but I can safely say I never saw such gallantry, such real heroism as I did that night on the ice. How those men ever traveled over ten miles of snow, ice, and crevasses will always remain a mystery to me.[6]

In the maddening hugeness of the place, through that crystal clarity of the air before the fog set in, Conger and Howell watched, imprisoned by the distance and obstacles, as the six men struggled toward their own salvation.

Howell's only regret was that it took them so long to reach them. Everyone aboard the *Pine Island* had been doing everything in his power to find the missing men.

Caldwell knew that. It was evidenced in the condition, and the spirit, of the men he brought down from the mountain. They still had plenty of fight left in them, Howell said in the interview.

"The job of survival, ninety-nine percent of the time comes down to refusing to quit. That's what made him [i.e., Caldwell] a good leader. He knew we would be out there looking for them the first chance the weather cleared."

But the men weren't out of the woods yet. They were all about a mile from where Howell and Conger had stashed a cache of survival supplies. Open water, where the *George 3* was waiting, was a little farther still. The fog was thick with newly formed snow, softly falling around them now in puffy flakes.

This covered their tracks back to the edge of the sea ice. In the darkening Antarctic twilight they followed the faded tracks for a while, aided in their search by the sound of the *George 3*.

ABOARD *GEORGE 3*, 11 P.M. Things were getting dicey at this point, in Litz's recollection. The big plane's auxiliary power unit wasn't functioning. Electricity needed to contact *Pine Island* had to be conserved since they had dedicated some of their power to monitoring the slow dance of the icebergs around them.

They revved up the engines periodically to inject additional juice back into the batteries and "crept" away from the bergs, maintaining their seventy-five-yard proximity to the rescue point by using paddles and sea anchors as a scum of sea ice began forming on the lake.

It had been nearly four hours since they had seen Howell or Conger. Soon after hearing the gunshot, Litz gazed out a window toward the shoreline and told Mincer he thought he had Howell in view.

A huge, dark figure stood in the shadows. Litz could just barely make it out. It must have been at least six feet tall, he guessed. Who else could it be? The men traded binoculars. Indeed, someone was staring back at them, but it wasn't Howell.

It was an enormous Emperor penguin, just standing there on the shore of ice, watching the airplane in a trance of numbed curiosity. Soon the gigantic seabird was joined by about twenty members of his tribe. Litz assumed the larger, commanding-looking bird had been their equivalent of Iron John Howell—no one to mess with.

ON SHORE, JANUARY 12, 1947, MIDNIGHT TO 7:30 A.M. Howell, Conger, Caldwell, Kearns, McCarty, Robbins, Warr, and LeBlanc found their way and were received by the penguins. The men kept warm as best they could and waited for the weather to clear.

The penguins walked right up to the intruders and inspected them with their customary tuxedoed belligerence. Who were these shabby interlopers? their manner seemed to ask. Hadn't they been informed that this Antarctic send-off was a black-tie affair?

It was a surreal moment of comic relief. In their exhaustion the men had the impression they had stepped into a cocktail party.

It seemed to a delirious LeBlanc—who could do nothing more than stare with one eye out of his coverings, hoping to God they would be able to leave the ice—that the largest of the penguins was eyeing him, personally. The bird stood there and watched over LeBlanc, as if full of pity for him. It was an eerie feeling.

Sometime during the early morning hours, LeBlanc asked Conger to take a picture of the big penguin, and this photo later became a cherished memento of the crash, handed down to his children.

In the early morning the fog had finally cleared enough to allow the men to transport the survivors one at a time between the ledge of ice and the *George 3*.

By 10 A.M. all were aboard the *George 3* except for Caldwell. He came aboard last, cradling the bottle of whiskey, as Conger paddled the life raft alongside the airplane. It was slightly more than twenty-four hours since they were first seen by Chief Pharmacist's Mate W. A. Long aboard Lieutenant Ball's plane, *George 2*.

Litz reached down to help Caldwell, but Caldwell politely refused his hand.

"That's all right. I can make it on my own, son."[7]

And the ship's captain with the cracked vertebrae in his neck, injured ankle, broken nose, and shattered teeth hoisted himself aboard.

LeBlanc was ministered to by one of the two pharmacist's mates aboard. He asked the young pharmacist mate to remove his shoes, which the man did. LeBlanc, staring through the mucous membranes covering his eyes, looked down at his feet, which still appeared to be covered in black leather. He asked the man again to remove his shoes.

"I have, Frenchy," came the reply. Frenchy LeBlanc's feet and his lower legs had died. He drifted off to merciful sleep in one of *George 3*'s bunks.[8]

Sometime during the one-and-a-half-hour flight back to *Pine Island*, Conger took a picture of the men, huddled around a bleary-eyed Caldwell as he related the tale of how they had crashed, lived on the ice, and been rescued. Kearns leaned back against the bulkhead, now humming with the familiar sound of the big R-2800 engines. McCarty, Warr, and Robbins listened as the captain spoke, their adrenaline slowly giving way to exhaustion.

18 ABOARD *PI* AGAIN

ABOARD PINE ISLAND, 11:20 A.M. Doc Williamson was ferried out to the *George 3* as soon as she touched down. He remained aboard her, looking after LeBlanc while the *Pine Island*'s crew set the hook to haul her inboard.

Williamson immediately informed the ship to prepare his clinic for LeBlanc and have men at the ready to bear the stretcher to the clinic. Like Howell and Conger, he had been appalled at how bad the man smelled. Not that bathing would have done him any good over the last two weeks. He was decomposing.

The men covered LeBlanc in soft blankets and attempted to bandage some of the wounds on his face until Williamson could get a good solid look at his legs.

In his article McCarty recalled how tender the entire crew was with LeBlanc.

LeBlanc was the first to be disembarked. Six seamen carried him. When they set him down the wind blew the blanket from the stretcher and the [sailors] looked down at Frenchy's burned, scarred face. [A] young man broke down.

"God . . . we worked like bastards but we got there too late! He's dead!"

Frenchy opened his eyes. He smiled. It must have been hard 'cause his skin was so cracked and burned and he said, "No fella, you did just fine! Thanks a lot!"[1]

The young man turned to a photographer snapping pictures and said, "That was worth more to me than a Congressional Medal," as LeBlanc went past.

Caldwell stepped aboard a platform hoisted up on a forklift, and as he was lowered to a waiting George Dufek, he clasped his friend's hand and said, "Wasn't the slightest doubt that you'd get us."

Before the men had the chance to wash or change clothes, they were escorted through a gauntlet of snapping cameras to a briefing set up in *Pine Island*'s flight ready room.

Kearns was handed a cigar. In that customary way of the 1940s navy, all the men were treated to Lucky Strikes, cigars, coffee, and a couple more shots of Old Crow in hot cups to stem their aches and pains.

The entire flight department and some select members of the crew filed into the room as Dufek, Schwartz, and a navy chaplain, Lt. Everett J. Le Compte, former pastor of the Central Presbyterian Church of Joliet, Illinois, interviewed Robbins, Kearns, Caldwell, Warr, and McCarty.

Navy photographers snapped photos of the interview while the balance of Flight Crews 1 and 2 looked on. Many of the men in the photo appear grim faced and tired.

Dead center behind Caldwell, watching over the proceedings, is Howell. Slightly to the right and behind him, Litz can be seen, saddened by the realization that his friend Lopez isn't among the survivors.

The men then convalesced in the commodore's cabin. Dufek gladly gave up his quarters for the crew of the *George 1*. After showers and shaves, and after a film crew toured through, Le Compte interviewed each man alone for personal impressions of his ordeal. These impressions were included in a lengthy dispatch to the fleets and back to Washington., D.C.

Le Compte even interviewed LeBlanc briefly as Williamson looked over his wounds.

The direct quotes provide a window into the roiling emotions the survivors were experiencing at that moment.

Captain Caldwell, whom the men now referred to as the Man of Iron (distinguishing him somewhat from Iron John), received the highest praise from all.

LeBlanc said, "During this experience I have met the finest man I have ever known, Captain Caldwell."

"Captain Caldwell seemed never to sleep. He always had an ear cocked for the sound of an airplane," said McCarty.

While devouring his feast of steak, pie, and ice cream in the commodore's cabin, McCarty broke down, overcome with emotion.

"Captain Caldwell promised me all this when we got back. . . . I never thought [it] would be so soon."

Kearns said of Warr and Robbins: "I can't say enough for their courage. Their spirit and ingenuity were amazing."

Warr had this to say when asked what it was like to see the *Pine Island* again: "It was the most beautiful sight I have ever seen. By the way, I would like to look this ship over, so don't anybody say a thing about flying for the next three weeks."

Although they didn't know it, Warr and Robbins had also been injured, by frostbite. Both men's toes and fingertips were damaged. A space heater and a fan were set up near their beds to thaw the extremities. Robbins later commented that it felt like his toes were being roasted alive as the warm blood began to circulate again and repair the damage.

They thought they would be on the job for the remainder of the cruise, but the navy had other plans. They were all to be sent home for a massive press conference. They were now front-page news.

McCarty's scalp began to heal as soon as it was treated. Kearns was another story. The difficult breaks in his arm would require serious attention. They would need to be "reset," as Williamson informed him—in other words, rebroken.

He also had a bone chip in his cranium where his head had impacted the frame of the cockpit window. The doctor wondered how Kearns had been able to walk at all, given the extent of his injuries. The dizzy spells that he, Caldwell, and McCarty experienced were the classic signs of concussion, Williamson told Kearns.

Most concerning to all and another apparent miracle was the condition of Frenchy LeBlanc. Williamson did not have the facilities to treat his burns or his frostbitten legs. The flier would have to be transported home as soon as possible.

In later years LeBlanc would tell his children of the level of concern that Williamson had. While he never admitted it to the patient, he did relate it to Dr. Leonard Barber, who took over LeBlanc's care from Williamson. Barber in later years told Frenchy how close he came to death.

According to the family, Williamson felt from the get-go that he was looking at a man who was essentially dead—the patient just didn't know it or flatly refused to accept it. Williamson felt that death would be likely to come at any moment. The massive loss of body weight from lack of food and from dehydration, the crust of angry burns and scars that covered most of his body, the fact that his legs were essentially dead below the knees, threatening blood poisoning—any one of these afflictions alone could kill a grown man.

It was an affront to reality that LeBlanc was not only alive, but lucid from time to time, capable of carrying on a conversation and even joking about his sorry state. From a medical perspective it couldn't be happening, yet there lay Frenchy breathing, talking, even joking. As Williams tallied the unbelievable damages on his patient's chart, the balance sheet said that LeBlanc had died days ago.

J. D. Dickens was equally amazed by how much a man in LeBlanc's shape could extend himself. Approaching LeBlanc, who was lying on a gurney, he asked a pharmacist's mate about his friend and plane commander. Was he awake?

LeBlanc by now was totally covered in bandages. It was hard to tell when he was conscious and when he wasn't.

"Is that you, Dick?" LeBlanc asked.

"Yes, it's me, Frenchy."

"I'm glad you didn't go, Dick. I'm glad you weren't there. It was a bad one."

Dickens was struck to the heart with the selflessness of Ralph LeBlanc, assuaging his worst fears: that he had somehow abandoned his buddies, that he should have been there, that things would have worked out differently if he had been aboard. LeBlanc gave him total absolution and put his worst fears to rest immediately.

The way he said it, it was as though he had anticipated the conversation, thinking about others, their problems and feelings, when he himself was at death's door.

Dickens asked him point-blank if his presence aboard would have changed the outcome of the crash. LeBlanc coolly replied, "Oh, hell no, Dick. There weren't nothing you could do."

The way LeBlanc said it, the two men might have been standing beside a calm lake somewhere with a can of beer in one hand, a fishing pole in the other. When Dickens was interviewed for this book, the memory of the conversation with LeBlanc brought tears to his eyes.

The crew who had rescued LeBlanc and all the men were immediately given a well-deserved break from routine. If Warr didn't want to be asked about flying for the next few days, the *PI* crew also didn't want to repair, hoist, fuel, and launch another PBM for a while. Schwartz issued the orders for suspension of flight operations until further notice. He congratulated the men he had driven hard to find the missing aircraft.

Ensign Jones made use of the rest to pen two more letters, which, along with all crew mail, would be sent to the *Philippine Sea* by way of the *Brownson*, due to arrive on the 17th. The *Brownson* would also take possession of the survivors for immediate transport.

Jan. 14, 1947

Dear Mom, Dad and Ray:

I'm a pretty happy guy right now. A couple of days ago we found the survivors of our lost airplane. It was my crew that found them out there. We had been 3½ to 4 hours out when we spotted their signal smoke. I was flying the plane at the time they were spotted. You should have seen the crew shouting and jumping for joy. Of course these men below us were pretty happy too.

They were living in the wreckage of their plane and two tents on a slope about 1,000 feet above sea level. We dropped lots of food, a radio, some medicine to them. Then we laid out a course for them to the sea where another plane landed to pick them up. We circled around them for about 7 hours dropping messages and generally watching over them. Five of the men were walking around and the sixth man was seen in a sleeping bag. He was pulled to the coast in a sled. Which was salvaged from the wreckage. It was quiet [sic] a site [sic] watching them start their trek to the coast pulling the sled with the injured man.

I lost a buddy in the crash. Ens. Max Lopez was killed in the explosion along with two other men. The plane was flying low in storm after storm with very little visibility. They didn't know they were over land. The plane hit the top of a snow-covered ridge and skipped into the air in full control. Bill Kearns was flying and he says he put full throttle to it and started to

pull up when the plane exploded in the air. The plane was carrying about
2,500 gallons of gas. . . . Bill went out the co-pilot's hatch taking it with
him. How he wasn't killed I don't know. The pilot, "Frenchy" LeBlanc was
strapped in the seat and knocked out in the crash. He was very badly
burned. In fact, I didn't recognize him. He had lots of will in him to live
these two weeks without medical attention. His feet were badly burned and
frostbitten. I have talked to him and he is very brave and in good humor.
He put out his hand, shook mine and said "Thanks."

The three dead men were buried near the plane. Their names were
printed on the wing in yellow paint for searchers to see.

The day after they were found the men were back aboard ship. The men
say that the Captain was a man of iron. He treated them swell and really
looked after them. . . .

I hope you are all well and not worrying about me. I'm in good
health. . . . So long for now.

Love, Howard.

The following day, sometime before his evening watch, Jones inventoried and boxed up the possessions of his pal Max Lopez for ship-
ment back to his family in Newport, Rhode Island. He included a note
to Lopez's mother relaying his sympathies for her son's death.

19   HOMEWARD RUN

USS BROWNSON, JANUARY 18, 1947   Comdr. Harry Gimber insisted that Lt. (jg) Ralph "Frenchy" LeBlanc be given his own personal quarters for the trip to the *Phil Sea* after five of the remaining survivors were transferred from the *Pine Island*, via launch boat, somewhere two hundred miles northwest of Cape Leahy.[1]

Robbins recalled that the smell of gangrenous flesh was so overpowering, he couldn't imagine the men of the *Brownson* removing it quickly from the skipper's quarters.

For seven days the *Brownson* steamed through pack ice as though she were an icebreaker, damaging her bow in the rush to get the survivors, most of all LeBlanc, to the *Phil Sea* for proper medical attention.

During the crossing Robbins and Kearns would both take turns sitting at LeBlanc's bedside, reading from the Thomas Eggen classic, *Mister Roberts.*

This 1946 novel was about a junior-grade lieutenant who was the executive officer aboard a fictitious cargo ship in the Pacific during World War II. The "JG," Roberts, played sane man to the comically idiotic captain, whom the other men covertly referred to as Stupid, as though the insult were either a rank or job title aboard ship. The book was hugely popular among young navy men in the late 1940s, and was later made into a movie starring Henry Fonda as Mr. Roberts and James Cagney as the captain bent on adhering to the most idiotic of regulations and on avoiding warfare at all cost.

LeBlanc, now covered in medical tape and bandages except for one eye, would hold a hand up periodically, asking for a particularly humorous passage to be read again. A muffled staccato moan and a tear falling from his eye would let the reader know the funny passage had again found its mark.

Amazingly, the transfer of the men from the *Brownson* to the *Philippine Sea* went off without a hitch. The men were hauled over using a high wire. The four in better health were held on the line with a breeches buoy, a device consisting of a life ring with a pair of canvas "breeches" attached beneath a pulley. The breeches buoy was perfected in practice during the previous century by the U.S. Lifesaving Service. Somehow the men managed to haul LeBlanc in a gurney between ships. The transfer went so smoothly, LeBlanc didn't remember how he came aboard the *Phil Sea*; he slept throughout the high-wire act.

By January 25, the Central Group had landed, with great difficulty, at the Bay of Whales, had unloaded their cargo, and was completing the tent city known as Little America IV.

The tent city itself was erected a mile in from the thick shelf ice where the ships *Merrick*, *Mount Olympus*, *Yancey*, and *Northwind* were moored with lines and "deadmen"—phone poles sunk into the snow and fitted with slip-toggles to lines attached to the ships.[2]

During the unloading on the 21st, Antarctica claimed a fourth

American life. Seventeen-year-old Vance Woodall, a seaman second-class from Louisville, Kentucky, aboard *Yancey* had been riding behind a tank-style pull tractor on an empty skid. As the tractor bounced around and burrowed for grip, Woodall became tangled in the metal tracks. He was killed instantly.[3]

Back on *Pine Island*, Dufek and Sessums on the 19th had crashed a second Sikorsky beside the ship. They were rescued, but it was becoming obvious to the entire task force that these helicopters were dangerous to operate in extremely cold temperatures and could prove instantly fatal in dense fog.[4] The pilot's only clue to precisely how badly his rotors had iced up came as he approached the deck of the ship. When he couldn't control the wild descent to the flight deck, he discovered with seconds to spare that his propellers were coated with ice. There was no choice at that point but to "ditch," or impact on the deck. It had happed to Dufek and Sessums twice, as the fleet was now aware.

The *Brownson* stood close off from the *Phil Sea*, and would later serve as a weather station and potential rescue craft for the R4Ds that were slated to take off for Little America any day now. The *Northwind* motored out to a position somewhere between the *Phil Sea* and the Ross Ice Shelf to serve as another potential rescue ship; it waited there for the launch. All that was missing was clear weather.

By now the men of *Phil Sea* had gotten to know the man who was responsible for the whole show in the first place, Rear Adm. Richard E. Byrd.

Since Panama, Byrd had begun taking "constitutional walks" on the *Phil Sea*'s considerable flight deck. Men formed a growing cadre of admirers that huddled around the admiral, to provide human windbreaks for him as they listened to him expound on everything from the current weather to past experiences at both poles.

Neither Robbins nor Warr were among this group, although they certainly would have been instantly welcomed by Byrd, to whom the word *enlisted* was a euphemism for a hands-on man. Byrd would have valued and admired Robbins and Warr as much as he would have any fleet admiral for the job they did in the Antarctic. But Warr and Robbins became fascinated with the gigantic ship's radio operations and Command Information Control (CIC) centers. They were like kids in a candy store, with so much to explore and learn.

More than once Kearns was invited on one of these constitutional walks following a cordial lunch with Byrd in the ship's officers' mess.

The elder statesman of the Antarctic demonstrated immediate kindness and understanding to Kearns following the crash. After all, Byrd knew what it was like to find oneself trapped in whiteout conditions and narrowly escape death. He also knew what it was like to crash-land an airplane on the ice. He told Kearns, as he had told reporters in Panama, and as he wrote in *National Geographic* in October of the following year, that generally explorers were introduced to Antarctic conditions incrementally; the men of the *George 1* had been smacked in the face with those deadly conditions without experience and yet somehow had managed to muddle through and survive.

If Kearns was feeling a bit down at this point, it is perhaps understandable. LeBlanc was informed that he was going to lose his lower legs. They didn't know yet how his severe burns would be treated, or even if they could be. Doctors might never be able to remove the hideous burns from his face.

Lopez, Hendersin, and Williams were dead, which was announced and hashed over again and again on every news broadcast Kearns heard. He had been at the controls when the plane crashed. More to the nail of the matter, he was feeling damned by the faint praise of those who said that it could have happened to anyone. He had no one to talk to about it.

But what it definitely did not mean was that he should burden someone else—least of all a heroic admiral—with what he was going through. Like any good pilot, Kearns was no fan of squishy introspection. He was uncomfortable with situations that required it. Like many sailors, aviators, and soldiers of his generation, Bill Kearns was raised to take the manly way out when faced with extreme mental stress: deal with it, all by yourself. Sometimes that meant silence; sometimes that meant drink.

How could he approach Frenchy with anything but a good word and a smile on his face when LeBlanc was dealing with so much more? He didn't feel he could chat with Robbie or Warr about it, nor with McCarty for that matter.

Fifty-seven-year-old Byrd seemed to understand what Kearns was going through and tried to shake him out of the doldrums in at least two fatherly chats.

Byrd was the first and only person during those hours of waiting to launch the R4Ds to the continent and return home, who sensed the case of survivor's guilt that descended on Lt. (jg) Wiliam Henry Kearns, Jr., like a lead elephant.

Kearns went on to appreciate the admiral's kindness in later years, ferociously defending him against all detractors, wherever and whenever he encountered them.

In the five days the ship sat idle, waiting for weather to change, a depressed Kearns went so far as to avoid the admiral once—not for anything the man said or did, but because Byrd would invariably invite him to walk topside with his group after they dined together. It was a request he could not turn down.

Ever ahead of his time, Rear Adm. Richard Byrd, as Kearns quickly learned, was also a true health nut who ate like a rabbit. When he "messed," his lunches consisted of carrot soup, celery, tomato juice, lettuce, and the like. He expected those around him to follow suit. Kearns was becoming accustomed to the steak, gravy, and mashed potatoes that flight officers received in their own mess hall.

"I was in a great deal of pain, and it hurt like hell to walk around up there. I hid from him so he couldn't invite me to lunch, because after lunch there was also the walk to contend with."

In the two brisk walks he had taken with Byrd, Kearns found he was still in very rough shape and in need of rest more than anything else.

Phil Sea was indeed a good place to hide. Since it was peacetime, the usual complement of soldiers and marines was not to be found aboard. In some sections of the ship, hallways resembled the streets of a ghost town. The fliers commandeered the forward section of the vessel, where they could relax and get loud without disturbing the "real" crew.

A member of that "air group" attached to the *Phil Sea* was Lt. Gus Shinn, a proud "driver" of R4Ds. Shinn, like Kearns, remembered well his long walks with Byrd on the deck of the *Phil Sea*.

"He was a very nice man and in extremely good health for someone who was fifty-six or fifty-seven at the time," Shinn said.[5]

Shinn would be the third pilot off *Phil Sea*, en route to the continent. He would take off about three hours after Byrd and his escort plane had safely landed at Little America. Shinn also remembers that Byrd recognized usable publicity whenever and wherever he encountered it.

"He was a promoter, there's no doubt about it," Shinn said.

Kearns also saw this side of the admiral. But in contrast to those who believed Byrd to be stuffy and overly serious about himself, Kearns knew the admiral was conscious of his own showmanship. Kearns was told by Byrd at least one of the tricks of the trade in promoting Antarctica as a testing ground for explorers seeking adventure. During one of their walks Byrd turned to Kearns with a smile and told him that he had a story to tell that would be good for Antarctic explorers and would-be explorers everywhere.

He said, "Lieutenant, remember when you get back home, the last thing the public wants to hear is that it was a nice sunny day and everything was fine."

Fortunately, Kearns knew he wouldn't have to embellish anything in relation to the crash of the *George 1*. Some of their days on the ice indeed had been sunny, but burying your friends in the snow, watching another being eaten away by burns and elements, and waiting to find out whether you would live or die seemed far from nice.

In the early-morning hours of January 29, Kearns was called to the bridge of the *Phil Sea* by Capt. Delbert Cornwell and a flight officer. He was told to report to the *Brownson* in order to serve aboard her as an observer. *Brownson* would rush to rescue any of the survivors should an R4D take a plunge on takeoff. It was an honor he didn't expect.

By late afternoon Kearns found himself miles away, aboard "868." There he was, called to the bridge by Comdr. Harry Gimber for another unexpected surprise.

"Lieutenant, they want to know how long they need to get all six planes off the deck," Gimber said to Kearns.

The *Phil Sea* needed a certain amount of space in which to steam into the wind while releasing Byrd's planes. They had to look for an area with a suitable length of open water. They also wanted to make sure each aircraft kept a safe distance from the wake of the one preceding it, but they also needed to get each plane off in a hurry as bad weather was creeping in. Kearns was asked to render an opinion as one of the few men who had flown in these conditions. Once again, men in planes were placing their lives in his hands. It was a huge vote of confidence.

"At least thirty-six minutes, total," came the answer after a few moments. "They'll need six minutes a piece."

His best guess turned out to be precise. The Admiral of the Antarctic was "going home." And, after transferring back aboard *Phil Sea*, so were Bill Kearns and the crew of *George 1*.

PHILIPPINE SEA Sometime before the ship reached Panama, Frenchy LeBlanc had the balance of his right shin and foot amputated. The leg had been frozen beforehand, and he was given copious

amounts of morphine to deal with the pain leading up to the operation, which was conducted by the *Phil Sea*'s medical officer, Capt.
Leonard Barber, USN.

But just before the operation, as they were preparing to anesthetize
him again, he asked, "Don't give me any more dope, Doc, will ya
please?"

Rather than morphine, which clouded his thinking, he asked for
someone to talk to. Through the operation he held a corpsman's hand
and told him jokes. The young man could just make out some of
them, muffled by Cajun and the bandages. But the delivery, and of
course, the ones he did catch, doubled him over. The medical staff had
never seen anything like it. Barber became totally taken with his patient. LeBlanc likewise bonded with his doctor. He became convinced
that Barber was the man to look after him and asked the doctor not to
leave him.

At one point Barber let on just how close LeBlanc was to death, ad-
mitting that even now odds were not in his favor.

"What do you think about that, Lieutenant?"

"No, I don't think I'll die, Doc."

"That's what I wanted to hear."

After the first operation, Barber also wanted to remove part of
LeBlanc's frostbitten left hand. LeBlanc had another request.

"No, Doc, please. Can't we wait one more day?"

Granting his request and noticing the hand was going to get better,
Barber made it his mission to see that LeBlanc survived, and he obtained permission to follow him through his treatment after he returned stateside.

Others similarly touched by the spirit of Frenchy LeBlanc included the crewmen of the *Phil Sea*, who became his blood brothers
by donating pints of blood for his numerous transfusions, as well as
the crew of the *Brownson*, who radioed their best wishes for LeBlanc's
continued recovery.

Following additional medical attention and liberty in Panama, Mc-Carty, Kearns, Robbins, and Warr were given a chartered flight to Washington, D.C. LeBlanc was sent to San Diego for additional operations following the removal his remaining lower leg, then on to the navy hospital in Philadelphia, Pennsylvania. Dr. Leonard Barber went with him.

20 NEWS CONFERENCE

DEPARTMENT OF THE U.S. NAVY, WASHINGTON, D.C., FEBRUARY 21, 1947, 3:00 P.M.   Following an eight-hour flight to Washington, four of the surviving crewmen of the *George 1*—LeBlanc and Caldwell not present—were greeted at Dulles International Airport by snow on the ground and a limousine for their hop across town to navy department headquarters.

The tired men were photographed as they came down the steps to the tarmac. The navy photo clearly shows a mixture of relief and annoyance on some of their faces. Fatigue is written in the eyes of Robbins and McCarty, who had probably told their story a hundred times or more at this point and were preparing to tell it again, officially, for the combined press of the nation. Robbins said in an interview that if he seemed annoyed in the photo, he was. It had just dawned on him that because of the fame of his ill-fated mission, and the press conference he was about to attend, he would not be afforded liberty in Rio de Janeiro. That had been one of the main payoffs promised him for his part in the mission. Also, he wanted to be able to tell his grandchildren he had "rounded the Horn," and he hadn't done that yet. He was looking forward to wearing his hat backwards and spitting into the wind—the sailor's rite after rounding the southern tip of South America.

Kearns is seen smiling reflexively and grimacing in pain at the same time. Warr, somewhat giddy with all the fuss and publicity, has a boyish, bemused grin on his mug.

The briefing was arranged by Undersecretary of the Navy John L. Sullivan. Several stories had appeared in papers across the country about the crew, and yet the media was crying for more news as the men returned home. Now the reporters wanted an even-greater level of detail. Seizing the opportunity to promote the navy, Sullivan did not disappoint them.

The cameras flashed in the young faces, and for a moment the men felt like Hollywood starlets as they were escorted to a table facing the newshounds.

Participants included Rear Adm. Felix L. Johnson, Rear Admiral Sullivan, the press, and a public relations officer, Captain Chambliss.

Part of the verbatim transcript[1] follows:

CAPTAIN CHAMBLISS: All in, sir:
UNDERSECRETARY SULLIVAN: Okay, fellows, let's sit right down here.

Ladies and gentlemen, here we are. I know you have been delayed in taking these photographs. We are very happy and proud to present to you these four fine young, typical American youngsters. They are all yours. Take them away.

Do you have a statement you would care to make, Lieutenant?

LIEUTENANT KEARNS: Well, sir. I didn't expect to return to Washington and see snow on the ground.

UNDERSECRETARY SULLIVAN: This has been arranged at great personal expense for your benefit.

LIEUTENANT KEARNS: We hope the citizens don't think we brought it with us from Antarctica.

THE PRESS: You should have seen it here three weeks ago.

LIEUTENANT KEARNS: I wish I had been here three weeks ago. (Laughter.)

UNDERSECRETARY SULLIVAN: Is there a brief statement you would like to give us about your misadventure?

THE PRESS: A sort of narrative, you know.

LIEUTENANT KEARNS: Well, our flight was a reconnaissance flight and photographic mission over the Antarctic Continent from Cape Dart on Thurston Peninsula, photographing to the eastward as much of the coastline as we could possibly do with existing weather conditions. Our takeoff time was 2:30 in the morning, December 30. We were three hours and ten minutes from takeoff time when we sighted the continent. The weather was extremely bad—very low ceilings from six hundred to one thousand feet with intermittent snowstorms, squalls, and very poor visibility. It was very variable. At times the visibility was zero-zero—absolutely no sight beyond the plane itself. Then, at other times, it would open up, and we could see parts of the cape. Previous flights over the area had reported good weather, so we continued in hopes we would get better weather conditions.

As I said, when we did sight the continent, knowing the weather to be bad, we wanted to remain over the sea area. So we altered course to fly to eastward and parallel to land. We proceeded on this course about ten minutes. I was at the controls at the time. Lieutenant LeBlanc, the patrol plane commander, was coding a message. The weather became worse. Visibility dropped to absolute zero. So I started to turn to the left, to seaward, when it appeared to me that I had flown right into a snow squall. There was no visual reference to the ground. Just coincidental with that, we hit a snow ridge. The initial impact was not very great in itself. I did recover control immediately afterwards. I applied full power and put the plane in a climbing left-hand turn, and we exploded. I can't tell you much after that.

I was blown from my seat—but I think the man to take it from here is Machinist's Mate Warr. He was the first man to recover. He had quite an interesting experience. He was my flight engineer and the crew chief.

UNDERSECRETARY SULLIVAN: Go to it, fellow!

MACHINIST'S MATE WARR: I don't have much to say about it. The only thing is that I wasn't far away from them. I was pretty weary, and I was crying because I didn't see anybody around. The plane was on fire. I started looking for the other guys, and the first one I found was Robbie—Robbins. There he was, half-dazed, on one knee and one foot. So, between the both of us we started looking for the rest of the survivors. We found the captain and Mr. Kearns. Mr. Kearns heard Mr. LeBlanc call, so we went into the fire and got Mr. LeBlanc out of the seat.

THE PRESS: He was still in the plane?

LIEUTENANT KEARNS: Robbins and Warr pulled him out. I just unfastened the safety belt.

THE PRESS: You were still in the plane?

LIEUTENANT KEARNS: No, I was blown clear of the plane. Lieutenant LeBlanc, the patrol-plane commander, was strapped in his seat and was unable to get out by himself. He was very badly burned.

THE PRESS: How far were you scattered from each other when you started out? Did you have to look far?

UNDERSECRETARY SULLIVAN: How far from the plane were you?

MACHINIST'S MATE WARR: I was the farthest one. I was

about one to two hundred feet away in the opposite direction. The rest of them were all in one group except McCarty. He stayed in the tail section of the plane when it happened. He was still back there. We found them all. As I said, Robbins was the first, then the captain. Then we started putting them in the only shelter we had vacant. That's the time we found Mac.

UNDERSECRETARY SULLIVAN: What was your shelter?

MACHINIST'S MATE WARR: The forward section of the tunnel of the plane, just like the waist section, which didn't blow up, but it was a place to get out of the snow.

We got in there and opened up the parachutes to cover the entrance. We started nestling down pretty good then.

THE PRESS: What equipment did you have to keep yourself warm?

MACHINIST'S MATE WARR: You can tell the equipment we had in there, the supplies and all.

LIEUTENANT KEARNS: Well, we had our Arctic survival equipment: four tents I believe, two-man tents; one toboggan-type dog sled; 180 pounds of concentrated rations—pemmican, alpenstocks; ice creepers—

THE PRESS: What are they?

LIEUTENANT KEARNS: Crampons for the bottom of your feet.

UNDERSECRETARY SULLIVAN: For the bottom of your shoes.

LIEUTENANT KEARNS: Yes, sir.

—9 sleeping bags; 2 spare blankets; 2 four-and-a-half-gallon breakers of water; about 200 small tins of Spam—concentrated emergency life rations; 2 six-man life rafts with all the accessories; fishing equipment.

THE PRESS: You weren't anywhere near water—not near enough to use it?

LIEUTENANT KEARNS: We could see water from our position, but our life rafts wouldn't do us any good without paddles.

THE PRESS: You say that all this was saved, or was this what you carried?

LIEUTENANT KEARNS: That's what we carried and what we recovered. We recovered all that.

THE PRESS: Most of the plane was destroyed?

LIEUTENANT KEARNS: Yes. This was stowed in the waist compartment of the plane, lashed to the overhead, and that part of the plane was not burned.

THE PRESS: What about a radio?

THE PRESS: You wouldn't have been able to survive without this, do you think?

LIEUTENANT KEARNS: No, not for very long. We did recover some of the food from the flight rations—rations for the flight itself.

UNDERSECRETARY SULLIVAN: Where were they?

LIEUTENANT KEARNS: They were stowed in the galley, but Robbins and Warr recovered the food the day after the crash. It was scattered around in the snow. We figured that we had recovered 90 percent of the flight rations that we had for the flight.

THE PRESS: Ninety percent?

LIEUTENANT KEARNS: Yes.

THE PRESS: Did your radio get smashed so that you had no way of signaling to the people where you were?

LIEUTENANT KEARNS: Well, we recovered part of the radio, but our batteries were cracked and would not put out sufficient voltage to get the receiver working. Robbins tried for several days, but we lacked the four volts from the necessary twenty-four. We did discover the Gibson Girl emergency transmitter.

UNDERSECRETARY SULLIVAN: Was that effective?

LIEUTENANT KEARNS: No, sir, it was not, due to the fact that we were over land area and the range of that was cut down greatly.

AVIATION RADIOMAN ROBBINS: It's supposed to be good from ten to fifteen miles according to the manual. The ship—the fellows were flying right above us and couldn't pick us up at all at five

hundred feet, so evidently it may have been the unit itself. It's hard
to say.

THE PRESS: How long did you expect to be there before you
would be picked up? As soon as, you know, they would come out, at
least, to look for you?

LIEUTENANT KEARNS: Captain Caldwell, who was the commander of the *Pine Island*—he was aboard, and in our talks we were
discussing when we would be picked up. We fortunately computed
the exact day when they would come and find us, and we were found
on that day.

THE PRESS: What day was that?

UNDERSECRETARY SULLIVAN: How many days after your
crash?

LIEUTENANT KEARNS: Well, sir, it was the day we could see
clear weather over the continent and over the water area. The first
clear day that they had good weather over the water area, we knew
they would come.

UNDERSECRETARY SULLIVAN: You heard them over there
before that?

LIEUTENANT KEARNS: No, sir.

UNDERSECRETARY SULLIVAN: Had they been above you?

LIEUTENANT KEARNS: One plane came within thirty miles
of us.

UNDERSECRETARY SULLIVAN: How many days after the
crash?

LIEUTENANT KEARNS: The sixth day after the crash.

UNDERSECRETARY SULLIVAN: How soon after the crash
did they start their search?

LIEUTENANT KEARNS: Immediately, sir—at the first available
opportunity they could launch planes from the tender.

THE PRESS: Did I understand you to say you had computed the
figure in advance that this particular day they would find you, or that
you know [sic] it would be first day the weather cleared?

LIEUTENANT KEARNS: We knew it would be the first day we had clear weather.

THE PRESS: Did you have some forecast that it would be clear that particular day?

LIEUTENANT KEARNS: No, we didn't compute that it would be the thirteenth day, but the day we had clear weather over the sea area and the land area. As it happened, it was the thirteenth day that was the first day when the weather was clear.

UNDERSECRETARY SULLIVAN: You fellows don't think thirteen is an unlucky number now, do you?

LIEUTENANT KEARNS: No, sir. (Laughter.)

THE PRESS: Could you tell that they were looking for you? How and when did you first know it?

LIEUTENANT KEARNS: Well, we naturally assumed they were looking for us. We have confidence in the men aboard the ship *Pine Island*, and we knew they would be out for us at the first available opportunity they could launch planes. I think all of us have a great deal of confidence in Lieutenant Ball, the pilot of the first plane that sighted us, and Lt. Comdr. Howell, the pilot of the plane that picked us up; also the officers and men of the *Pine Island*.

THE PRESS: This plane that came within thirty miles of you— that didn't spot you, did it?

LIEUTENANT KEARNS: No, it didn't.

THE PRESS: When was the first one that spotted you?

LIEUTENANT KEARNS: The thirteenth day.

THE PRESS: How did you know they had established contact, that they had seen you, and all that sort of thing?

LIEUTENANT KEARNS: They first passed us at 6:20 A.M. in the morning, and, after waiting all that time for rescue, we were caught unawares. We hadn't prepared a black smoke signal. We were relying on our smoke grenades, which, we should have known, were white smoke and against a white background—were useless. They passed over and disappeared over the horizon. We assumed that they would be back when returning to the ship. So Chief McCarty and Robbins here took our life rafts, [and] Robbins removed powder from the various pistol shells, took some gasoline from the remaining bomb bay tanks, and poured it inside the life rafts. When the plane finally did return to our vicinity again, we ignited the gas, and it caused a big column of black smoke to rise up to about three hundred feet into the air. They sighted us, dropped their left wing, made a turn, and came about one hundred feet from the wreckage. They stayed with us for about six hours, dropping equipment, circling and marking a trail from our position to this ice-free lake in the shelf ice to which we would have to march in order to be picked up by the seaplane.

Mr. Secretary mentioned something a while ago about the cause of the explosion. That was due to rupturing of the fuel cells after the initial impact, and friction along the hull most likely ignited the gasoline fumes, and we exploded over two thousand gallons of gasoline.

The press went on to grill the men about the conditions they faced, what pemmican tasted like, the strains of their long march out of hell, and the improving condition of Lt. Ralph LeBlanc.

Warr and McCarty spoke infrequently. Mostly, the answers were given by the lieutenant from Boston. At one point Robbins described his showdown with the skuas and his distaste at seeing them "just sort of waiting around."

Toward the end of the lengthy conference, McCarty spoke fitting words about Captain Caldwell:

I think we all realize that we were pretty fortunate to have a man like Captain Caldwell on the hop with us. He did a lot for our morale.

This tribute was seconded by all.

Robbins, who got to know the men of the *Brownson*, and heard the story of their hours spent risking everything to get close to the coast, said:

> I would like to say something about the *Brownson*. She was the only ship that immediately took heed to our having gone down. She took it on her own and pushed in within 150 miles, I believe, and that was pushing into that ice. The skipper wanted to build a helicopter deck. I believe he could have honestly pushed on in to get us. Then the Pine Island would rather have waited until they sent out a plane to find out what the situation was. But I think he did a wonderful job in his efforts. That whole ship was right down in there in it. . . .

And with that, the flight department's Crew 3, attached to USS *Pine Island* during Task Force 68, Operation Highjump, walked into history for a time.

The men remained in Washington during that week and socialized briefly, but Robbins and Warr were soon off to Philadelphia to see LeBlanc in the hospital. Kearns would remain in D.C., trying to push through his application to become a fully commissioned officer in the regular navy.

21 THE REST OF THE STORY, THE REST OF THEIR LIVES

Capt. Henry Howard Caldwell maintained command of his ship, *Pine Island*, throughout the remainder of his cruise despite the navy's initial suggestion that he come home with the younger sailors. He fought for the right to keep command of his ship and was rewarded with the nod despite his injuries. The neck injury would go ignored until later in life, when the evidence of the hairline fracture was revealed in a medical exam. He limped throughout the cruise, reportedly aided by an Ace bandage on his swelled ankle, which gradually healed. His chipped teeth were crowned with fillings on board.

Standing beside him on the bridge were Capt. George J. Dufek and Comdr. Isidore Schwartz, who with his diligence had improved his stature among the crew. Dufek and Schwartz's incessant, ghostly companion, the vexing Mr. Murphy, also remained aboard.

Hampered by weather, the Eastern Task Group was conceding repeated losses to a continent that seemingly did not want to be photographed from Cape Dart to Marguerite Bay. Flight operations did not commence again until January 23 but were quickly cancelled due to weather.

On the 26th, the two PBMs left for the continent, and the SOC *Albatross* searched for leads through the pack, marking the first time all available aircraft were airborne at once in the mission. The event was dutifully recorded in the ship's log.

The ship was ordered to explore the ice over the Marguerite Bay area, in the nook of the Palmer Peninsula in early February. Dufek and a landing party from the *Brownson* attempted to make landfall at Charcot Island on February 10, but records show that a barrier of ice prevented it from happening.

On February 13, Dufek experienced yet a third brush with fate. As he was transferring from the *Pine Island* to the *Brownson* in the breeches buoy, the ships took opposing rolls that slackened the line and dunked him. The line then tightened and snapped, hurling the task group leader aloft. Dufek then plummeted thirty feet to the water below. Comdr. Harry Gimber was credited with skillfully dropping his fuel lines, knifing his destroyer around to rescue Dufek in the nick of time.

As he was rushed to a hot shower and packed into bed with hot water bottles following a record-breaking eleven minutes in the freezing water without any kind of exposure suit, Dufek reportedly cursed the so-called Phantom Coast.[1]

He would go on to become one of the most beloved and famed figures of exploration in his own right. Commanding operations during Deep Freeze I through IV, he was the pioneering rear admiral who founded the Amundsen-Scott South Pole Research Facility. Sadly, this facility, which he knew as home for many months, now lies crumbling beneath the crushing weight of ice and the newer facilities above it.

Men who flew in air groups to Antarctica following Highjump recall Dufek as an eccentric, courageous warrior of exploration and one of the most hearty, entertaining men to have around for the spirit and good cheer he brought into the mix of ice, wind, and waiting.

Today he has an Antarctic land feature bearing his name. Located on the edge of the Ronne Ice Shelf, the extrusion of granite, which resembles Stone Mountain, Georgia, or Gibraltar, Spain, was aptly named the Dufek Massif.

After fighting through heavy seas to map this area, the aviation department received some of the most spectacular views of the mission, but they only flew two flights over the icy Weddell Sea. During these last flights of the *George 3*, flown by Howell, Mincer, and Litz with Dickens aboard as flight engineer, the crew had its own narrow escape from death.

Litz and Dickens remembered that somewhere over the pack ice en route back to the *Pine Island*, the port-side engine cut out, then the starboard quit. At that moment, the men were descending through a cloud bank, and as fate would have it, the plane was also icing up. Howell told the crew to brace for a hard landing.

Everyone scrambled midships except Howell and Dickens, who continued working the problem while the crew sat down in the center aisle and locked arms and legs like kids on a sled racing downhill.

"Marx, the first class machinist mate, was sitting in front of me, and he said he got that 'fluttering sphincter' feeling," Litz recalled.

The airplane descended rapidly from two thousand feet. The aluminum shell began to rattle as Howell angled her down, preventing her from stalling. Everyone prepared for the worst: a hellacious dead-stick landing on the pack ice, miles from *Pine Island*. But Dickens repaired the vapor lock that prevented the proper transfer of gas from the fuel cells to the engines, and then the seaplane sputtered to life. Howell pulled out of the rapid descent with a few hundred feet to spare, as Dickens recalled, and calmly climbed back on course to *Pine Island*.

Dickens, Litz, and others of the remaining crew were treated to more adventures. Sometime during the rush to round the Antarctic Peninsula en route to the Weddell Sea, or perhaps en route to the Falklands after that, the *Pine Island* bent her port-side screw after dinging a propeller on an iceberg. Dickens and Litz both recalled that Dufek had steamed through a dangerous garden of ice to save time during a late-evening watch. She could only make half speed after that, and began shuddering "like a dog shittin' bones," said Litz. In Panama a new propeller replaced the dented one, according to the official report.

This error aside, and with weather conditions worsening, the men of Task Group 68.3 looked forward to the moment when Dufek would pull the plug on the remainder of the trip. Facing the prospect of losing another seaplane in the increasingly bad weather, with no hope of rescuing the men for a year or more if they were forced down on the continent, he turned to Caldwell and said, "To hell with this, Henry . . . let's get out of here."[2]

On March 3, the ship headed northwest toward Rio de Janeiro for some well-deserved shore leave before departing for Panama and necessary repairs.

According to eyewitnesses, Dufek enjoyed his shore leave nearly as much as his men did. Blame it on the Bossa Nova and his joy at surviving three swims in twenty-eight-degree water—the future admiral was seen returning to the *Pine Island* after an all-night street festival, having danced from dusk till dawn. With his "dress white" coat unbuttoned and his thinning hair tousled above a beaming smile, Dufek was piped aboard and came on his flagship in his bare feet. Not a word of reproach was heard.[3]

Howell and company were given the honor of flying dignitaries from the Brazilian navy around the statue of Christ overlooking Lago and Ipanema Beach.

Howell retired from the navy as a captain, as did James Ball. Howell raised a family, and now, in his early eighties, he heads an engineering firm in Johnson City, Tennessee. Before he left the navy, he trained flight crews from Great Britain in the finer points of taking off and landing on a sea-tossed carrier deck. Richard Conger became a successful Antarctic explorer in his own right and has at least one Antarctic feature named in his honor.

Litz settled down to married life, spent years in advertising, and even was the publisher of a skiing magazine. He now lives in New Hampshire. He has fond memories of Caldwell.

Litz said that in Panama, shortly before they went separate ways after Highjump, he was standing on the hangar deck looking down along the quay and noticed Caldwell walking with an admiral in command of the Naval District. Caldwell looked up, saw Litz standing there, left the admiral's side, and climbed the steps to have a word with him.

"He made his way to where I was, thanked me for my part in the operation, then rejoined the admiral."

Later in life, when Litz was in school elsewhere, he happened to attend a naval academy lacrosse game. He saw Caldwell, then the Annapolis athletic director, sitting with other VIPs. Because of his ingrained deference to rank, which wasn't appropriate in this case since Litz wasn't on active duty, he couldn't force himself to impose a handshake on Caldwell. But as he was leaving the arena, Caldwell limped forward through the crowd and grabbed him by the elbow.

"What? You were going to leave without saying hello?" Caldwell had spotted Litz among a large crowd, and with difficulty owing to his previous injury, he bulled his way through.

"There haven't been many heroes in my life, but right at the top of that list is one H. H. Caldwell," Litz said. "He was a true leader who always had the safety of his crew uppermost in his mind."

Dickens, like Howell, who is also now in his early eighties, went back to middle Georgia, raised a family, and began his own upholstery business, which still keeps him busy today.

Two days before Dufek and the Eastern Group finally capitulated to the oncoming winter, the remaining 190 men stationed with Byrd at Little America IV boarded the icebreaker *Burton Island* for transfer out of the Bay of Whales. The *Yancey, Merrick, Mount Olympus, Northwind, Currituck, Cacapon, Canisteo,* and *Henderson* likewise were all on various treks for their homeward run.

The *Merrick*, already damaged in earlier clashes with the ice, took the brunt of Antarctica and had to be towed out of Antarctic waters by *Northwind*. A new rudder was fabricated for her in New Zealand, but she was soon decommissioned and placed in the naval reserve fleet until the following year, when she was refitted and recommissioned.

Also slightly damaged was the *Mt. Olympus*, after rolling during a wicked storm in the "Screaming 60s."

As for the men of the *George 1*, in many ways the accident touched their lives even more deeply than marriage, kids, or career. Litz put it this way: "Some of us peaked at twenty."

CAPT. HENRY CALDWELL   The courageous captain who helped keep his men thinking positive, and seeing his command through to the end, continued his naval service. By many standards he already had a full career before Highjump. He had graduated from the naval academy in 1927 and commanded Air Group 12 in the Pacific, earning the Navy Cross, the Bronze Star, and the Navy Flying Cross.

After Highjump he returned to the naval academy as the director of athletics, and later, having seen duty as fleet air commander in Jacksonville, Florida, and having raised a large family, he retired as a rear admiral. In December 1979 Caldwell gave an extensive interview for the *Jacksonville Times Union* from his Ortega Forest home. The story ran on the thirty-third-year anniversary of the day of the crash. About his time on the ice, he told the reporter, "I resolved that in the future when I wanted cream and sugar in my coffee, I would have it." He died in the mid-1980s of natural causes.

LT. (JG) RALPH "FRENCHY" LEBLANC   Under the watchful eye of Lt. Comdr. Leonard Barber and Chief Pharmacist's Mate First Class Charles Frye, Frenchy continued to heal.

Continuous transfusions, fifteen of them coming from the men of the *Philippine Sea*, kept him alive following his operations until, perhaps as long as a month later, he stabilized and the bleeding stopped.

His left hand was spared but damaged. He was one of the first patients in medical history to undergo skin grafting in lieu of plastic surgery. The recovery period was long, but he maintained his sense of humor.

During his convalescence LeBlanc was held, sometimes against his wishes, at the navy hospital in Philadelphia, Pennsylvania.

A Philadelphia newspaper reported sometime after February 4 that LeBlanc was visited by his parents and his girlfriend, Anna Wiman of New York City.

But the relationship was to be short-lived. According to family members, around the time they drifted apart, LeBlanc and his gal were on a picnic during a weekend "liberty" from the confines of his hospitalization.

On the way back into town, Ms. Wiman's car suffered a flat. Frenchy, then wheelchair bound, had to ask another young man to change the tire for her. It troubled him and wounded his pride. LeBlanc was going through his own "blue period." He felt like a science experiment gone wrong in a bad B movie. He let her move on.

LeBlanc was fitted with prosthetic limbs and vowed to walk from the hospital unaided by crutches or a walker of any kind. He was told that that was highly unlikely.

Robbins and Kearns both recalled visiting LeBlanc in Philadelphia, and were amazed at the fury with which the Cajun attacked the problem of life as a double amputee—a condition that he considered a temporary inconvenience, an annoyance and nothing more. After all, he was Frenchy LeBlanc. For hours he would walk on a treadmill rubbing the nubs below his knees raw against his prosthetics, muttering that he'd "be damned" if he wouldn't walk out of the hospital unaided by wheelchairs, crutches, or walkers. Robbins said that Frenchy pushed himself so hard that his nubs bled, blistered, and bubbled like pork rinds before they finally calloused over.

Though the prosthetic limbs were very cumbersome, they represented the state of the art in 1947. A thick waist belt was attached, suspenders fashion, to the two plastic legs. Rubber and foam-molded cups served as stirrups for the stumps. The entire contraption was not only uncomfortable but also produced a great deal of strain on LeBlanc's hips and knees.

He bore it just as he had borne his massive burns and scars—with admirable stoicism. The permanent leather shoes never left the plastic foot-shins he was given. In the center of the shins, there was a hole running into the hollow prosthetic limbs to allow air to circulate beneath the toughening nubs. Almost immediately, LeBlanc began finding entertaining uses for the "holes" in his shins. Leaving the butt ends of a few cigarettes to smolder beneath his pant legs, he had only to lift the cuff of his pants above the sock to create the illusion that he was a smoking-hot commodity from head to toe.

Ironically, it was his ironclad sense of humor that kept LeBlanc in the Philadelphia Naval Hospital for longer than his medical needs required. The navy asked him to stay on for a few months so that his charm and contagious sense of mirth could work their magic on navy men who had lost their arms or legs or had their spines snapped during World War II.

At one point LeBlanc, on his prosthetics and a pair of aluminum crutches as he pushed another double amputee in a wheelchair, repaired to a nearby liquor store to buy some sorely needed spirits. Alcohol was strictly verboten, and LeBlanc, accustomed to his navy ration, was about to lose his cool. Having secured the liquor, the men returned to the hospital, and, rather than face front-entrance inspection carrying sacks of liquor secreted in their pajama robes, they attempted to climb four or five flights of stairs, with a now powerfully arm-strong LeBlanc hauling backwards the wheelchair-bound man who carried the liquor in his lap.

LeBlanc would haul two steps, set the crutches down on the railing, plant his prosthetic feet, haul his man with an iron right hand and gnarled left, lean him back toward the incline of the stairs as the wheelchair driver balanced in mid-wheelie (the rubber wheels and the sticky rubber matting on the stairs precariously securing him), grab his crutches, lift himself two steps, lean down, grab the handles of the wheelchair, and haul away again, gaining another two steps. And in this palsied fashion, the veteran navy flier and his charge were making progress up the first flight. But it was not to be.

Either some crucial operation in the procedure—for instance, setting the brake, or leaning the man back—was omitted, or the crutches dangling from the railing slipped from their posts. Whatever the case, down the stairs and out the door of the stairwell bounced LeBlanc's charge. He continued across the sidewalk and out into midday traffic, holding a lap full of liquor and screaming bloody murder. LeBlanc, arms over feet, went clacking after him, bellowing, "Hey! Hey! Watch out now! Look out for that fella!" to the oncoming tide of buses and delivery trucks, which screeched to halt as the pajama-clad veterans passed.

The far curb stopped their progress. The traffic-snarling performance brought out the police. Fortunately, no one was hurt, and there didn't seem to be any proper citation that the cop could draft that would cover all the bases. The punishment definitely fit the crime— the veterans were taken back upstairs to the amputee ward without their booze, which lay in glass shards and puddles all over the blazing hot sidewalk.

LeBlanc returned to St. Martinsville, Louisiana, soon thereafter. His father, Albert, tried to make the young man as comfortable as possible. At this point in his life, LeBlanc didn't like to be alone, and sometimes it was difficult to accommodate him. He wanted people around him at all times. And if he couldn't dance properly anymore, he wanted there to be music. Lots of it, and at all hours if necessary.

With the aid of a few good friends, he built a small social club adjacent to Albert's house and shop. He and his friends would drive over to Lafayette once a week, purchase a keg or two, bring the beer back to the clapboard structure, play pool, and sip suds for hours on end.

LeBlanc charged twenty-five cents a serving, just enough to recover the cost of the beer itself, and made new friends as the crowds grew. He let the good times roll. Friends recalled that LeBlanc was forever saying, "That's the girl I'm going to marry," about any woman he was semiseriously interested in.

In Mary Daigle, however, a young woman who decided she didn't want to be a nun after all and quit the convent soon after her twenty-third birthday, he found a kindred spirit.

She was not only a beautiful young girl from St. Martinsville who shared his love of song and dance, she also had a highly developed sense of humor.

This time, when he said, "That the girl I'm going to marry," he meant it. Mary was approached by Ralph's sister, Vienna, for their first date. She told her own sister that she was considering going out with LeBlanc, who was now famous throughout the nation, not to mention the state of Louisiana.

"Yeah but, he ain't got any legs?" her sister incredulously replied.

Like her future husband, Mary saw the glass as half-full, not half-empty. She said, "Yeah, but it looks like he got everything else."

LeBlanc quickly became a leader of his adopted town of Breaux Bridge, serving two terms as alderman on the city council. He later became the tax collector for the St. Martinsville Parish School Board, where he spent most of his career.

Quoted in the same article Caldwell had been interviewed for in 1979, LeBlanc said many of his coworkers at the school board still did not know he was a double amputee. Those who did often found out in ways that were humorously embarrassing.

One evening LeBlanc was preparing to leave his office when, halfway out the door, he realized that he had left his car keys in his desk. He turned quickly, catching the door in his right hand, but as he pivoted to hold the door open, his right foot came off. It now lay a few feet away. If he hopped over to retrieve his foot, he would lock himself out of his office and his car. He didn't think he could "pogo" over to his desk and grab the keys, though, without falling out of his second leg. He envisioned himself flopping around like a fish on a deck, or crawling around the halls of the dusty old building on his hands and stumps until the next morning.

There he stood in the hallway, undecided and amused at his predicament, until a young woman rounded the corner and was nearly floored by the sight of the school board administrator who stood with his foot yards away from his vacant pant leg, a huge smile on his face. LeBlanc couldn't resist the comic potential of the moment.

"Can you give me a hand here?"

She huffed off to find a janitor, convinced LeBlanc was having a laugh at her expense, scaring the hell out of her with some juvenile Halloween prank. The janitor helped LeBlanc out of his humorous conundrum the two of them laughing so hard it was difficult for the janitor to keep LeBlanc from falling over as the leg was reattached.

Ralph and Mary LeBlanc had four sons, Albert Paul "Buz" II, Patrick John, Leonard Rex (named after Leonard Barber), Brent Clark, two daughters, Janice and Corrine (named after Dr. Barber's wife, Corrine), and twelve grandchildren.

In exploring their own sense of humor, handed down from both sides, Ralph's children often found comic good use for Dad's prosthetic legs. The boys would sneak up to the couch on a Saturday afternoon and covertly load down Dad's legs by slipping marbles through the holes in his shins. That way when LeBlanc got up to tread the hallway toward their room, they could hear him coming. Along with the sound of the pennies and marbles rattling around inside his legs was an outraged message in Dad's colorful Cajun slang: "Damnit all, I told you boys stop putting them things in my legs now!"

In retribution Dad would terrify his sons' friends by showing them the hole in his leg at picnics and barbecues, saying, "Go ahead—stick your finger in there." The kid would do it only to feel the creepy movement of Ralph's unseen finger attacking from the other side, and often end up fleeing with giggles and screams.

"That's my mouse. That's what that is! He lives in there."

At wedding receptions or funeral wakes—it didn't really matter which—Ralph would ignore the "pinched ole biddies" admonishing him with disapproving stares and do his "smoking man" routine for the kids, sending them into fits.

Buz, LeBlanc's son, remembers the first time he slept over at a friend's house. The baseball game was on television. It was about 7 P.M., and six-year-old Buz began to wonder what was wrong with this family. The father was still up walking around. Mystified by his friend's puzzled look, the neighbor child asked, "What's wrong, Buz?"

Buz leaned over. "Ain't he gonna take off his legs?" His own father had made so little of his problem that it seemed a natural part of the day: at 7 P.M. or thereabouts, a grown man had a right to slip off his legs and lean back in the easy chair. Wasn't this what all fathers did?

Ralph's son Patrick went on to attend Annapolis and later became a navy pilot in the Pacific, flying F-14s. On the side of his canopy, his handle read "Frenchy II." One of his biggest fans and most frequent visitors was retired navy chief Jim Robbins. Pat now flies for American Airlines, based in New Orleans.

Buz took to aviation as well but didn't get as far. In an interview he said he washed out of the navy's program. An officer had made this notation following a training flight: "NAFD . . . No Apparent Fear of Death." He made a career for himself in law enforcement before pursuing his lifelong dream of becoming a history professor. He is studying for his degree through Louisiana State University. He recently married and lives with his wife, Angel, in Lafayette.

Ralph LeBlanc died at his home on Poydras Street, Breaux Bridge, Louisiana, in the summer of 1994, surrounded by his sons. One of his sons remarked, "Well, I guess he's getting his legs back."

AVIATION RADIOMAN JAMES H. "ROBBIE" ROBBINS   Jim married his sweetheart on April 3, 1947. Before doing so, he took her to meet Frenchy LeBlanc in the Philadelphia Naval Hospital.

Through bandages, LeBlanc told Dolly Dale what a wonderful prize she was getting in James Haskin Robbins.

For the next twenty-two years Robbins rose through enlisted ranks, serving in Bermuda, Hawaii, and Midway Island. He continued serving on PBMs until 1950. During that time he and Dale were blessed with a son, James E. Robbins, and later four grandchildren and two great-grandchildren.

Robbins retired from the navy as a chief in April of 1965. He immediately received a letter from Adm. Henry Howard Caldwell. Caldwell addressed him warmly and opened with a joke about all their games of Salvo together down there in that "strange and inhospitable land."

But Caldwell's tone soon grew more serious:

Many times I have wondered just why we six were chosen to return and our less fortunate shipmates were forced to remain behind. Perhaps it was just our turn at the wheel of fortune or divine destiny, but there was one factor that intervened in our behalf that can be attributed to neither of the foregoing.

To be sure, I am referring to the survival training you received while you were an Eagle Scout. The use you made of that practical training surely was primarily responsible for pulling us through. All of us that survived owe you an unpayable debt that will never be forgotten.

Following his own retirement, Caldwell became active with the Scouting groups in the Jacksonville area. This mountain of a man, admired among football players, decorated war veterans, captains, aviators, and admirals on seven seas, admitted to kids involved in Jacksonville-area scouting that his lifelong hero was a former aviation radioman second class named James Haskin "Robbie" Robbins.

Frenchy Leblanc also sent Robbins a letter of warm regards upon his retirement, thanking him for what he had done for them all. He told Jim, "I thank God every day." (that Robbins had been there).

The LeBlanc and Robbins families continued their association, which endured throughout the years, beginning in the mid 1960s after Robbie's retirement. Corrine LeBlanc Depuy long thought of Jim Robbins as Uncle Beer for the fact that, whenever this charming man and his wife were around her father, he had a cold can of Budweiser in hand as he laughed and smiled away the afternoon.

In April of 2002, Jim lost his beloved wife, Dale. He now lives in Palm Desert, California, close to his son, James, his daughter-in-law, Marilyn, and their children and grandchildren.

MACHINIST'S MATE WILLIAM WARR   Bill Warr returned to Reading, Pennsylvania, and married his schoolteacher, Jean Zwoyer.

Soon thereafter they had a baby boy named Thomas. Bill worked as a roll grinder for Carpenter Technology Corporation, a local steel mill, over the next thirty years, but his marriage to Jean was rocky, according to his second son, Todd.

Todd said that after his father divorced, he married Geraldine Habel of Reading. Todd was born January 11, 1963, sixteen years to the day after the remaining crew of *George 1* was found alive on the ice.

Bill remained married to his second wife for seventeen years before trouble again crept into his marriage, brought on by excessive
drinking that Todd said was a direct result of the crash and that was
exacerbated by a gnawing case of survivor's guilt that stalked him for
the remainder of his life. Whether he knew it or not, he was not the
only survivor thus afflicted.

Todd had this to say about his dad and his experience in Antarctica:

"I remember him talking of wishing he could have done more for
the injured men, and of feeling guilty that he was relatively un-
hurt. . . . My father was a quiet man, especially when it came to talking
about himself. I remember my mother saying the whole incident left a
lifelong mark on him that he was never able to get over."

Bill Warr died in February 1980 after a weeklong bout with pneu-
monia. He is buried in Lauderdale Cemetery, just outside Reading.

Todd continued his father's legacy of assisting aviators in need. After working in a local steel mill himself and graduating from high
school, he joined the army as a flight operations specialist. Having
served in Germany, Hawaii, and Korea, and after a stint with the Fed-
eral Aviation Administration, he now works as an air traffic controller
at Washington National Airport. If you've landed there recently, you
now share in the Highjump legacy. It's likely that Todd Warr helped
guide your pilot home.

Todd married his own sweetheart, Diane Taylor, on St. Valentine's
Day 2003. They are raising three children together, Jessica, Troy, and
Justin, from her first marriage.

CHIEF PHOTOGRAPHER'S MATE OWEN "MAC" MCCARTY   Mac
disappeared from view, as far as the remaining crew of the *George 1*
was concerned, soon after publishing his account of Highjump,
"Dead Man's Diary," in the May 13, 1947, edition of the *Saturday Evening Post.*

Upon receipt of the royalty check for the publication, McCarty divided the money up and sent a share to every other member of the surviving crew. According to Bill, Robbie got a deserved double share, five hundred dollars. It is likely that Mac gave Robbins his money from the sale of the manuscript.

It is known that Mac returned to his wife, Gloria, and their children in Sonoma County California, but following that, he faded from contact with respect to the other members of the Highjump crew. Through the grapevine of shipmates, Robbins said he heard that Mac had died in the 1970s of health problems unrelated to the plane crash. His last meeting with Mac had been brief. Robbins said that Mac seemed troubled. He hadn't heard from anyone, and he wanted to know if everyone had received their checks. They had.

There is so much more that is known today about the effects of concussion than there was in 1947. Documentation shows that if a head injury is serious enough, it can change the victim's personality, often rendering him or her depressed and unable to cope during times of stress.

It is the opinion of this author that Mac unknowingly went through such a transformation during those days on the ice. The impact of that change upon his performance, which compared unfavorably with his earlier work in the Pacific, must have been a lifelong mystery to him.

In times of such stress, people fall into easily identifiable roles. Mac's role, while somewhat that of an injured skeptic during those days on the ice, also made him the outstanding chronicler of the ordeal. Without his faithful, objective account, in which at times he even criticized himself, the later accounts—including this one—would not have been possible.

Mac's words provided a time line for the moments after the crash; using it, any subsequent author or reporter could question and prod the shifting memories of the remaining survivors. If Mac felt disappointed with his handling of the situation, about his inability to help during those first days on the ice, and if that caused him pain in later life, history itself still owes him an eternal debt of gratitude for his selfless efforts in taking down what was done and said, on whatever meager supplies he managed to scrounge. When it came right down to it, that was who he was anyway—a chronicler, a photographer. In the absence of a camera, he began writing, giving navy officials vital information concerning the psychology of survival techniques, not to mention an indication of the precise caloric requirements for life in Antarctic environs, since he so faithfully described exactly what kept he and the other crewmen alive day in day out.

LT. BILL KEARNS, JR.   Bill was admitted to the naval hospital of Bethesda, Maryland, soon after his news conference. Following several painful operations to set the bones of his right arm and shoulder, he entered a difficult, if less lengthy, period of rest and rehabilitation for his injuries.

In recent years he recalled that during his stay in Bethesda he received mail frequently from Lopez's mother, Clarice.

"She blamed me," Bill said. "She blamed me for killing him."

Kearns said he tried to find the words to console her, to describe in his own letters what had happened in a way that would make her understand the dangers they all faced, and to express the fact that Val Lopez was one of his best friends in the world and that he missed him like a brother. He wrote three letters to her, none of which changed her mind. In some part of his young mind, he suspected he deserved her rage. So he let her keep it.

After a few weeks Lieutenant Kearns asked a navy chaplain from Newport to visit Mrs. Lopez and do what he could for her. Through the chaplain, Bill asked her to forgive him. Her letters ceased immediately.

News coverage may have had a lot to do with her attitude—that and letters from Lopez's other friends aboard ship who factually and forgivingly described what had never been denied: Bill Kearns was flying the plane when it crashed.

An Associated Press article by Alton Blakeslee, dated January 12, 1947, ran in the *Boston Sunday Post*. On the inside pages, editors had thoughtfully included breakout pieces detailing the lives of two New England boys, Lt. William H. Kearns, Jr., and Ens. Maxwell A. Lopez.

By editorial standards their choices for placement were factual, thoughtful, and creative—not insensitive in the slightest. Nevertheless, they may have had an unintended effect. The flight school pictures of both fresh-faced, smiling youths, the one on the left a survivor, and the one on the right deceased in the crash, stood side by side, just a few inches apart. Above the picture of Bill was this heading: LT. KEARNS AT CONTROLS WHEN PLANE EXPLODED. Below the picture of Lopez was this headline: LOPEZ OF R.I. KILLED.

Only a bereaved mother can know what it feels like to see such an item in the newspaper. During the weeks following the crash, there were hundreds of these articles all across the country. The radio brimmed with updates on the Byrd Expedition as it returned home. Then, as today, word and reminders of such a famous loss must have been inescapable for Mrs. Lopez and for Maxwell's younger brother, Richard, as well.

Hendersin's wife, Lillian, visited Bill in the hospital. But she did not blame the young pilot. She understood that her husband's job had been a risky one. The meeting was cordial and brief. Kearns was grateful for the kindness she extended to him.

He didn't know Mr. Williams, and perhaps having been scalded by the blame of one family member, he wouldn't risk being blamed by another. But every night as he tried to sleep, he thought of Williams, of his cries, of what he had been through. He thought of Hendersin and Lopez too. He didn't report the stabbing stomach pains he knew to be ulcers, or the nightmares, or the icy sense of guilt he was feeling.

With hopes of being accepted as a junior-grade lieutenant in the regular navy under full active-duty status, he didn't discuss what he was going through with anyone. By early March he was released from the hospital. On extended leave he was told to remain around Washington for a few days, for a meeting with President Harry Truman.

Truman wanted to congratulate Navy Marine Corps Medal recipients Kearns, Warr, and Robbins for pulling Lieutenant LeBlanc from their burning airplane. But the call never came. It's not surprising. Truman, now busied with reelection concerns and a growing conflict with North Korea, didn't even meet Byrd when he returned to Washington on April 13. He sent naval secretary James Forrestal in his stead.

In late March, Kearns wrote an eight-hundred-word account of the crash and rescue for the *Boston Globe*. The amount of space given the item, and the two-month intervening period, are indicative of the intense public interest in all things related to Highjump.

Kearns soon entered the Georgetown School of Foreign Service and began dating a witty twenty-four-year-old, Mary Louise Gallen, whose father, Capt. Frank Gallen, had served with Kearns's father, William, during their days in the U.S. Coast and Geodetic Survey.

Bill had never met a girl like her. She was at once lively, bright, and mirthful, and yet a discussion with her could turn deadly serious. The transition could happen in a flash. It is said that aviators love a challenge, and Bill had found his. Mary said that her father, a master mariner, traveled from port to port throughout his duty. Mary's childhood spanned the entire East Coast, from Cocoa, Florida, to Portland, Maine, and also the Caribbean, and across the Pacific Ocean.

When Kearns was awarded his Navy Marine Corps Medal, more than a year after Highjump was over, his fiancée, Mary Louise Gallen, was at his side. Kearns, Warr, and Robbins were less than twenty-five years old, and each had contributed a lifetime of effort to his country at one of the most crucial junctures in its history.

Bill and Mary Louise were married in June 1949. In their wedding party were navy lieutenant commander Beverly Britton and several friends from the D.C. officers' club. During the day, Bill worked in the offices of newly appointed naval secretary John L. Sullivan, and at night he attended classes at Georgetown. His petition to enter the navy as an officer was given review after review.

During that period the navy was downsizing, and junior-grade naval reservists were being shown the door—not because they weren't appreciated, but because there was little for them to do at the moment.

In the meantime Britton, who had been a reporter in Richmond, Virginia, began talking to Bill about his experiences and how news-worthy they were. For his own part Bill was learning more and more about Antarctic exploration. The very inconsistencies in different maps and charts of the cold continent began to intrigue him. He wanted to know how and why certain places were named.

During his free time, he looked up his friend from *Phil Sea*, Rear Adm. Richard Byrd, who was more than happy to fill in the gaps for him. Kearns began reading all he could about Palmer Land in particu-lar. He was fascinated by the English and Norse heroes of exploration who had pioneered there. What came out of all this intellectual wan-dering was an outline for a book that he and Britton would complete for Harper Publishers, called *The Silent Continent*.

Kearns took the name partially from "Spell of the Yukon," a Robert Service poem that he and Lopez had admired, and also from his own impressions of a place where you can find "silence that blud-geons you dumb."

"When the wind was down, it really had been so astonishingly silent," he said. It was the sort of silence that generated expectation from the slightest whisper of snow brushing upon snow. It created para-noia or bliss, depending on your mood when you let it creep into you.

His commission in the navy never came. But by now he had Mary Louise at his side and a career as a writer and news correspondent to think about.

In late 1950, just as he was completing his book, Kearns took a job as a bureau chief for McGraw Hill publishing in Detroit, Michigan.

The Silent Continent, published in 1955, sold well in the first printing and showed respectable sales overseas. Kearns would often say that the book was a labor of love, but not a very lucrative one: it sold far better overseas than at home, and he often joked that he and Britton received one royalty check in the amount of thirty-five thousand yen, which in 1960 dollars worked out to the price of a ham sandwich.

Along the way his children, John, Ginny, and Barbara, flourished and grew. In 1960 Bill was offered a job with *Time* magazine, where he would spend most of his career in advertising. While he was with *Time* Kearns and his family moved to Philadelphia. David Kearns, the author of *Where Hell Freezes Over,* which you're reading now, joined the team in April of 1963.

Bill's association with aviation, Antarctica, and the navy dwindled, but his military service was inspirational to his children. America, along with all the other nations allied in the Antarctic Treaty of 1959, sent observers every year to various member-nation outposts near the South Pole, ensuring that they were not involved in military operations. In 1967 Bill Kearns was offered and gladly accepted the chance to serve as an observer for the U.S. Navy in the Antarctic, arriving at McMurdo Station in January of that year.

Bill's son John went on to win an appointment to the U.S. Air Force Academy. For a number of years John Kearns flew large aircraft, including the KC-135 "Strato-tankers" and the high-tech surveillance plane known as AWACS. He retired from the air force in 1996 as a lieutenant colonel and now flies for Delta Airlines. He lives in Provo, Utah, with his wife, Nancy, and their children.

Through John, Bill Kearns has seven grandchildren and two great-grandchildren. He has seven more grandchildren through his daughters, Virginia and Barbara, and his youngest son, David, and his wife, Donna.

Bill was divorced from his wife, Mary Louise, in 1976. Many factors went into that, but the psychological impact of the crash on his life cannot be discounted as a contributing factor.

However, for every negative effect of the airplane crash, there was a positive result that outweighed it. Professionally, Highjump was an irrevocable mountainside to his military service. In 1950 he couldn't fly for the navy anymore. So rather than wallow in this disappointment, he threw himself into studies during night school, and he eventually went on to enjoy a career that spanned endeavors in the written word from reporting to advertising to publishing.

Moreover, the large extended family he had might never have existed if the crash of the *George 1* never had taken place.

In 2004, Sylvia, Bill's second wife, accompanied him to the reunion of the *George 1* crew and their many rescuers. The party was held at the home of retired rear admiral Henry Caldwell, in Jacksonville, Florida.

Those present also included Robert Howard "Bob" Jones, Richard Conger, Ralph "Frenchy" LeBlanc, Jim Robbins, and J.D. Dickens, who has never missed a gathering of Highjump veterans.

Captured on film, devoid of rank, and framed together while relaxing in a steamy Florida backyard, they are men glad to be alive after all these years, and happy to be in each other's company once again.

In late 1999, Bill was invited on an all-expenses-paid cruise to Antarctica aboard the Orient Luxury Liner cruise ship, *Marco Polo*. His price of passage was a lecture covering the *George 1*.

On the afternoon of February 3, 2000, with his wife proudly watching from the audience, Bill took the rostrum and delivered his account of the crash in his customary manner, pausing once or twice when his infrequent baritone tremble betrayed emotions that he had never completely dealt with and for that reason didn't want to force on a relaxed audience.

As the cruise director and captain had carefully planned, *Marco*

Polo's hull touched the same waters that held *Pine Island* when she finally rescued her six lost boys less than three hundred miles north of Thurston's shore. As he spoke, the slate gray sky, visible through port and starboard windows, filled with sleet and fog, perfectly mirroring conditions fifty-three years earlier when *George 1* took off on its final flight. The impact of the moment caught Kearns by surprise. He stopped for just a second or two to gaze out the window as it all came rushing back to him. Then he continued the story.

When he finished and the applause died down, three women in the audience approached him with tears in their eyes. They weren't related to Williams, Hendersin, or Lopez, and they hadn't much to say other than thank you, but their manner conveyed deep appreciation for the great story and all he had endured. While they could have done this at any other time during the cruise, something made them come forward to take my father's hand then and there.

Bill Kearns now lives in Sarasota, Florida. His wife, Sylvia, died in 2001. The grandchildren who live closest to him, Fiona, Emily, and Sean, visit him once a month.

USS *PINE ISLAND* (AV-12)   Following its Antarctic service, *PI* saw duty in China, Korea, and Vietnam. She received service medals for both the Korean and Vietnam Wars in addition to the one that she was awarded during the later stages of World War II.

The men who served aboard her have an eerily common impression. There was something about her, a personality—a benevolent, warm, and friendly spirit that was formed early in her service and lingered throughout it. Surely some of that came from her successful efforts to rescue six needy men during Operation Highjump.

Away from war she had many different functions, from hauling water to Hong Kong to accommodating scientists aboard her in the Galapagos. She even took up station as an observation platform during nuclear weapons tests in the Pacific Testing Grounds. Atomic veterans served aboard her during the detonations of Operation Redwing in April and May of 1976. Her commanding officer had been Capt. W. A. Stewart, USN.

George Bailey, of Alliquippa, Pennsylvania, a radarman who served aboard her later, during Vietnam, wrote the following website message dedicated to the USS *Pine Island*: "When she was decommissioned it was like taking your best friend to the cemetery. . . ."

That decommissioning took place in 1967 when she entered the U.S. Maritime Administration's reserve fleet, where she remained through 1970. She was disassembled not long thereafter.

OPERATION HIGHJUMP   By some standards, Operation Highjump was a mixed bag of successes and disappointments. More than seventy thousand photographs were taken of the continent. A healthier percentage of those photographs came from the Western Task Group, which throughout the entire mission experienced better weather than did the Eastern Task Group.

But those photographs could tie in to very few known points of reference: ground points that provided a baseline for assigning scale and location to each feature for the purpose of creating maps. So, from a cartographer's perspective, the operation wasn't immediately successful. Yet those ground points found in successive mission and photographs from Highjump were utilized and referred to by the navy and scientists on up until the 1970s.

As a cold-weather exercise Highjump was extremely successful. Crews at sea and at Little America learned what they would face in the polar realm and how to deal with it. Aviators learned from the crash of *George 1* how far they could push their efforts into worsening conditions.

Perhaps the most significant scientific discovery of the mission was an area called Bunger's Oasis. Bunger Hills' Oasis, its later name, is a three-hundred-square-mile expanse of dry valleys dotted with enormous lakes that are free of ice during the austral summer. It was found smack-dab in the middle of an ice-covered area the size of Texas in eastern Antarctica. The discovery was made in early February 1947 by patrol plane commander Lt. David Bunger, flying from the USS *Currituck*. Bunger and his crew landed in one of the lakes, photographed what they saw, and collected a water sample from the lime green waters.

Numerous similar dry valleys and lakes—the result of glacial separation, salt-brining, and bacterial growth, according to Dr. Paul Siple—have been found all over Antarctica. Scientists continue to ponder and study the exact processes of evaporation and ablation that have contributed to the creation of these ice-free, mineral-rich areas.

But the human imagination endures. To this day an assortment of reality-challenged theorists have construed the many ice-free lakes as proof positive of everything from a hollow earth to alien invasions. Even more miraculous is the fact that Elvis has not yet been mentioned.

Two factors are at work here: one, wild copy sells, and two, the common person can't very well traipse off to Antarctica to see for himself what's out there or to disprove the wild claims. The wilder theories owe their longevity to the misinterpretation of flowery reports by newshounds during Operation Highjump. These reporters were bored stiff with sending dispatches about the apparently limitless extent of the Antarctic ice shelf then being mapped by *Currituck*. Ever the promoter, Byrd did little to reverse the speculations when he added his own colorful flourishes describing these "oases."

One thing accomplished by the men of Highjump: a monument. In 1997 the fiftieth annual reunion of the men of Highjump was held in Washington, D.C. Garey Jones, son of *G2* navigator R.H. Jones, made the arrangements. Collections were held for a monument commemorating every U.S. explorer to perish in Antarctica. The first three names are those of crewmen of the *George 1*, followed by Vance

Woodall, of Louisville, Kentucky. The monument now stands at Mc-Murdo Station.

ANTARCTICA   Through America's involvement in creating the Antarctic Treaty in 1959, the country secured her interests while avoiding a rehash of the problem of who had been there first. In 1947, Great Britain had been convincingly asserting her provenance, using everything from Antarctic philately, place names, and charts to the good works of heroes such as Scott and Shackleton. Likewise, Norway had a convincing case that predated even Amundsen, as did Russia, Argentina, Chile, and New Zealand.

The treaty, which was eventually signed by forty-three countries, ensured that no one would technically own the land. At the same time it gave America the leeway to maintain interests on it, establishing her bases at the pole and as she chose thereafter, and using not only her own resources but also military and private resources from allied nations as well.

The treaty's prohibitions against any part of Antarctica being used for military purposes seemed to assuage everyone's fears.

The treaty was a tribute to Byrd, who wrote many times his deepest wish: that the continent would be preserved for all mankind, for all time.

During that time, the navy continued quietly mapping and surveying the continent with efforts Windmill (47–48) and Deepfreeze I–IV (55–60), carrying out the first three objectives of Highjump and paving the way for research facilities from all nations allied in the Antarctic Treaty.

The navy quit the Antarctic battle, whose nature has always been economic, in 1996. In his statement before a congressional subcommittee in July of that year, navy undersecretary Robert B. Pirie, Jr., said:

> The United States began its post–World War II involvement with Antarctica with Operation Highjump in 1947 . . . the largest expedi-

tion ever to explore the continent and surrounding waters. . . . Today the National Science Foundation has three permanent stations . . . 2,500 scientists, support personnel, and visitors require transportation to the permanent stations as well as to isolated field camps around the region. . . . The post–Cold War draw-down of funding for ships, aircraft, and other weapons systems put severe pressure on the navy. . . .

The result, Pirie concluded, was to turn navy functions for managing Antarctic interests over to the National Science Foundation.

For transportation post 1993, commercialized Antarctic base-support systems were backstopped by the New York Air National Guard via the LC-130s.

The giant landing craft, flown by the Air Guardsmen to this day, are fitted with skis very similar in design to those pioneered by Byrd's aircrews, landing on runways laid with construction techniques that were designed and pioneered by pilots and crews from Highjump.

The first three Americans to test the limits of Antarctic air operations to the point of the ultimate sacrifice remain where they fell from the sky, in an unmarked grave covered in snow. They are held within the protective embrace of the *George 1*'s wing, perhaps forever.

22 BRINGING THEM HOME?

LANDSAT-7, IN ORBIT 438 MILES ABOVE THE SOUTH POLE   On the second day of 2001, shortly after 9:30 A.M. local time, the U.S. Geological Survey's satellite, LANDSAT-7, pulled a routine swing through the blackness of space over Antarctica.

It floated directly above an island called Thurston, located on the northwestern coast of James Ellsworth Land. This was the last landmass it would record before passing over the tip of South America prior to its 10:00 A.M. rendezvous with the equator.

Thurston loomed vacant and blisteringly cold—a collection of empty peninsulas bound together in a tenacious mitt of ice. The frozen sheets, which meshed beneath the plains of wind-driven and compacted snow, crept downward from an elevation of about four thousand feet to a slowly melting ledge jutting well out into the Bellingshausen Sea to the north.

And from there a barrier of jagged lily pads, slushy brash, and mini icebergs stretched on for a dozen heartless horizons, a three-hundred-mile jigsaw of pack ice during the warmer months, growing to more than a thousand miles during the long Antarctic night.

Meteorologists often condemn their wind gauges and thermometers to death when they leave them behind on Thurston. The instruments seldom are able to provide a full measure of the lowest temperatures or the highest winds. If they are recovered, ballistic ice chunks, some the size of fists, are often found impacted in the gear. Usually, the best these instruments can send back are incomplete data sets for a few days before they are submerged in dunes of shifting snow.

Scientists pay close attention to the images rendered by LAND-SAT. The satellite enables them to locate dangerous structural weaknesses in glacial and shelf ice. The scientists use its images to plot their missions so as not to kill themselves from ignorance when they pay Thurston Island an infrequent visit. But something was amiss in the natural order that particular morning as LANDSAT faithfully recorded all below with an unwavering eye. The data it received contained "less than one percent cloud cover." For a rare moment, Thurston, of all places on earth, was picture-perfect and cloud free, revealing her precious detail. She sat there as if posing for the camera—liberated from wind-driven snow or fog, clear of even the wispy vapor tendrils that usually rise from openings in the pack ice.

The only music commemorating the moment came from electronic signals returning to Earth through soundless space. An on-board computer digitized the image, shifting colors for human masters so that the water below was rendered black, the solid ice became a pleasant, relief-yielding light blue, and the minimal clouds present were converted into furrows of pink cotton candy, barely obscuring a small portion of the island's southern slopes. That image was buried among thousands of files within the LANDSAT-7 Worldwide Reference System.

But somewhere on this file, diced down into binary bits of data stored in a massive computer, is the evidence of a plane crash. The telltale ice has cracked and furrowed around mountaintops photographed on January 11, 1947, pointing the way toward a ruined U.S. Navy Martin PBM-5 seaplane—the *George 1*, which exploded in midair on December 30, 1946, just after 6:00 A.M. after sending her last message to her mother ship, the USS *Pine Island*.

Somewhere, below meters of crushing ice scanned by the USGS satellite, beneath the airplane's starboard wingtip, await the frozen human remains of *George 1*'s navigator, Ens. Maxwell Albert Lopez, USNR, who loved Robert Service's poetry of the Yukon—a young man who wanted to be a polar explorer just like his leader, Rear Adm. Richard E. Byrd. Below that ice also are the stranded remains of Aviation Radioman First Class Wendell K. "Bud" Hendersin, USN, whose family would mourn him sixty years later, still without a clear knowledge of the specifics of his death. And Aviation Machinist's Mate First Class Frederick Williams, USN, a replacement flight engineer with a pleasant Tennessee accent, who died two hours after the tragedy, moaning in pain, is also still locked there in time and ice, perhaps a look of betrayed astonishment written in his eyes.

The idea of retrieving three lost airmen from the snow and ice of Antarctica has deep meaning for all veterans, and particularly for the families of those still missing. Wouldn't you do everything in your power to retrieve the body of a loved one who died violently in a mission for his or her nation? You would demand it. The idea of their sleeping away the ages in Antarctica would not be acceptable.

Ken Terry is the head of the Missing Persons Section of the Navy Casualty Assistance Branch, located in Millington, Tennessee. This navy annex is only a few miles from the rolling farm country where Fred Williams's sister, Lucy, lives, tucked near the Arkansas border just outside of Nashville.

Terry joined Navy Casualty as a retired major in the U.S. Marine Corps in 1998. He began his military career as an enlisted private in 1970, training as an aviation ordinance man for F-4 Phantoms during

Vietnam. He was later selected for advance training and was put through the Citadel in Charleston, South Carolina, with the government picking up the tab. He came out from there in 1976 a second lieutenant in the marine corps. He then served at various posts throughout the Far East and the United States.

When I met him in the summer of 2002, I assessed him as a man in his early fifties, fit and trim, sober as a judge, thoughtful as a priest, methodical, by the book, and extremely patriotic. When he addresses you about the missing loved ones that he hunts for day in and day out, and talks about their families in his low baritone, you begin to realize that to him each case really is not only interesting, but special, in need of attention.

And Terry knows that for every pine tree in the forest that surrounds the marine corps base at Camp LeJeune, North Carolina, there is a fallen marine, a downed naval aviator, or a drowned sailor. While he's well aware that a considerable percentage of military remains have never been repatriated, to him each individual missing person represents someone he has known in the service over the years, or someone else very similar. They're not missing bodies to Ken Terry, they're missing people who if they are found can bring very real and tangible resolution to their living loved ones.

The case of the missing members of the *George 1* was only one of the thousands that fell to Ken Terry when he took over his present job. Yet, if you walk into his office and ask him a question about the *George 1*, he quickly moves a hand to a desk drawer, and out comes the file. The immediate impression you get is that of a great detective who can lay his hand on his favorite case blindfolded. The *George 1* is the unsolved mystery he toys with like a hobby, fascinated and compelled by it in his spare hours, consuming his mind's energies in his quiet time as he drives to work every morning and as he travels home every night.

In the early 1980s retired navy chief Jim Robbins wrote down his own account of what happened during and after the accident in a straightforward thirty-page story. He was convinced that it would be important someday. He knew his impressions were different from those of McCarty and Kearns and wanted to see them published.

Writing the document was also a cathartic exercise of sorts, in that he still was troubled by dreams of Williams calling his name, seeking his help and solace in an Antarctic blizzard without end.

While Kearns was working for *Time*, Robbins even asked him about helping to get the story read by some publishing big shots. But at that period in the publishing business, there didn't seem to be a market for such an account. Patriotism was not a hot commodity, so Robbins let it drop.

In the mid-1990s Robbins began familiarizing himself with computers and the Internet. He contributed his story to a web page, www.south-pole.com, created by an outstanding Antarctic philately buff named Gary Pierson, who was also a HAM radio operator and a member of the American Society of Polar Philatelists.

Robbins's story, entitled "Antarctic Mayday," is now a special feature on the website. It was used as a basis for the accurate painting by aviation artist Stan Stokes, who lives a few miles from Robbins in southern California.

By 1996 Robbins had already begun writing letters to his congressional representatives, inquiring why the bodies of Hendersin, Lopez, and Williams had not been returned stateside.

In 2000, Wendell Hendersin's sisters, Joanne Hendersin-Olson and Betty Hendersin-Spencer, were led by Dale Spencer, Betty's son, to Robbins's account on the website. It was an emotional moment for the family.

A nephew, Charles Hendersin, now joined his relatives and began making his own inquiries in an attempt to gather more details about Wendell's death. The family had known that their beloved Bud had died tragically in the service of his country, as the original message from Vice Adm. Louis Denfeld informed them in 1947. But what they didn't know was precisely how he died.

Robbins's account filled in the gaps in a brutal recap that, for all the blunt honesty and precise description it contained, was exactly what they needed, and they remain forever grateful to him for it. They hadn't known that subsequent navy missions to Antarctica had been ongoing for many years, without any concerted effort to collect the first three men who had perished there. They didn't understand that the National Science Foundation was there year round now, and that scientific missions to Thurston had, albeit unknowingly, come within a few miles of where Bud's remains lay.

All this they would learn, along with Robbins, as they each began contacting their local and congressional representatives.

And then, when Ken Terry took over as section head at the Millington Annex, he was given the family's findings, their requests for information, and more.

He was immediately taken with Jim Robbins's story. And who wouldn't be? Just as when he was a young enlisted man working tirelessly to return his living shipmates home during his time on the ice, the retired navy chief, late in life, was fighting to bring back the three left behind for a full-honors military burial.

But the professional marine was also a realist. Contrary to the marine corps and navy mottos and oaths that grace the ideal world, in the real one, from time to time, fighting men and women get left behind. The military doesn't like it. It's not supposed to happen, but bodies, battered and bruised, sometimes buried with the enemy they fight, are forgotten in dense jungles, on hillsides where their planes disintegrated on impact, inside mass graves, as on Iwo-Jima, or at sea within the hulls of ships as yet unfound.

Terry began reading up on Highjump, fascinated by this strange expedition bookended by World War II and Korea. One aspect of the operation that intrigued him was how similar the crash seemed to later plane crashes and cases of missing airmen in Greenland and the

Arctic—cases that had received not only national attention but some minimal recovery work as well.

The LA-9 case was the most similar. On January 12, 1962 (fifteen years to the day after the *George 1* crew was rescued), a U.S. Navy P2-V crashed on the Kronborg Glacier in Greenland while flying a reconnaissance mission from the Iceland Naval Station at Keflavik in Iceland. This time, twelve good men were killed. The wreckage was found three years later by a British Geological Survey team. By September of that year a U.S. Navy icebreaker was mobilized, and ten unidentifiable sets of human remains were recovered. A group interment of these remains was held at Arlington National Cemetery the following October. In August of 1995, more remains, along with wreckage, were found by a helicopter crew, which did not make any recovery efforts. Pressure from fellow members of Patrol Squadron 5 made the recovery of the last two men of LA-9 a priority, and in August of 2004 the navy sent a sixteen member team to southern Greenland under the command of Capt. Tom Sparks. They were successful in retrieving the bodies of the remaining fallen aviators and in returning them home.

"I hope this gives the families and friends some comfort and closure," Sparks said to members of the press.

Terry's immediate question about *George 1* when he read the file was why efforts were not made in the Antarctica crash. Why was Antarctica so much more difficult to return to than Greenland?

Learning more about that desolate area gave him answers. The immense distances, the lack of scale with which to measure them, the pack ice, the altitudes, the slashing and jagged topography, which prevented access by air, land, or water, Antarctica's violently capricious seas—all these factors answered him. He became fascinated at what the story said about these men who had attempted to go to that land in 1947 and take pictures of everything. How nuts-brave or how bold could you be? These guys from Highjump apparently set the bar.

The missing men of *George 1*, along with six similar cases Terry had been handed when he took office (the LA 9 included), didn't seem to fit any of the criteria with which all the other twelve thousand files could easily be described as worthy of funding. "Nonhostile peacetime mishap" is the official classification, but even that doesn't quite fit or capture all of it, he felt. He couldn't even be sure it was categorized correctly. The expedition happened as a direct result of the Cold War, and there was a definite military component to Highjump if you looked at its objectives.

Terry began asking around. The families needed answers, and the records, stored in boxes in Suitland, Maryland, and in the Washington Navy Yard, weren't easily located. How much would it cost to go get these guys' remains to begin with? What were the safety aspects of that operation, and who, precisely, would be in charge of it?

Months went by as they awaited answers. In the meantime Hendersin's sisters received the official reports from the crash. These reports had originally been denied them under a technicality of the Freedom of Information Act that was later cleared up. It took a year and a half, letters from the sisters to Sen. Russell Feingold (Democrat-Wisconsin), then from Feingold to the JAG offices, to CILHI, from CILHI to Ken Terry, and back again to Hendersin's sisters.

The accident report was a two-page statement of the facts in the case, with parts deleted that were related to the severity of Lopez's injuries and other details of the crash. Otherwise, it was a pointwise critique of plane commander LeBlanc's decision to proceed with the flight in worsening conditions, and copilot Kearns's error during the whiteout at having mistaken the side of a hill as clear airspace.

Classification of accident causes: P.E. [Pilot Error] Judgment or technique.

SPECIFIC ERRORS: Patrol Plane Commander [LeBlanc] should not have continued through unfavorable weather under the circumstances of flying near unreliably charted terrain which was known to be mountainous.

In the same report:

> Pilot [Kearns] was not able to accurately determine his exact altitude above terrain before impact of plane . . . it is believed the pilot at the controls misinterpreted the snow-covered side of a mountain blending into the overcast as clear air space and inadvertently flew into the ground while attempting to leave the area.

The report gives a corrected position of the crash location at latitude 71 degrees 33 minutes south, longitude 98 degrees 45 minutes west. The plane was traveling at 118 knots when it exploded and crashed on the snowy hillside, nine hundred feet above sea level.

The normal mantle of obfuscation, protecting pilot and copilot from any public antipathy that this regrettable error might have generated, had worked over the years. Yet still the assessment conveniently lays it all on these two young men of 1946.

It was a harsh, but technically correct, judgment from the navy, and they both lived with it for the rest of their lives. It's a tribute to their generation that both quietly accepted that assessment and merely went forward, striving to lead productive lives, displaying that characteristic self-pity-be-damned stoicism for which the World War II generation is famous.

To approach the judgment another way, even the most experienced and well-equipped military pilots of today face peril from Arctic and Antarctic whiteouts—peril that is only mitigated by the most advanced technology we have. Take it back to 1946, heighten the odds of calamity by giving pilots aging bombers and gear designed for balmy, pacific conditions, then tell them they have a limited time to fly over and photograph everything in Antarctica. Stoke their patriotism and machismo, already honed to a razor's edge through the war, and give them an unrealistic deadline. It's not hard to see that an early flight in Highjump was destined to encounter trouble on a large scale.

Small consolation was this final report to the Hendersin relatives after Senator Feingold's diligent prodding, aided by the inquiries from Iowa Republican congressman James Leach, Republican senator John McCain, and Democratic senators Tom Harkin and Richard Durbin that were to be forwarded to Wendell Hendersin's sisters.

Back in Missing Persons, a typical government employee might decry the inquiries and point to a stack of other files. "You see them? I have to sort through all that. Now, you tell me which is more important—your case from 1947 here, or that stack of Vietnam cases right over there?"

Not Ken Terry. By now he was as interested as anyone in seeing how this all played out. Not only because of his growing fascination with Highjump, but also because the need to bring these men home would be weighed against the search for missing naval fliers, sailors, and marines from the Vietnam War. It was specifically for the missing of that war that Terry's job had been created. Everything within his job title told Terry that this *George 1* thing was a closed case. But the sisters and Chief Robbins demanded action. The letters kept reverberating in him. He didn't own an icebreaker or one million dollars in cash to fund an expedition to Antarctica. The taxpayers did. It was their government that would have to allocate special funds to get the three servicemen back home.

And this could set a precedent not only for contemporary nonhostile losses, but for losses going back to the Revolutionary War. If the remains could be verified in history books and by the Museum of Naval History, weren't they "ancient remains"? If it was the job of his office to find the result of "hostile losses" under what the law deemed a "full accounting effort"—if the remains could be found, they have to be restored to the family, pending extreme hardship of safety and cost—then how did the law apply to this case, which kept bouncing back to him?

With all these heavy hitters clamoring for action to placate their constituents, Ken Terry couldn't ignore the case. And by now he didn't want to.

In a letter written to me in July 2002, Joanne Olson states: "We have asked for Lopez's and Williams's families' location but they claim they can't tell us that. We think they do not want any more people pressuring them, and of course that's exactly what we want."

In a subsequent interview, Terry admitted that could be one interpretation of the unwillingness to share family information, but, again, there are laws protecting servicemen and their families from precisely these kinds of inquiries. These are laws Terry cannot bend or break.

Additionally, he said that as of July 2002 the navy had not contacted the Lopez relatives about recent inquiries into the case, nor the Williams relatives—one residing but a few miles from Millington—precisely because they did not want to stir hope that the remains could even be located. No congressman or senator would be foolish enough to do so either. It could turn out to be nothing more than an exercise in cruel futility.

Hendersin's sisters approached Terry by way of their elected officials after reading Robbins's account on the web. Robbins applied pressure by way of Sen. Dianne Feinstein (Democrat-California), who made the original inquiries back in 1996.

Terry said in an interview: "To complicate the issue, the case does not fall within the mission responsibilities for the U.S. Government's 'Full Accounting Effort,' which was specifically established to address unaccounted for hostile combat casualty cases from World War II through current conflicts. Further research is ongoing to determine whether current personnel recovery policies would also apply to the recovery of ancient remains associated with Unaccounted for Non Hostile Casualty Cases."[1]

He could have left it at that. He didn't.

Owing to his desire not to let any fallen serviceman down, he began toying with the question of how one would even locate the men. Maybe satellite data could do it. He contacted officials at the U.S. Geological Survey, where the nation's most up-to-date survey maps are kept.

Terry decided in early 2001 that there should at least be a meeting that included someone from the U.S. Geological Survey to discuss the surviving family members' concerns. Jerry Mullins, deputy chief of geographic sciences for USGS, set the meeting up and tasked scientists with the job of pointing out where to look. The meeting was set for USGS Headquarters in Reston, Virginia, on May 16, 2001. Present were officials from USGS, the National Science Foundation, NASA's Goddard Space Flight Center, and the army's CILHI (Central Identification Laboratory Hawaii).[2]

During the months previous to the meeting, USGS scientists sorted through their database, finding a satellite image of Thurston Island, taken from LANDSAT-7 on January 2, 2001. It was so clear, they knew right away it would be useful in at least highlighting where they thought *George 1* might be.

According to a USGS fact sheet, each LANDSAT-7 snapshot of the Earth, taken from 438 miles up at roughly a dead overhead angle from the center of the page, produces an image that covers an area 115 miles wide by 106 miles long. These impressions are amazingly clear and deceptively beautiful. More than artwork, they are chock-full of data in addition to the information they contain in the visible wavelengths.

On board the LANDSAT was an enhanced thematic mapper. Thanks to this device, which was developed by Raytheon Corporation of Santa Barbara, California, each image contains 3.8 gigabits of data, or the equivalent of fifteen sets of encyclopedias at twenty-nine volumes per set. The average size of any encyclopedia is about an inch and a half across the spine. Most encyclopedia pages in my day were thin and had up to 400 words per page—that is to say, times 600, times 29, times 15. These figures provide an idea of how much data one image from LANDSAT-7 holds.

Seemingly invisible land features are buried within all that information, nested down deep—too deep for visible detection, but certainly within a computer's capability. Resolution narrows down to just less than fifty feet, providing definition to every rocky outcrop in the wilderness or every building in a metropolitan setting.

In 1947, when Ball's photographer, James B. Payne, or whoever it was, took his three shots of the crash site, there was no way he could have known just how crucial those three to five mountaintops/nunataks he thoughtfully added for scale would prove to be in 2001, or how they would be used.

Coming up with an equation and tasking the computer with all the data, right down to the focal length of those cameras used by Ball's crew, USGS scientists were able to narrow down the crash location, and the location of the *George 2* at the time the photographer snapped his photos, to a circle less than two miles in diameter, with a high degree of certainty falling in the very center.

One can only marvel at the diligence and the level of dedication that this group of scientists displayed at solving this part of the puzzle. After all, they weren't related to these men and weren't even alive when the *George 1* crashed. It's not only a testament to their dedication as professionals, but a demonstration of the adhesive power of the *George 1*'s story. Their combined report was submitted by USGS scientist Dr. Daniel R. Sechrist.

Assuming the protruding mountaintops had not been moved by unseen geologic forces, the next question became how far downslope the wreck site had slid in the intervening period, and how deeply it had become buried beneath the ice.

Dr. Robert Bindschadler, of NASA's Goddard Space Flight Center, is a noted Antarctic field researcher who on eleven expeditions, over twenty years, has measured and calibrated how fast various types of glacial ice accumulate and flow. He delivered the rest of the puzzle with equal specificity.

The ice covering the wreck could be anywhere from 100 to 200 meters thick, he reported. Given only the known information on snow and ice accumulation in that area, and no information on ice calving or compaction, which would have to come from subsequent surveys, he said it might have slipped downslope anywhere from 73 to 600 meters.

But when these speculations are combined with the information from the photos and the satellite, there's every reason to believe that the ice block containing the *George 1* and the remains of Lopez, Hendersin, and Williams has not yet calved off into the Bellingshausen Sea.

Oddly enough, these most recent satellite images show a pocket of open water hugging the coast of the Noville Peninsula that could even accommodate the landing of a Martin PBM-5, if an operable one still exists. This ice-free lake is shown clearly in the LANDSAT image. It awaits the block containing the dead naval aviators and their plane precisely downslope from the estimated position of the *George 1* if in the interim they are not rescued. As a result of warm currents upwelling along the coast, pushing pack ice seaward, the lake now eats away at the ice cliff that Caldwell, Kearns, Robbins, McCarty, and Warr traversed with LeBlanc in tow.

Through further research, Ken Terry said that, based on estimates given him by Jerry Mullins and his team, recovering the last three crewmen of the *George 1* would take place in two missions. The first, whose object would be merely to pinpoint the wreck with ground-penetrating radar, would cost upwards of $750,000, including a five-man team working on and off a U.S. Coast Guard icebreaker.

The next phase of the operation, digging down through all that ice with jets of hot water to access the airplane wing, finding the bodies, and returning them to the States, could cost one and a half million dollars or more. Mullins said a proposed cold-mining event could take place in stages. Such a search was completed in Greenland by a private enterprise that recovered and is reconstructing several U.S. Army Air Force P-38s and B-17s. The planes were abandoned after being forced down in a disorienting whiteout of 1942 along the Labrador Coast. They were located with ground-penetrating radar in 1992. Some of them were recovered by using a device called the gopher. Manufactured for the expedition by a private company from Tucker, Georgia, the device, called Super Gopher III, bore through more than two hundred feet of ice to locate the target aircraft *Glacier Girl*. A fifty-foot-wide cavern was then carved out of the ice as the plane was sliced into sections and then hauled up the shaft. *Glacier Girl* was reassembled and flown in October of 2002.[3]

Mullins said that more than likely it "would be possible" to burrow down to the *George 1* and retrieve the remains of Lopez, Hendersin, and Williams, using precisely the same technology. He said the fact that the *George 1* had crashed at one thousand feet and now resides beneath the ice less than ten miles from the coast, in an area that experiences pockets of open water during the austral summer and is thus accessible by icebreaker, the job could be done. He cautioned, however, that the Department of Defense would have to say whether or not it should be done.

Rep. Mark Kirk of Highland Park, Illinois, has taken up the call, owing to continued correspondence with Betty Spencer. Kirk voiced support for the project in an article in Spencer's hometown paper, the *Daily Herald* of Chicago.[4]

There may yet be interest in recovering not only the men's remains, but those of the aircraft itself for display in a museum.

In early 2002 Ken Terry submitted a report to naval secretary Gordon R. England, including his findings on the case of *George 1*, awaiting review for approval. In September of 2004 e-mails began circulating between Captain Sparks and members of the bomber squadrons. These indicated that the navy had secured the funding for the recovery of the *George 1* crewmen, Hendersin, Lopez, and Williams.

At this writing, the recovery effort is being considered for January of 2005, with a backup date of 2006.

If the expenditure is approved and he gets his way, Ken Terry said he wants to be there in Antarctica when the missing men are found.

So now I spend free moments writing my own solicitous e-mails and making phone calls, seeking higher contact into the world of the U.S. Navy—a world my dad left more than fifty years ago.

If it can be arranged, I would like to stand on the slopes of Thurston Island, Antarctica, during that solemn moment and bow my head on behalf of my father as Lopez, Hendersin, and Williams are finally rescued from the ice.

The Last Word

DIFFERENCES OF OPINION
AND FOR THE RECORD

No two people will experience or remember the same event quite the same way. At this writing, the last two survivors of the crash are Bill Kearns and Jim Robbins, both of whom are in their early eighties. Bill is my father. He lives about one hundred miles from me in Sarasota, Florida, making it rather easy for me to interview him in person, via e-mail, and on the telephone.

Jim Robbins, of Palm Desert, California, has graciously made himself available via phone and e-mail. Despite the disagreement he has had with my father about some of the facts, he has always strived to give me compelling accounts of what he remembers. Another great resource has been Gene Litz, who submitted to phone and e-mail questions from his home in New Hampshire and made a great third-party interpreter of events, helping me to identify the men in the photos, as well as giving me his point of view from within the rescue plane where he and the others waited for word from the ice shelf. It's a point of view that has not been revealed until now.

There are two incongruities in the accounts given to the press and to me by both my father and Robbins. They disagree on the altitude at which the crash occurred, and also on the time—two hours or four, or none at all—that elapsed between a reported first flyover by rescuers and a second flyover when the men were finally spotted by the crew of the *G2*. According to Kearns, speaking in an interview for the *Palm Beach Post*, the crash took place at about three thousand feet. Robbins said that this is wrong, that it was more like one thousand feet. Again, while Kearns says that there was a two-to-four-hour time lapse between the first flyover by their rescuers and the second, when the men in the plane saw the survivors, Robbins maintains there never was a "first" flyover.

Here is a seaway into how these differences were brought to my attention. Also, this is as good a place as any to answer the question posed to me twice by reporters, "Why did you write this?"

In 2000, when I was still working at a local newspaper in Sebastian, Florida, doing columns about local war vets, I featured my dad, Bill Kearns, in one of them. And why not? He lived only a few miles south of the area we covered. It was after I compared his accounts with those of other veterans from the World War II era that I decided I had to write a book about the Antarctic crash. As I gathered steam, I asked myself, "Wouldn't it be great if because of publicity for the book, the recovery of the bodies of the three men who died was somehow prodded along?" There's really no way to know if in all the digging I did, I helped to make this happen. I hope I did. I have known the story of the *George 1* since I was a very small boy. In fact, when I was a kid, I thought that all fathers had gone through similar calamities "back in the day." I thought that they all expounded on it of a Sunday afternoon over a bit of Scotch. I thought that they had all been in the navy and all had their own respective plane crashes, wherever they might have occurred, and that they all talked about how they had gotten out of it by subsisting on peanut butter and keeping burn victims alive until help arrived.

Not so. There was something about this *George 1* thing that always seemed especially compelling—and not just because it was a story about my father. Perhaps what intrigued me most was the part about fighting the cold and those deadly internal enemies, fear and panic.

When I told what I felt to other writers and reporters, they immediately said I wasn't biased because of my father; rather, my instincts were right: this was a special story. They also said it was haunting to be aware that three good men remained behind. In doing my research I found Jim Robbins's account through www.South-Pole.com. I had met Frenchy LeBlanc when I was boy, but as far as the rest of the crew went, I knew only their names and nothing else. I wanted to get their points of view and match their words against my dad's memories, which he had shared with me over the years.

Meanwhile, Dad had answered a letter in the *Palm Beach Post* in which someone had taken potshots—as Dad saw them—at the character of Adm. Richard E. Byrd. Dad rose to the bait, recounting what he knew of Byrd as someone who was loyal and clear-eyed. True, Byrd was a bit of a showman, he said, but he was a leader who was deeply committed to the men under his command—so much so that he even made moves to help them further their careers later in life, whether these were in journalism or polar exploration.

Before Dad knew it, there was a photographer from the *Post* at his house and a reporter on the phone taking in his story for a huge feature article soon to run called "Fire and Ice." (I remain forever jealous of this title and the amount of information digested by the *Post* in less than a week.) To nail it all down, the reporter, Douglas Kalajian, came to Bill's home and spent the day going over the details.

Doug noticed some of the discrepancies between Bill's and Robbie's versions of events as well. Robbie steadfastly maintained that they crashed the plane at one thousand feet, and Bill said the altitude was more like three thousand. Doug wasn't there, so he included both points of view in the interview. Later, in covering the material, he happened upon the question of this first flyover. Not so, said Robbie to Doug: He had said the same to me: There was no "first" flyover, because there was no second one. They were seen on the first pass, and that was the end of it. Any attempt to say otherwise bordered on an insult to his honest account, he said. Well, in both cases—in my father's case of remembering the crash at three thousand feet, and Robbie's recollection of only one flyover—the present-day accounts go squarely against what was recorded and what the survivors themselves said within hours of returning to USS *Pine Island*. The most recent memories also go against numerous well-documented accounts written down by scribes such as Owen McCarty, who was also a survivor. Indeed, they both go against an article written by Bill Kearns in the *Boston Post* within months of his return to the United States. The very minutes of the press conference relate the account of the first flyover. You can find them in chapter 20 of this book.

Furthermore, in the briefing of the *G2*'s crew, after they had seen that the crash victims were on their way to a recovery point and after they had left the area, the following is written in the report for the Eastern Task Group, Annex I-(c), page 9:

MARINER GEORGE ONE FIRST SIGHTED BY W. A. LONG, CPHM MONROE N CAROLINA ON THIRD LEG OF SEARCH FLIGHT . . .

The report is very clear. The ship had been moved over the course of the previous two days one hundred miles west of where *G1* took off. That gave the *G2* a more direct due-south course to the coast. *G2* took off at 7 A.M. and sighted the crew and the smashed remains of *G1* just after 11 A.M. on the third leg of the search. *G1* took a little over three hours to reach their crash site. *Pine Island* moved closer to a due-south shot to Thurston, cutting down on the need for a southwesterly approach to the last radio contact position of 71 degrees, 22 minutes south, 99 degrees 30 minutes west. They cut off the hypotenuse of the triangle, so to speak. It would take less than three hours to get there, not more. Once they reached the last reported position, they began their search pattern, consisting of three legs, before sighting the men. Which they did, a little over four hours into their flight. From just after 11 A.M. to 4:20 P.M., they circled the site, dropping markers and supplies. Then they headed back to the ship, landing at 6:35 P.M., a little over two hours later. All agree that the sky was very clear and that the air was calm.

Records clearly show that the PBM *G2* had sufficient gas when she took off—a total of twenty hours, worth—and had left early enough and was in the vicinity of the crash long enough to make a first pass over the site, and that it was hailed on a subsequent passing. Again, *G2*'s crew reported to Dufek and Schwartz that

GEORGE ONE CRASHED ON BARRIER OF EIGHTS' PENINSULA AT ALTITUDE OF 1000 FEET ON APPROX COURSE 130(,) TRUE MOUNTAIN TOPS SIGHTED ABOUT 25 MILES SOUTH OF CRASH SITE PLANE WAS VERY DIFFICULT TO SEE AND SIGHTING GREATLY ENHANCED BY SMOKE OF SURVIVORS' FIRE.

So why are the memories of these two men in disagreement with those of their younger selves and with the record? Such disagreement is to be expected from men sitting in their living rooms and reliving events that happened a half century ago. Having raised families, gone through divorce or marital tumult, and endured the deaths of friends and loved ones, having seen children succeed, fail, and succeed again, and mature and grow, these men view the distant past without the crystal edge of clarity, especially when it comes to times and dates.

Yet seemingly miniscule bits of conversation—for example, about the way an iceberg looked in the distance, the feeling of teeth chattering with cold, the sound of ice pelting the hull of the ship seconds before it exploded—all come into sharp focus and contrast. Even faced with documentation—the very news articles that he himself authored—he stammers and asks, "Now how the hell did I remember it the other way?" It is a phenomenon that fuels the speculations of conspiracy theorists who thrive on conflicting accounts such as these—particularly when they involve mysterious places such as Antarctica. Such differences can alter history and start arguments that last for years. They are explained, unflatteringly, as the result of getting old. These inaccuracies detract not one iota from the outstanding, at times superhuman things both men did, particularly Jim Robbins, who not only walked through fire shoulder to shoulder with Bill Kearns and Bill Warr, but also shone as an idea man and an informal leader, who applied blood, muscle, and bone when Bill Kearns, wracked with pain, no longer could move and others similarly dazed and confused by the crash were also incapacitated. Furthermore, Robbins repeatedly risked his life to lend company to a dying man. . . . Well, there are no words to equal that act, are there? Some things Robbie accomplished in the act of saving himself and his shipmates as a nineteen-year-old aviation radioman continue to amaze me, one of the chief beneficiaries of his guts and courage. He enabled my father to live, and thus permitted my family to exist, along with Frenchy's family and Caldwell's family and Warr's family and his own family. In my mind these things Robbie did for all of us have earned him the highest rank, no matter how strongly he disagrees with me on those two hours or how angry he gets at the smaller details I have laid down in this account.

He and my dad quibbling over these details are like teenage boys competing on a football field, and that makes me think that perhaps there's something healthy and good about their bickering. The fight lives on inside them. In many ways we're left dealing with a junior officer and an enlisted man, each for his own reasons in awe of the other. I asked a third-party witness what she remembers of the relationship between Robbins and my father. Mary Louise Kearns—Mary Louise Gallen at that time—attended the premiere of *Secret Land* in 1949, in Washington, D.C. She remembers her fiancé, Bill, being recognized by Admiral Byrd. Bill came up to the microphone and asked that a spotlight be shone on a real hero who saved his entire crew. She also remembers that Jim Robbins rose to acknowledge applause from the audience. While indeed it must have been difficult for Bill to have a man of lesser rank outperforming him and even a navy captain, it is my opinion that my father meant no disrespect for Jim Robbins and to this day remains thankful and accepting of the fact that Robbins did the work of six men combined. It might have been harder for Robbins, who outshone everyone, to come back to the navy from Antarctica and salute junior officers from the reserves, not to mention sitting through a press conference and remaining quiet in deference to rank while the man he saved told the story.

We can only imagine the entirety of what was said during the first and second sightings of the rescue plane. It must have been the most maddening experience anyone can imagine—certainly worse by far than anything described here. Would they get another chance? Was the plane coming back, or was that it? Were they going to sit there and slowly die? Two long hours, at least, perhaps even three . . . who knows what curses or sobs fell out into the air? Who knows how these men behaved at this crucial moment when they were stretched beyond pressure, fear, and sanity? The last two left alive aren't spilling all of it.

However they acted, Robbins, by all accounts, finally got the fire lit, likely with help from McCarty (who remembers using a lighter) while Caldwell calmed everyone down—now at that moment seemingly beyond all hope, demonstrating leadership through a moment of pure, white panic—after speaking with Kearns about flight patterns. (Robbins recalls this conversation. How did it happen if they had no previous cause to be talking about search patterns?)

Precisely what was said will remain behind among the harsh and ghostly echoes of the Silent Continent.

And perhaps that's exactly as it should be.

ENDNOTES

1: THURSTON ISLAND

2: OPERATION HIGHJUMP: TASK FORCE 68

1. http://www.trumanlibrary.org/calendar/main.php?currYear=1946&currMonth=11&currDay=14.
2. British foreign office spokesman Mallory Brown, "British Are Firm on Antarctic Area," (special to) *New York Times* (Dateline: London, December 28, 1946), 1-A.
3. Byrd, "Why We're Going Back . . ." *American Weekly* (July 4, 1955), 11–12.
4. U.S. Navy, *Report of Operation Highjump* (June 10, 1947), 2–3.
5. Phone interview with Capt. John D. Howell, USN Ret. (March 2002).
6. U.S. Navy, "Standard Aircraft Characteristics" (fact sheet), NAVAER 1335F (January 1949 rev.), PBM-5s "Mariner."
7. U.S. Navy, "AN 01-35ED-1" (fact sheet and cutaway view), NAVAER 1335F (January 1949 rev.), PBM-5s "Mariner."
8. Lisle A. Rose, *Assault on Eternity: Richard E. Byrd and the Exploration of Antarctica 1946–47* (Annapolis, Maryland: Naval Institute Press, 1980), 49–50.

3: USS *PINE ISLAND*

1. USS *Pine Island* configuration and information on *Currituck* class seaplane tenders from USS *Currituck* Association. http://av7.8m.com/page9.html.
2. Interview with John D. Dickens, Thomaston, Georgia (June 2002).
3. Bill Kearns interview (January 2002).
4. Kearns interview (January 2002).
5. "Spell of the Yukon," from *Spell of the Yukon and Other Verses by Robert W. Service*, http://www.artdamage.com/service/yukon/spell.htm.
6. Capt. Finn Ronne, USNR, at Arlington National Cemetery website. http://www .arlingtoncemetery.com/finnronn.htm.
7. Phone interview with Capt. John D. Howell (February 2002).

4: PANAMA AND THE RIDE SOUTH

1. U.S. Navy, *Report of Operation Highjump*, Annex I(o) (1947), 1.
2. Interview with Litz. The presence of the actor in Panama was confirmed in separate interviews with Kearns and children of Ralph P. LeBlanc. That Errol Flynn often transited the canal en route to Jamaica from Catalina during the late forties was confirmed by the actor's daughter, Rory Flynn, in a June 2002 e-mail to the author.
3. U.S. Navy, *Sailing Directions for Antarctica*, H.O. No. 138 (U.S. Navy Hydrographic Office: Washington, D.C., 1943), 21–25.
4. Al Muenchen, *Flying the Midnight Sun: The Exploration of Antarctica by Air* (New York, New York: David McKay Company, 1972), 98.

5: THE *GEORGE 1*'S LAST FLIGHT: A RIDE THAT WOULD COST THEM PLENTY

1. U.S. Navy, *Report of Operation Highjump*, Annex I(o) (1947), 5.
2. Re: loss of first seaplane of the Western Group. *The Secret Land*, U.S. Navy and MGM documentary film (1948).
3. List of flight crews for 1946–47, USS *Pine Island*, Operation Highjump Expeditionary Records, courtesy of Byrd Polar Research Center, at Ohio State University, Columbus, Ohio.
4. Owen McCarty, "Dead Man's Diary," *Saturday Evening Post* (May 17, 1947), 16.
5. U.S. Navy, *Report of Operation Highjump*, Annex I(o), *Pine Island* (1947), 4.
6. Interview with Buz LeBlanc, July 2002.
7. U.S. Navy, *Report of Operation Highjump*, Annex I(o), *Pine Island* (1947), 4.
8. From the minutes of the press conference, Department of the U.S. Navy, Washington, D.C., February 21, 1947, confirmed in the accident report, description of the crash from copilot's perspective. Minutes courtesy of Bill Kearns.
9. McCarty, "Dead Man's Diary," *Saturday Evening Post* (May 1947), 15.

6: DAY 1 ON THE ICE

1. From Bill Warr's interview with navy chaplain Everett LeCompte and press conference, Washington, D.C. (February 21, 1947).
2. Robbins in *Antarctic Mayday* http://www.south-pole.com/p0000153.htm (1981) and subsequent interviews: "First thing he said to me is 'Robbie, we're all screwed up.'"
3. William Warr interview with Chaplain Everett T. LeCompte aboard USS *Pine Island*: "The Captain lost his pants. . . . We were always having our jokes [about it]." Additional *Jacksonville Times-Union* (December 29, 1979), 1-B, interview with Caldwell re: cracked ankle and neck. Reporter, Joe Caldwell.
4. McCarty, "Dead Man's Diary," *Saturday Evening Post* (May 1947), 16.
5. Robbins, *Antarctic Mayday* and in interview. "He kept calling out to me. Everyone knew me as Robbie. Mine was the only name he knew."
6. From phone interview with Jim Robbins.
7. U.S. Navy, *Report of Operation Highjump*, Annex I(c) (1947), 5–6.
8. Ibid.
9. Ibid.

7: DAY 2

1. http://trumanlibrary.org/calendar/viewpapers.php?pid=1842.
2. British foreign office spokesman Mallory Brown, "British Are Firm on Antarctic Area," (special to) *New York Times* (Dateline London: December 28, 1946), 1-A.
3. http://www.solon.org/Constitutions/Japan/English/english-Constitution.html.
4. http://www.jhu.edu/~jhumag/1199web/invent.html.
5. McCarty, "Dead Man's Diary," *Saturday Evening Post* (May 1947), 16.
6. Ibid.
7. Bill Kearns interviews.
8. Bill Kearns interviews.

8: DAY 3

1. Bill Kearns interviews.
2. (Timetable of meals provided throughout.) McCarty, "Dead Man's Diary," *Saturday Evening Post* (May 1947).

9: A LITTLE KNOWLEDGE IS DANGEROUS, FEAR IS CONTAGIOUS: DAY 4

1. U.S. Navy, *Report of Operation Highjump*, Annex I(o) (1947), 5.
2. Interview with J. D. Dickens.
3. Interview with Buz LeBlanc.
4. Rose, *Assault on Eternity* (Naval Institute Press, 1980), 127.

10: ABOARD SHIPS: DAY 5

1. Rose, *Assault on Eternity* (Naval Institute Press, 1980), 95.
2. Fred Sparks with Edward P. Morgan, "The Icebergs Bear Down," *Collier's Magazine*, New York: June 14, 1947), 28.
3. http://www.oceanwanderers.com/SouthGiantPetrel.html.
4. Rose, *Assault on Eternity* (Naval Institute Press, 1980), 32.
5. Fr. William J. Menster, *Strong Men South* (Dubuque, Iowa: Stromen Publishing, 1949), 89.
6. Fred Sparks, "Admiral Holds Out Hope for Missing Fliers," *Boston Globe* (January 3, 1947), 1-A.
7. Sparks and Morgan, "The Icebergs Bear Down," *Collier's Magazine* (June 14, 1947), 32.
8. Alton Blakeslee, "Antarctic Rescue Is Completed," Associated Press from USS *Mount Olympus* (January 12, 1947). It remains unclear whether the article is from the *Boston Globe* or the *Boston Herald*. Article localized to Newport, Rhode Island, in sidebar: "Mrs. Lopez of 402 Spring Street this morning received official word . . . from Vice Admiral Louis Denfeld, chief of naval personnel." Lists surviving brother, confirmed in separate article, Richard, attending Rogers High School, Newport.

11: SKUAS: DAY 6

1. Skua story confirmed in accounts by Kearns, McCarty, Robbins, and in February 21, 1947, press conference.
2. U.S. Navy, *Report of Operation Highjump*, Annex I(o), 5.
3. Robert H. Jones (letters), courtesy of Emil Buehler, National Museum of Naval Aviation, Pensacola, Florida.

12: FORMAL BURIAL SERVICE FOR LOPEZ, HENDERSIN, AND WILLIAMS: DAY 7

1. Account of the burial was given by Kearns and Robbins in separate interviews.
2. U.S. Navy, *Report of Operation Highjump*, Annex I(o), *Pine Island* (1947), 5.

13: MURPHY'S LAW: DAY 8

1. U.S. Navy, *Report of Operation Highjump*, Annex I(c), 6.
2. McCarty, "Dead Man's Diary," *Saturday Evening Post* (May 17, 1947), 17.
3. Robert H. Jones (letters), courtesy of Emil Buehler, National Aviation Museum, Pensacola, Florida.

14: SALVO: DAY 9

1. U.S. Navy, *Report of Operation Highjump*, Annex I(c), 7.
2. McCarty, "Dead Man's Diary," *Saturday Evening Post*, 18.
3. U.S. Navy, *Report of Operation Highjump*, Annex I(o), 5.
4. McCarty, "Dead Man's Diary," *Saturday Evening Post*, 136.
5. Robbins, *Antarctic Mayday* and in interview.
6. Bill Kearns interviews.

15: SPIRITS DROP: DAYS 10, 11, AND 12

1. U.S. Navy, *Report of Operation Highjump*, Annex I(c), 7.
2. Separate interviews with Jim Robbins and Bill Kearns.
3. U.S. Navy, *Report of Operation Highjump*, Annex I(c), 8.
4. McCarty, "Dead Man's Diary," *Saturday Evening Post*, 136.
5. McCarty, "Dead Man's Diary," *Saturday Evening Post*, 138.
6. Ibid.
7. Flight logs for the *G2* courtesy of Buz LeBlanc from the Byrd Polar Research Institute.
8. U.S. Navy, *Report of Operation Highjump*, Annex I(c), 8.
9. Ibid.
10. Ibid.

16: SIX ALIVE! SIX ALIVE! DAY 13

1. U.S. Navy, *Report of Operation Highjump*, Annex I(c), 8.
2. Quote from the personal log of Robert Howard Jones, courtesy of his son, Garey Jones.
3. The *G2* flight log.
4. Menster, *Strong Men South* (Stromen, 1949), 72.
5. Jim Robbins in phone interview.
6. McCarty, "Dead Man's Diary," *Saturday Evening Post*, 143.
7. U.S. Navy, *Report of Operation Highjump*, Annex I(c), 9.

17: RESCUE: DAY 14

1. Phone interview with Litz.
2. U.S. Navy, *Report of Operation Highjump*, Annex I(c), 9.
3. Litz in e-mail to author.
4. Rose, *Assault on Eternity* (Naval Institute Press, 1980), 87.
5. Rose, *Assault on Eternity* (Naval Institute Press, 1980), 88.
6. McCarty, "Dead Man's Diary," *Saturday Evening Post*, 143.
7. Phone interview with Gene Litz.
8. Rose, *Assault on Eternity* (Naval Institute Press, 1980), 92.

18: ABOARD *PI* AGAIN

1. McCarty, "Dead Man's Diary," *Saturday Evening Post*, 143.

19: HOMEWARD RUN

1. Robbins phone interview.
2. Menster, *Strong Men South* (Stromen, 1949), 104.
3. Menster, *Strong Men South* (Stromen, 1949), 113.
4. U.S. Navy, *Report of Operation Highjump*, Annex I(o), 7.
5. Interview with Gus Shinn at National Museum of Naval Aviation, Pensacola, Florida (July 2002).

20: NEWS CONFERENCE

1. From press conference held February 21, 1947, Department of the U.S. Navy, Washington, D.C.

21: THE REST OF THE STORY, THE REST OF THEIR LIVES

1. Al Muenchen, *Flying the Midnight Sun: The Exploration of Antarctica by Air* (New York, New York: David McKay Company, 1972), 98.
2. Rose, *Assault on Eternity* (Naval Institute Press, 1980), 167.
3. Interviews with Gene Litz and J. D. Dickens.

22: BRINGING THEM HOME?

1. Interview with navy BUPERS MIA section director Ken Terry, Millington, Tennessee (July 2002).
2. Phone interview with USGS Geographic Mapping Division leader Jerry Mullins (January 2003).
3. http://thelostsquadron.com/coldmining1.html.
4. Russell Lissau, "Lost on the Ice," *Elgin and Fox Valley Daily Herald*, and for Associated Press (January 19, 2003) F12 and AP Wire Service.